THE
FONDAS

BY PETER COLLIER WITH DAVID HOROWITZ

The Rockefellers
The Kennedys
The Fords
Destructive Generation

BY PETER COLLIER

When Shall They Rest?
Downriver

THE
FONDAS

A HOLLYWOOD DYNASTY

PETER COLLIER

G. P. PUTNAM'S SONS   NEW YORK

G. P. Putnam's Sons
Publishers Since 1838
200 Madison Avenue
New York, NY 10016

The author gratefully acknowledges permission to reprint the following:
Lyrics from "Fat Angel" by Donovan Leitch. Copyright © 1966, 1967 by
Donovan (Music) Ltd. All rights controlled by Peer International Corporation.
International copyright secured. All rights reserved. Used by permission.
Passage from F. Scott Fitzgerald letter. Excerpted with permission
of Charles Scribner's Sons, an imprint of Macmillan Publishing Company,
from *The Letters of F. Scott Fitzgerald,* edited by Andrew Turnbull.
Copyright © 1963 Frances Scott Fitzgerald Lanahan.

Library of Congress Cataloging-in-Publication Data

Collier, Peter.
The Fondas : a Hollywood dynasty / Peter Collier.
p.   cm.
Includes bibliographical references and index.
1. Fonda, Henry, 1905–1982. 2. Fonda, Jane, 1937– . 3. Fonda, Peter, 1940– .
4. Motion picture actors and actresses—United States—Biography. I. Title.
ISBN 0-399-13592-8
PN2285.C56   1991   90-46808   CIP
791.43′028′0922—dc20
[B]

Book design and composition by The Sarabande Press

Printed in the United States of America
1   2   3   4   5   6   7   8   9   10

This book is printed on acid-free paper.
∞

In memory of my mother, Doris Collier, who came to Hollywood to make a different, more artful life for her family

THE
FONDAS

GREENWICH, 1950

The death of Frances Fonda—and that is what her husband Henry always called it, a "death," not a suicide—was not really unexpected. The pretty forty-two-year-old onetime socialite had begun to walk in the deep shadows in the months since she had moved her children from the idyllic homestead in the Hollywood Hills to a rented house in Greenwich, Connecticut, so they could be with Henry, whose smash hit *Mister Roberts* was beginning its long Broadway run. As one family friend put it, "She had a strange look—faraway eyes and a fixed smile. It was the look of someone who has just been told the bad news."

At first a sense of displacement had affected them all. Jane, a scowling tomboy recently turned ten, refused to make friends, and eight-year-old Peter, already frail and difficult, had scrawled "I hate the East" on the wall of his new bedroom. But soon the local newspaper was reporting Jane's success staging pet shows with her old Hollywood friend Brooke Hayward, also living in Greenwich now, and, in smaller type, the honorable mention Peter had received for his achievement in art at the year-end ceremonies of his new school.

Only Frances was still disoriented. She had been born in the East and had relatives scattered throughout the area, but all her roots seemed to have been sheared off.

Those close to the Fondas knew that the unhappiness caused by the move east was only a symptom. The disease was her marriage, which had been slowly decaying since Henry returned from the Navy at the end of the war. Neither of them would admit it. In fact, Frances had come to Greenwich believing that they could start over, once they were away from Hollywood and its pressures. But from the moment of her arrival, the feeling was of an ending rather than a beginning. Always moody, Henry was openly resentful when he had to spend time with her and the children. For months they had been alone apart from each other; now they were alone together.

"Hank doesn't satisfy me sexually anymore," Frances sadly admitted to a friend soon after moving east, making it clear that the problem was that he lacked not the ability but the interest. In fact, while she withered from neglect, he was blooming. In the summer of 1949, after she had been in Greenwich about a year, he finally told her what she already suspected: that he had fallen in love with another woman. The object of his affection was Susan Blanchard, Oscar Hammerstein's stepdaughter, who, at twenty-one, was young enough to be *his* daughter. With that frigid midwestern honesty that charged his character off the screen as well as on, he told Frances that given what he was now experiencing with Susan, he wasn't sure he had ever really loved *her*. He moved out of the Greenwich house just before Christmas 1949 and announced his intention to divorce and remarry.

Frances vowed to win him back and for a week or so summoned up a brittle gaiety. But soon she sank back down into one of her manic troughs, saying sadly to a friend, "I can't fight this. Hank is not in love with a person. He's in love with youth. I am not youth. . . ." Her family and friends reassured her: She was still an attractive woman and would find love again. Frances didn't disagree with them, but they sometimes found her looking in the mirror, studying the image that stared back blankly at her as if it belonged to a familiar stranger. "Just look at me!" she said. "No one will want me again!" She began to worry that she might be going crazy.

The spring of 1950 was the worst time the Fondas could remember. Henry came up to Greenwich on the weekends to spend time with Jane and Peter, but these were silent, guilty outings that seemed grudging rather than special. Their afternoons at a local amusement park developed into awful homilies on the price of celebrity as Henry screamed obscenities at the autograph seekers and hustled the kids from one sheltered area to another.

At home it was worse. Jane and Peter were increasingly mothered by governesses and housekeepers and finally by their maternal grandmother as Frances gave herself over to psychotherapy, an activity that took all of her attention without cutting any of the pain.

Victimized by moods ranging from febrile optimism to mute despair, absent even when she was there, Frances finally allowed her mother to commit her to Craig House, a sanatorium in Beacon, New York, in the middle of the night on February 3. She received intensive psychiatric treatment over the next several weeks and appeared to improve, at times resembling once again the confident and vivacious woman who had captivated Henry Fonda almost fifteen years earlier. But the physician in charge of her case, Dr. Courtney Bennett, was worried by her violently shifting moods, which swung from giddy peaks of excitement to valleys of shadow. Fearing that she was suicidal, Bennett had her closely watched at the sanatorium, and in mid-March, when Frances arranged for a driver to take her home to see the children, the doctor insisted that a pair of nurses accompany her.

When she arrived home for what would be her last visit, Frances looked particularly radiant—hair lustrous, skin aglow, voice filled with fey animation. Jane saw her from an upstairs window. Later she admitted that she hadn't wanted to see or speak to her mother. Peter was with her and she forced him to hide too. He wanted to go to Frances, but Jane wouldn't let him budge during the time their mother was calling out for them.

Downstairs, Frances kept up the flow of small talk while calling the children, joking about the way her "keepers" followed her wherever she went in the house. Finally she darted into the bathroom, commenting archly as she locked the door, "At least I can go potty by myself." Alone at last, she took a double-edged razor blade from the medicine cabinet and hid it in the backing of a framed photograph of Jane and Peter that she brought out of the bathroom with her; she said she wanted to take the photograph to Craig House and put it on her nightstand there as a reminder of the normal life she would soon resume. Once again she called out for the children. When they failed to answer, she left, Jane watching silently from the corner of an upstairs window.

On April 14, Frances Fonda's forty-second birthday, a Craig House nurse named Anne Grey entered her room at seven in the morning with the usual wake-up glass of orange juice. The patient was not there. The nurse looked around and saw a note propped on the dresser: "Mrs. Grey, do not go into the bathroom, but call for Dr. Bennett."

The doctor came running to the room. When he opened the bathroom door, he found Frances splayed out on the floor in a pool of blood. She had inserted the razor blade into the flesh below her ear and pulled it hard across her throat, opening a wound that gaped like a second mouth. Feeling only the suspicion of a pulse, Bennett quickly packed towels around her throat in an attempt to control the bleeding. He tried to revive her, but it was too late.

Henry was in New York about to go to a publicity interview when Sophie Seymour called with the news. He choked out words of shock and pain, and then caught a train from New York. When he arrived, he and Frances's mother arranged for a hurried funeral service that afternoon at a local mortuary. They agreed that they would be the only mourners. Later that afternoon, while her body was being cremated, the children were told Frances had died of a heart attack.

She was gone, vanished almost without leaving a trace. The family photographs of her disappeared from the mantel. It was almost as if she had never lived.

In the years to come, this death would be one of those things not to be discussed around the Fondas. Yet it was always a defining point in their lives—the event that, even more than Henry's celebrity, made them different from other people; the dagger at the heart of their relationship which each of them would, at various times, twist sadistically and ineffectually try to withdraw. And as this family of a star became a family of stars with unparalleled impact not just on American film but on American culture as well, those who knew the Fondas best were aware that the forlorn and unappeased ghost of the dead wife and mother remained an audience of one in the projection room of their lives, watching the outtakes nobody else could see.

I

I hope you won't be disappointed. You see, I'm not a very interesting person. I haven't ever done anything except be other people. I ain't really Henry Fonda! Nobody could be. Nobody could have that much integrity.

—Henry Fonda

ONE

|||||||||||||||||||||||||||||||||||

Henry Fonda was the sort of man who always prided himself on plain speaking and on keeping his ego on a short string. To be an actor, he once said, was no different from being a butcher or bricklayer. Yet he always remembered the exact moment he embraced his destiny. It was a warm summer evening in 1926 and he was just twenty-one; he had flunked out of the University of Minnesota a few months earlier and returned home to Omaha, Nebraska, ready to fit himself into the conservative expectations that had enfolded his family for generations. He had moved back in with his parents and had found a good job with a local business. He was only a credit clerk, but his boss told him that if he applied himself in the years ahead there were prospects for advancement.

Then a friend suggested that he while away his after hours by getting involved in the local community theater. Partly out of boredom, but also believing that the stage might help him combat his almost pathological shyness, Henry became part of the Omaha Community Playhouse, doing everything from set design to ticket sales. Sometimes he rehearsed with the other actors. He was soon stagestruck, although he didn't admit it to his mother and father or his boss.

Impressed by his tongue-tied good looks and the candor that

shone through his laconic self-effacement, the director of the playhouse, who had used Henry in minor roles, finally asked whether he would like to play the lead in *Merton of the Movies,* a popular play about a young grocery clerk in a midwestern town who dreams of being an actor, goes to Hollywood, and blunders onto the set of a director who sees greatness in his youth and naiveté and makes him a star. *Merton* was the life story he wanted to have. Henry jumped at the opportunity.

On opening night he worried that he might be sick. But when he stepped onto the stage, he entered a special zone of clarity. There was an eerie calm within the spotlight; in playing his character, he felt he was something more than himself.

Fonda never forgot the climactic moment of the play—the scene in which Merton kneels on the floor in front of his cot at the rear of the grocery store where he works. "Oh, God," he prays. "Make me a good movie actor! Make me one of the best! For Jesus' sake, amen." As he said the words, words he knew were not yet bound in a polished delivery or a commanding stage presence, he was moved by the spectacle of his own performance. The skin prickled at the back of his neck. He suddenly felt "more real" than he had at any other time in his life. He was speaking for himself as well as Merton. At that moment he knew he would have to be an actor, whatever the costs.

Later on, after his prayers had been answered and he had discovered the truth of Oscar Wilde's maxim that there are two types of tragedy in life, not getting what you want and getting it, this scene would acquire an almost mythic weight in his memory. But although he might have felt like Faust as his life became engulfed in tragic complexity later on, Fonda had not made a devil's bargain at the age of twenty-one. In deciding to be an actor, he wasn't asking for fame and riches, but simply for a release from the monotony he feared was not only around him but inside him as well.

Henry's life had hardly been unpleasant up to then. On the contrary, his boyhood had been part of a midwestern idyll, filled with the Norman Rockwell images that would soon define American middle-class consciousness.

Every Sunday afternoon, Henry's father brought their Hupmobile up alongside the house, removed the engine, and cleaned it in the basement "laboratory" he maintained in the tradition of Henry Ford and other amateur inventors of the Midwest. The car took them ice-skating in the winter and on picnics in the summer. Often it was parked right next to the vacant lot where the Fondas' solitary cow grazed.

Henry swam naked in the Omaha sand pits with his friends. They built clubhouses with lumber pinched from construction sites. He worked for two dollars a week during the summer and spent the money he made watching Charlie Chaplin, William S. Hart, and other heroes flicker through one-reelers at the local arcades.

He was one of the gang, yet he looked different from the robust, towheaded boys he grew up with. He was exotic by comparison, with slate-blue eyes, shiny black hair, and a mouth that seemed always to be chewing on puzzlement. His father, keeper of the family genealogy, told him the look came from northern Italian forebears who had migrated to Holland after being on the losing side of a local religious war during the Renaissance.

But the family had actually been in America longer than many who looked more typically American than they did. An ancestor named Jellis Fonda had arrived in New Amsterdam in 1642. One of his great-grandsons, Douw Fonda, had migrated into the wilds of what was now northern New York State in search of open land and settled on a spot by the Mohawk River; he gave the little town that grew up around him his family name.

During the Revolution, Fonda, New York, was sacked by the Indians who sided with the British. Douw was killed and scalped during the skirmish. His widow, Peggy, left to run the gristmill of the little town by herself, would not receive her reward until some two hundred years later, when her descendant Jane would pluck her out of the family tree in press interviews as an example of the fortitude of female Fondas.

By the early 1800s, as the social structure of upstate New York began to congeal, members of the family left the town of Fonda to seek their fortune beyond the Mississippi. One of them settled in Nebraska and began producing solid citizens such as Henry's father, William Brace Fonda, a hardworking printer who started his own business shortly after marrying a pretty, strong-willed young woman named Herberta Jaynes.

Henry was born in Grand Island, Nebraska, on May 16, 1905, the same year that the nickelodeon, early home of the moving picture, made its appearance in arcades around America. When he was six months old, his father moved the family to Omaha, where they would live in a succession of homes reflecting their growing affluence. They finally came to rest in a large white clapboard in one of the city's better neighborhoods. By then, Henry had two younger sisters, Harriet and Jayne, who doted on him.

He remembered his mother as an "angelic" woman formed by her Christian Science faith. There were never doctors in the household. When someone was sick, Herberta would call her mother, and "Grammy," as Henry and his sisters called her, a first reader and a practitioner in the Church, would come to the house and try to stage a triumph of mind over whatever was the matter.

Henry was more ambivalent about his father, a strict and self-contained man with an eccentric streak that made him one of the few liberal Democrats in town. Son of a man who had run away from home at the age of seventeen to fight with the Union forces in the Civil War, William Fonda did not give emotion easily. But Henry had trouble condemning him for this, because it was a trait he had inherited. He had also inherited other aspects of his father's character and, almost uncannily, his looks as well. Throughout his life he would sometimes glimpse a slice of his face in a mirror and think to himself, "That's my father!"

Much later, after he was a success, Henry was asked to make a personal contribution to a selection of readings about fathers. He said: "Fathers are men who look eight feet tall and walk with giant steps. I knew my father was the best kite flyer that ever lived." Henry would often fly kites with his friend Jimmy Stewart and feel inferior to William Fonda. He would also wish, as his woes with women deepened, that he had inherited his father's knack for marriage. He would feel measured and wanting by vivid memories of William and Herberta going out for ice cream sodas on warm nights and holding hands as they returned in lockstep, their shoes beating out a syncopated rhythm on the wooden planks of the sidewalks below his bedroom window.

Although small for his age until his last year of high school, when he shot up to his full height of slightly more than six feet, Henry was a good athlete. He was a Boy Scout. He passed his YMCA Bible study examination with honors. He got in one fight that he could remember, and after unexpectedly beating a tough Irish kid who had tormented him, he was carried home in triumph on the shoulders of his friends and lionized for days after by his sisters.

But as a result of his almost willful innocence, he was a failure with girls. Even after he began to fill out and to acquire his dark good looks, Henry was still ill at ease. His father drove him on his first date. Henry escorted the girl from her house, put her in the backseat of the car, and then tried to get in front, but he couldn't open the door because William Fonda was holding it shut to force him to sit with the girl. So he got into the backseat and huddled miserably in one corner. His uneasiness with women persisted long after his friends got him drunk on Prohibition bathtub beer and spent two dollars to rid him of his virginity at a local bordello; he always recalled the act as "repulsive."

Two events in particular stood out in the flat prairie sameness of his early life and seem to summarize the competing forces he felt were struggling for dominance in his character.

The first occurred when he was five years old. His mother came into his bedroom in the middle of the night and woke him. Figuring Henry's two sisters were too young to understand, she took her eldest child downstairs and then out the front door. As he stood shivering on the porch, she pointed up at a peculiar brightness lighting the darkness, almost as if fairy dust had been sprinkled at the bottom edge of the sky. It was Halley's comet. Henry had been hearing about it for weeks. Many people in town feared it and were stuffing towels under their doorjambs for fear that its tail would lash the earth with poison gases when it drew near. But here was his mother pointing out the veil of brilliance clinging to the horizon, laughing with delight and talking about it as if it were for him alone. "It comes once in a lifetime," his mother said.

The other event occurred when Henry was fourteen, on an evening when the mood at the dinner table had been somber be-cause of the news that a black man had been arrested that morning on a charge of raping a white woman. After the family finished eating, William told Henry to come with him. They got into the car and drove to the Fonda print shop, which was on the second floor of a large brick building in the center of Omaha. The smell of ink and solvent was heavy in the air, and an eerie stillness filled the vacuum left when the presses were shut down.

His father beckoned Henry to the window. Down below, an angry mob was surging against a thin line of policemen, some of them on horseback. Finally a group broke through and charged the city jail. They reappeared a short time later with the struggling black man, looped a rope over a lamppost, and hung the man without ceremony. While his feet still danced in the air they shot him repeatedly; then they cut his body down, hitched it to the back of a car, and dragged it all over town.

When Henry looked back on these events, unrelated except in his imagination, they seemed to be portents of the alternating patterns of light and darkness in his life—a life at which he often felt more a spectator than a participant. These events expressed the soft side of his mother and the harder side of his father, which would always be at war in him, a clash John Steinbeck, who became a friend, later tried to define: "Henry is a man reaching but unreachable, gentle but capable of sudden wild and dangerous violence. His face is a picture of opposites in conflict."

Straining only mildly against what seemed to be the conservative fate awaiting him, Henry went to the University of Minnesota instead of a school in Nebraska. He said he wanted to study journalism, but what he really wanted was to get away from Omaha for a while. His father sent an occasional ten dollars, for which Henry had to make a precise accounting. For the week of January 11 to January 17, 1925, for instance, he showed cash on hand of $9.58 on Monday and 95 cents on Sunday, having made expenditures on the intervening days for carfare, string for his ukelele, shoes, and history maps.

What he got from home was not enough to support him, and thus he got a job working with settlement youths, teaching them sports and keeping them so busy that they would stay out of trouble. He worked long hours, and there was little time left for school. He had a steady girlfriend, whom he saw on weekends. Later he admitted that although he went with her for two years, he never kissed her.

By the end of his sophomore year, he was no longer able to keep up with his schoolwork. He sat in a daze when the bluebooks were handed out for final exams. He had an unexplored artistic ability, and while the other students intensely scribbled answers, he drew pictures. He knew he had flunked out before the letter from the dean arrived.

He returned to Omaha not so much in disgrace as in uncertainty about what came next. At the end of a summer he had spent loafing, Dorothy Brando, a Christian Science friend of his mother's, called him. Mother of an infant son named Marlon, she was one of the founders of the Omaha Community Playhouse. She told Henry that the theater needed a juvenile for a play it was doing, Philip Barry's *You and I*. He agreed to try out for the role. He was so naive about the theater that when he auditioned he read the name of the character and the stage directions on the script as well as the dialogue.

Henry got the part and immediately developed cold feet. He hardly looked up during rehearsals; he mumbled. Yet there was an odd charge to acting that excited him. In an awkward attempt to describe the sensation, he said it was like playing cops and robbers: the thrill of pure make-believe; an escape.

You and I ran for about a week. But Henry stayed around for the rest of the fall season as a volunteer. Then came the inevitable talk with his father in which William Fonda told him it was time to get his life on schedule. Henry got a job with the Retail Credit Agency at $30 a week. He thought it would at least be interesting to do credit checks on people—a kind of detective work. But his job consisted of sitting in the office filing index cards. One day a call came from a director at the Community Playhouse who said the company had decided to open the new season with *Merton of the Movies*. Henry told his parents he'd been offered the lead.

"Absolutely not!" his father exploded. "You're not going to sacrifice your job for some make-believe world."

Henry said he would do both.

"You can't," William Fonda continued. "In no way can you do justice to both of these things. You've got a good job and a real chance for a future in business. . . ."

Henry threatened to move out to the YMCA, defying his father for the first time either of them could remember. Before the confrontation went further, his mother intervened and negotiated a truce. And so Henry would get up early and go to his job, and after quitting time grab a bite of dinner and go directly to rehearsal. He didn't talk to his father for weeks and hardly saw his mother and sisters.

Finally it was opening night. His family went to see him as Merton and afterward his mother and sisters threw a little party of celebration. His father held himself aloof in his favorite armchair, screened off from Henry and the Fonda women by a newspaper. Amid all of the congratulations, Henry's sister Harriet entered a criticism: "There was one scene in which I thought you didn't quite . . ." Before she could finish, William Fonda lowered the paper and spoke from across the room: "Shut up! He was perfect!"

Henry remembered it as the best review he ever got. Yet he had gone beyond needing his father's validation. Something had happened during his preparation for the role of Merton. It had occurred to him during the rehearsals, as he later said, when he had had a sudden epiphany. Acting was escaping a self you didn't particularly like and feared was boring; acting was creating other selves that you could live with.

Not long after his triumph as Merton, Henry received a call from a wealthy Omaha woman, Mrs. Hunter Scott. Her son, Hunter Jr., was about to leave Princeton after a brief and undistinguished career there. She didn't want him to drive back to Nebraska by himself and asked Fonda, whose family she knew, to go to New Jersey by train and accompany him on the trip back. As enticement, she offered to pay for a week in New York, including tickets to all the Broadway shows he wanted to see.

Henry immediately went into the office of his supervisor at Retail

Credit: "Sir, I've come to give notice. The business world is not for me."

His boss tried to dissuade him by offering a promotion and the prospect of someday heading a Retail Credit office of his own.

Henry was firm. "Thank you. Sounds very tempting, but I've made up my mind."

He landed on the Great White Way in the middle of an extraordinary season. Plays such as *The Front Page, Coquette,* and *The Constant Wife* were all playing at the same time. Henry saw them all, but since he was a populist liberal like his father, his imagination was particularly seized by *Gods of the Lightning,* a play about Sacco and Vanzetti. The feeling it created was so real that he came out of the theater scowling like a syndicalist at the uncomprehending beat cop who passed him on the street. On the way back to his hotel he thought about the spell he had been under and about the difference between an actor who the audience knows is acting and one who makes the audience forget. He uttered an addendum in his own voice to the prayer he had spoken as Merton of the Movies: "Please, God, don't let the wheels show!"

At the end of the week, Hunter Scott, Jr., picked Henry up in front of his hotel. There was a woman named Mrs. Davis in the car, along with her two teenaged daughters. The older one, Bobbi, was already pinned to Hunter, and so Henry became her sister's escort. They all drove to Princeton for one last evening before heading back to Omaha. When they had a moment alone, Hunter made a friendly wager with Fonda about which of them would get more kisses. He then convinced Mrs. Davis to let him and Henry show her daughters Princeton stadium by moonlight.

Left by himself with the younger sister, Fonda gave her a quick peck on the lips. The next morning, the girls left before he got up, but there was a note waiting for him: "I've told my mother about our lovely experience together in the moonlight. She will announce the engagement when we get home." It was signed "Bette Davis." When

Henry met her again a decade later in Hollywood on the set of *Jezebel,* he told her how he had hurried back to Omaha after reading the note, for fear that she would return to carry out the threat.

At home again, he got a job as an assistant director at the Community Playhouse. Then he heard that the actor George Billings, whose one-man show in which he played Abraham Lincoln toured country fairs and civic meetings, was now looking for a young actor to play Lincoln's secretary, John Hay. Fonda took the role and toured with Billings until he had saved enough money to go east again for summer stock.

He arrived at Cape Cod, first stopping in Provincetown, which Eugene O'Neill had made the center of avant-garde American drama. Wherever he went he was told the same thing: The plays being performed that summer had been cast weeks earlier in New York. Henry worked his way down the Cape from playhouse to playhouse. In Falmouth he took in a play put on by a group called the University Players and starring a Princeton undergraduate, Joshua Logan. After the performance, Fonda went backstage. He told Logan that he had appreciated the humor in the play. After talking about comedy for a few minutes, Henry gathered enough confidence to give Logan a look at a character he had conceived, "Elmer," a ten-year-old idiot boy who shyly imitated fish by wiggling his fingers. On the basis of this pantomime, Logan invited Fonda to join the troupe, offering him five dollars a week and room and board.

Over the four years of its existence, the University Players would introduce several actors, in addition to Fonda and Logan, who would go on to have a significant impact on American theater— figures such as Margaret Sullavan, Mildred Natwick, Myron Mc- Cormick, and Jimmy Stewart. But that summer of 1928 they were all still unknowns in plays that were, for the most part, equally obscure. Henry's first role, for instance, was as an Italian nobleman in *The Jest.* It turned out to be a disaster. As Logan later said, "When the suave Italian spoke with a nasal Omaha whine and moved like a human angle iron, we all wondered what we had gotten ourselves into." But Henry made it up in the next work, *Is Zat So?*, in which he played an over-the-hill boxer. He practiced fighting with another actor for a week in matches so realistic there were black eyes and bloody noses; the cops were even called one afternoon when the two actors were rehearsing in the alley outside the theater. A woman who reviewed the performance wrote: "The fight, to female inexperience, was thrilling." Logan gave an even better review in words that captured what would become Fonda's special power as an actor: "He wiped us all off the floor simply by seeming to do nothing."

It was a summer of discovery in which Henry struggled constantly against the persona of midwestern hayseed. In one incident that amused some of the more sophisticated University Players, he told about taking a young woman out on a date in her car and, in the middle of what was then called heavy petting, excusing himself, getting out of the car, and relieving himself of beer he'd drunk, by digging a shallow hole and lying down on top of it. Another contretemps occurred with a stage manager who showered him with attention. As Delos Smith, a member of the Players, recalls, "Henry was very flattered. Then one night he was walking back to the boardinghouse and this fellow followed him and tried to hug him. Henry was amazed."

After the summer was over, Henry went to New York, rented a run-down apartment, and began to pound the streets for work, becoming in the process, as Josh Logan said, the best-known unknown actor in New York. The casting secretaries got to know him so well that when he showed up they would look up and smile sympathetically before he even asked and say, "Nothing, Hank."

He finally got a job playing Sir Andrew Aguecheek in *Twelfth Night* in a children's theater in Washington, D.C. When he finished and returned to New York with about $200 in savings, he found that his landlord was about to kick out the friend to whom he'd sublet his apartment because of his nonpayment of rent. "It took every penny I had to get it out of hock," he recalled later. "My friend stayed on with me, and between us we cleaned out everything in the pantry. Then, during the next week, we didn't eat anything. Not *anything!* We drank water. That's all. Later on we'd be able to pick up a nickel once in a while and when we got one we'd spend it on rice—five cents' worth of rice swells up into quite a good-sized dish."

He didn't write home for help, because he figured that he had made a break and was on his own. "I was perfectly capable of taking care of myself, and if I did it so badly that I had to starve in the process, then that was no worry of the folks'."

When he returned to the University Players the next summer, there was someone new in the cast—a sparky strawberry-blonde from Virginia named Margaret Sullavan, known as Peggy. Descended from a genteel southern family, Sullavan had taken up acting just out of high school to escape the stultifying atmosphere of the South and the constricting propriety of her parents. The role in life she thought she was playing was that of Scarlett O'Hara, but it was really closer to Zelda Fitzgerald. A slightly out-of-kilter southern belle, the husky-voiced Sullavan had a deep need to be the center of attention, especially male attention. Her brittle wit was an effective weapon in her flirtations, but so sharp that it hurt when relationships went past the fencing stage. Fiercely ambitious, she announced to University Players director Charles Leatherbee, "By the time I'm thirty-five, I will have a million dollars, five children, and I will have starred on Broadway." Except for the fact that she had only three children, her prediction came true.

Henry had actually already met Sullavan. The previous year, while performing in *Twelfth Night,* he had traveled to Cambridge, Massachusetts, to help out a friend in the Harvard Dramatic Club who was putting on a musical and couldn't find an undergraduate to perform in a comedy walk-on scene. The bit part called for Fonda to walk across the stage in one direction while a girl walked across in another. As they passed he gave a lewd double-take; she paused long enough to slap him and then kept on walking. Sullavan, as the girl, delivered a rock-hard slap every time in rehearsal and performance. As Fonda commented later, "You would have thought I could only say, 'Who is this bitch? Get her out of my sight.' But it didn't work that way, see. She intrigued me."

Getting to know her better now, Henry was even more intrigued. Her irrepressible sense of fun contrasted with his own saturnine character. (He once said that she was the sort of person who, if she saw a water pistol, could not keep herself from grabbing it and shooting anyone near her.) Moreover, she was the first person he had met who was always onstage even when there was no play being performed. She had an intensity that altered the shape of time. Henry fell in love with her almost immediately. He understood that there was a touch of danger in her volatility—he described her to one of his sisters as "cream and sugar on a bed of hot ashes"—but when he was with her he felt more charming and interesting himself.

She was the first woman with whom he'd had a real physical relationship. But there was also the innocence of first love. People close to the University Players remembered the two of them as always together that summer, engaged in verbal duels like Beatrice and Benedict, or in slapstick acts in which they walked on their hands. Often they could be found on the steps of the box office just as the audience was beginning to assemble, Henry cross-legged and expressionless, Sullavan sitting atop his shoulders with her feet crossed under his chin. When the bell rang indicating that there were fifteen minutes until curtain, they would disentangle themselves and, laughing wildly, dash into their dressing rooms.

When the summer ended, Sullavan followed Henry back to New York. But she was further along in her career than he, and ready for a breakthrough. It came one afternoon in an interview with theatrical impresario Lee Shubert. She was sick with a cold, but Shubert was charmed anyhow. After a few minutes of conversation he told her that she was hired.

"What do you mean, hired? You haven't heard me read a part."

"You have a voice like Helen Morgan," Shubert said, "a voice like Ethel Barrymore."

"What I have is a bad case of laryngitis," she replied.

But Shubert wouldn't take no for an answer. He put her in the lead of *A Modern Virgin,* for which she won rave reviews.

Sullavan's success made Henry only more conscious of his empty prospects. The best offer he had was from the Omaha Community Playhouse for a round-trip ticket home and back and a starring role in one of its productions.

Coming into Nebraska by train, he was struck by how different things looked. In part it was the change within himself. But there was also the Depression. Storefronts were boarded up; farm machines were sequestered in repossession yards. He discovered that it was only the need for foreclosure notices that kept his father's printing business afloat.

There was an aftershock in their unresolved struggle when William Fonda asked him the obvious question: What was he going to do with his life? Henry replied, "I don't suppose I'll ever make a fortune, Dad, but things aren't bad enough to give up. I keep thinking, It's just around the corner, then it's going to happen."

After completing his stint as "guest celebrity" starring in the Community Players' version of J. M. Barrie's *A Kiss for Cinderella,* Henry used the other half of his round-trip ticket and left Omaha for good.

In the summer of 1931 he was in Cape Cod again with the University Players. When Sullavan's run on Broadway was finished, she arranged to rejoin the group too. She staged a grand entrance in the middle of a rehearsal. Henry, who had grown a mustache for one of his roles, was up in the rafters fixing the curtain.

"Hi," he called down.

She glanced up imperiously, said, "Fonda, shave off that damned mustache," and kept on walking.

They immediately picked up their courtship and took it to a new level of bravura. Being with Peggy made Henry do things that didn't seem part of his staid and stoical nature. Once, actor Cesar Romero, accompanied by his mother, came to meet Henry and Peggy backstage. Romero was talking to Sullavan when he heard his mother scream. He ran to her and asked what was wrong. She said that Fonda had been walking on the rafters and had tripped and somersaulted down. Just then, Fonda, who had taken the fall on purpose and landed on his feet, came walking over, looking at Sullavan with a smile on his face.

As one friend remembered later on, "The two of them fought and made up. They bought marriage licenses and tore them up. They wouldn't be speaking to each other in the wings, but they couldn't wait to get onstage and play their love scenes." Sullavan once threw a pudding in Fonda's face and stormed out of the company's rooming house; she crossed the sand of the beach and plunged melodramatically into the ocean fully clothed; Henry followed, wiping the pudding off his face as he walked into the water to rescue her.

Late in the fall they reached a critical stage where they had to make a decision about their future. A reporter who had seen their names in a marriage-license list in the Baltimore *Post* burst upon them at breakfast in the residential hotel where they were staying and demanded further details, and found himself in a scene right out of the zany domestic comedies of the day.

"What! Marry Fonda?" Sullavan cried. "Just look at him! Who'd want to marry him?" Then she flounced out of the room, with Henry behind. When she heard one of the other players tell the reporter that they had also gotten a license in Manhattan, Sullavan stuck her head in the room: "That's it. We're collecting them. We got one from New York and now we've got one from Baltimore. After we get some from a few more cities, we'll have quite a collection."

A few days later, on Christmas morning, they were married at the gloomy Kiernan Hotel in Baltimore. They were supposed to go off for their honeymoon in a used Stutz Bearcat Fonda had bought for the occasion, but the car got only two blocks before succumbing to a coughing fit. The newlyweds walked back to the hotel and moved into Henry's old room.

That spring they went to New York to be closer to Broadway. The arguments continued, now with a sense of claustral reality because they were married. Sullavan's temper could flare on any topic: the food they ate, her wardrobe, the parts they tried out for. To survive, Fonda fought back, point by point. After three months, he moved out of their tiny garden apartment in Greenwich Village and got his own room for what he thought would be a cooling-off period before they reconciled. One afternoon Fonda was standing outside a theatrical agent's office waiting for an appointment when he overheard the conversation of two other actors who didn't know who he was. One was asking the other if he'd heard about the torrid affair producer Jed Harris was having with Margaret Sullavan. As Fonda described it later, hearing this was like being hit in the stomach.

The bottom had dropped out of his life. He couldn't stay in his room. He walked aimlessly through the Village, his path inevitably leading to the apartment he and Sullavan had shared. He watched Harris go in and, leaning on a fence, waited hours for him to leave. But then the lights went out, the producer still inside. Fonda stood wiping the tears off his face, feeling more betrayed, rejected, and alone than ever before in his life.

Even before he filed for divorce, something had changed in Henry. It was as if his youth were over, the period in his life when he was still trying on personalities and wondering what he would be.

He pulled back into himself and, some felt, never really came out again. As Peter said later of his father, "His first marriage broke his heart so badly that he never recovered." It was the first in a long series of disasters with women that defined Henry Fonda's life.

Down and out in New York, Henry hit bottom in June 1932. His place in the University Players had been taken by a gangly architecture student from Princeton named James Stewart, who projected some of the same midwestern innocence as Fonda. The two actors quickly became friends. Elsewhere, summer stock was filled. Henry was reduced to working as a handyman in a theater in Maine; it was the same type of job he'd had with the Omaha Community Playhouse when he was younger. Noting his artistic talents in painting backdrops, people advised him to abandon acting and take up set design. For a time he considered it.

In the fall he returned to New York to live with Josh Logan, Myron McCormick, and Jimmy Stewart in a two-bedroom apartment on East 63rd Street, up the street from where gangster Legs Diamond was shot. The four called their place "Casa Gangrene," and all of them were desperately poor and did whatever was necessary to survive. On one occasion Fonda got Stewart to play his accordion on a Manhattan street corner while he passed a hat among those who had gathered to listen.

Yet through it all, Fonda's belief never wavered. He wrote his worried mother: "Don't despair. I have a feeling success is going to happen tomorrow." Indeed, his break came in 1934, just after the first of the year, when producer Leonard Sillman called him for an audition for a musical revue. Asked if he could sing, Fonda said no. Could he dance? No. What could he do? Fonda said he could do an imitation of babies aged one week to one year. It was one of his deadpan acts, like that of Elmer, the ten-year-old idiot boy who did wiggling fishes. The baby act left Sillman in stitches, and he hired

Henry for a revue to be called *New Faces,* which would costar another unknown, Imogene Coca. The show earned rave reviews, which Fonda carefully clipped and sent back to Omaha, along with news that he was now making $100 a week.

Henry signed on with Leland Hayward, a dashing young Ivy Leaguer who had become the most important theatrical agent in the country and who already represented established stars including Garbo and Astaire, as well as younger ones such as Margaret Sullavan. Hayward telegraphed Fonda that he wanted him in movies. Fonda telegraphed a one-word response: "No." Hayward cabled him again: "It won't cost you anything. I'll pay for your goddamned airplane fare and your hotel. . . . Don't be an idiot." Fonda gave in, and Hayward was waiting for him when he arrived from New York at the Burbank airport. They drove through the make-believe of Hollywood on the way to a suite Hayward had reserved at the Beverly Wilshire Hotel.

Producer Walter Wanger showed up. When Fonda left the room, Hayward browbeat Wanger into agreeing to sign him to a contract. "It's settled, then, isn't it?" Wanger said to Fonda when he came back in. "We'll start you at a thousand a week." Henry weakly shook his hand, incredulous at what he was hearing. After Wanger had left, he eyed Hayward suspiciously and made a comment that was quintessentially Fonda: "There's something fishy."

Things were beginning to happen quickly for him. Back in New York, the producer of a big new Broadway play, *The Farmer Takes a Wife,* offered Henry the leading role. Midway through the run, Wanger told him he had "loaned" him to 20th Century–Fox for the film version of the play at $5,000 a week; he would split the surplus with Fonda after paying him his $1,000 guarantee.

But not everything that happened was good. Herberta Fonda had been diagnosed as having a blood clot in her leg. Before Henry could visit his mother, William Fonda telegraphed the bad news: the clot had traveled to her heart and she had died. Henry knew that it was

Herberta's perseverance and denial of adversity, which he had inherited in good measure, that had seen him through. At his low point, after the breakup of his marriage with Sullavan, he had been aimlessly walking the streets of New York when he passed a Christian Science reading room. He had remembered his mother and her faith, and had gone in and sat for a couple of hours. The mood of bleak despair passed and he came out ready to pick up the challenges of his life once more. Now he was unable to share his triumph with her.

Henry traveled to Hollywood by train and began filming *The Farmer Takes a Wife* under the direction of Victor Fleming. After a few days on the set, Fleming took him aside and told him that he was mugging to the camera. Fonda was insulted. Then Fleming explained that he was still performing as if he were onstage—playing to the back row and balcony. Henry got the message. He summarized the lesson later: "No sense in using too much voice, and you don't need any more expression on your face than you'd use in everyday life." He already had a perfect film look—a steep jaw with a downturned mouth that could, when breaking into a grin, brilliantly contradict its own hint of gloom; eyes given intensity by a deep stare. Combined with these looks was an obdurate, aggressive shyness and a penchant for understatement that would make him one of the great film actors.

Henry saw a sneak preview of *Farmer* in Sacramento, where he was already on location for his second movie, *Way Down East*. He recalled the moment later: "Eventually this thing comes on the screen and it's me and I'm sliding down in my chair. Nobody knew I was there and I didn't want anybody to."

When he learned that his father was suffering from kidney trouble, Henry arranged for Fox to screen *Farmer* for him in Omaha. Afterward he and his father talked for a while. William spoke about getting well, and since he was only fifty-five, the prospects seemed good. He told Henry that after his health improved he'd like to get out of the printing business and buy some property on the edge of town and raise chickens. Henry said, "Dad, that's what'll happen. I'll set it up for you." He went off to New York thinking that setting up a chicken ranch together was a way to heal the wounds that still marked their relationship. Three weeks later his father was dead.

TWO

By the time Henry learned not to mug before the camera, the film industry had changed considerably from the days when he was a boy peering into nickelodeons. Revolutionized by *The Birth of a Nation,* the epic twelve-reeler that grossed $50 million on its first run across the country, the film industry had grown up practically overnight. The 1920s had been a period of shakeout and consolidation, as the great studios emerged to take over from the small-time operators who had founded the industry. Movie palaces like the Orpheum in Los Angeles and the Strand in New York replaced the converted barns and auditoriums where the first films had flickered onto bedsheets. A new generation of stars was born.

Since Cecil B. DeMille traveled there in 1913 to make *The Squaw Man,* Hollywood had been the capital of the new empire. It was the center of an industry; it was also another country, a never-never land populated by an overnight nobility. In addition to providing cheap land and a mild year-round climate, Hollywood was an open society. There was no encumbering past, only an undiscovered future. It was possible for would-be stars to change their names and personalities, even their faces, enter the Dream Machine of Hollywood and emerge born again. In Hollywood it was possible to go directly to the top of a social ladder whose rungs had not yet been permanently arranged.

Joseph P. Kennedy and others might dismiss the Hollywood moguls as "a bunch of furriers," but the immigrant Jews who built the great studios saw in the new industry not only a source of wealth, power, and social mobility but also a way of demonstrating fealty to their adopted homeland. The vision of America that emerged from Hollywood was of a utopia. Movies were not a mirror held up to reality, but a screen onto which was projected a national fantasy created by men such as Louis B. Mayer, so fiercely patriotic that he took July 4 as his birthday when he arrived from Russia. Mayer had made MGM the archetypal studio of the thirties, producing films that reassured the nation in the middle of hard times and fashioning a compelling ideology based on personal virtue, the sanctity of family, and the importance of loyalty and tradition. For Mayer, home was Judy Garland and Mickey Rooney singing and dancing behind the white picket fences of the middle America he helped create.

By the middle of the Depression, however, the authority of men like Mayer was being challenged by the campaign of Upton Sinclair. The socialist author of *The Jungle* and other muckraking works had joined the Democratic Party so that he could run for governor as head of a movement he called End Poverty in California. The EPIC platform was more radical than the New Deal (although critics said that the acronym stood for "Empty Promises in California") and was supported by fledgling unions in Hollywood. Studio chiefs were thus doubly anxious to defeat Sinclair because of what they regarded as his un-American political views.

Mayer commanded every employee at MGM making over $100 a week to contribute a day's pay to the campaign against Sinclair, and only a few (James Cagney, Charlie Chaplin, Jean Harlow) refused. Other studio moguls joined with him in threatening to close down if Sinclair were elected. They used their medium to work against him, filming fake newsreels in which well-dressed WASPs spoke favorably of the incumbent, Governor Robert Merriam, and criminal-looking extras speaking in staged Slavic accents endorsed the EPIC candidate. Hollywood's resident intellectual and eventual martyr, Irving Thalberg, was one of those who drafted the film industry's assault on Sinclair, which proved decisive in the November election. "Nothing is unfair in politics," Thalberg said. "We could sit down here and figure dirty things all night and every one of them would be all right in a political campaign."

When Henry arrived in town early in 1935, this bruising struggle was just ending. Hollywood was denying the social dislocation of the Depression with utopian fables and screwball comedies, and the movies were being carried by female stars. Shirley Temple was number one at the box office. But there were others—Garbo, Lombard, Harlow, and even Margaret Sullavan, who had established a reputation for her saucy pronouncements as well as her witty screen portrayals. ("If Katharine Hepburn and I could have our way," she told one writer, "we'd strip this town of its silly sham.")

Fonda arrived as a man without an image. He found that the creation of his public personality was undertaken by the publicists of Walter Wanger. Even when he was not acting, he had to act like a star. Once he was assigned to accompany Marlene Dietrich to a movie premiere. He drove to her place in a Ford he had bought secondhand, and waited nervously in her hallway for her to appear. When she did, it was a grand entrance down a spiral staircase. She spurned his Ford and insisted instead on going in her chauffeured limousine. Henry said only a small mouthful of words to her the entire evening, but he walked beside Dietrich down a corridor of popping flash bulbs on the way to the theater. That was what counted.

His friend Jimmy Stewart had signed a contract with MGM, and when he arrived in Hollywood they took a place together, a sprawling Spanish-style ranch house in Brentwood next door to Greta Garbo. Orson Welles met them at this time and told a friend, "I thought these two guys were either fooling everyone and having the hottest affair in Hollywood or were the two straightest human beings I ever met in my life. I came to the conclusion that they were the two straightest human beings I'd ever met in my life."

Often Fonda and Stewart spent evenings at home exchanging monosyllables as they pursued their favorite hobby, building model airplanes. But they also romanced their share of starlets. On one memorable occasion they invited Humphrey Bogart to one of their little parties, provided him with a girl, and then disappeared into separate bedrooms. After the evening was over and they returned from taking the girls home, Fonda and Stewart noticed that Bogart seemed depressed. They asked if he'd been disappointed, and he shook his head vigorously: "Anybody that would stick a cock in one of those girls would throw a rock through a Rembrandt."

After *Way Down East,* Henry did *The Trail of the Lonesome Pine,* the first outdoor film in Technicolor. It established the Fonda persona—resolute and idealistic and innocent. With the tensile strength beneath his implacable surface, he was the perfect westerner—speaking in a natural drawl that was hesitant and authentic; slightly stooped in posture, with a loping, cantilevered gait. What Hollywood's resident malapropist Samuel Goldwyn once said with accidental insight about Gary Cooper applied to Henry as well: "He is an unintentional actor." The two of them were among the first to realize that in the new medium of film, less could be more. Al Capp, then a young cartoonist, saw *The Trail of the Lonesome Pine* and modeled his character Li'l Abner on Fonda.

In 1936, Wanger produced *The Moon's Our Home,* which brought

Fonda together with Margaret Sullavan. Since their breakup, she had married director William Wyler. On their New York honeymoon in 1934, in fact, Sullavan had made Wyler jealous by forcing him to go see Henry in the stage version of *The Farmer Takes a Wife*. Their marriage had since hit the rocks, largely because Sullavan got more work than her new husband. The final blow to Wyler's ego came when he proudly brought home a weekly check for $2,500 and she trumped him by flourishing hers for $8,500.

Since then Sullavan had continued her climb, becoming one of Hollywood's biggest stars. Beneath the ditzy wit, there was a recklessness that got her into car crashes and household accidents and led one writer to say in a fan magazine that she was carrying "an uncanny eerie jinx." But for Henry she still embodied youth itself.

When they first met on the Lake Tahoe set of *The Moon's Our Home* there was a hesitant exchange.

"Hello, Peggy."

"They call me Maggie out here."

"Maggie? I'll still call you Peggy, okay?"

"Okay."

The publicists worked overtime on the fact that the divorced pair were working together again. Watching them on the set, one movie journalist wrote, "They approached each other warily. They smiled frostily, began to shake hands, faltered. . . . They clinched like two frostbitten snowmen bored with life." In fact, the frost soon thawed and they became inseparable once again. When Sullavan broke her arm, gossip columnists noted that Fonda was the only person allowed into her hospital room.

For her it might have been another flirtation, but for him it was a way perhaps to reopen the places in his heart he had locked when she first betrayed him. They were even talking about marrying again and looking for a house. But then Sullavan had one of her tantrums and the reconciliation was over as quickly as it had begun.

· · ·

On the rebound once again from the woman who would keep turning up in his life for the next twenty-five years, Henry sailed for England to do *Wings of the Morning* with the French star Annabella. During a break from filming one afternoon, producer Bob Kane rented a launch to see Eton, Windsor Castle, and other sights along the Thames. He invited Henry to join him, along with two young American women who were visiting England—Frances Brokaw and her brother's fiancée, Fay Keith. Unlike many other women he met, who demurely waited for him to make the first move, Brokaw boldly declared an interest in Henry on their leisurely boat ride. By the time it was over he had arranged to see her again.

In part he was struck by her looks. She was a petite blonde with a smooth forehead and high cheekbones that narrowed her eyes into a look of sensual irony. But he had seen more beautiful women in Hollywood. It was the frank and open manner that captivated him, the touch of class she conveyed, and also the way she aggressively engaged him. The story of her past, which came out in bits and pieces as he took her around London over the next few weeks, made her seem wholly different from any other woman he had met.

She had been born Frances Seymour, a member of an upper-class New Jersey family which had included Horatio Seymour, Ulysses S. Grant's opponent for president in 1868. Her maternal uncle was oil tycoon Henry Rogers, one of John D. Rockefeller's partners in setting up the great Standard Oil trust. But while her own parents were socially well connected, they were not rich, and after graduating from high school Frances had emulated some of the young men in her set by going to Wall Street to make her fortune.

She had met George Brokaw, a fifty-two-year-old former congressman who had inherited millions of dollars from his family. He had been married once before, to Clare Boothe, but while the social world into which he had introduced her provided a vantage point for her later acidic writings, the marriage itself had been a disaster. A drunk who hid gin in golfing trophies around the house, Brokaw was insipid and oafish between bouts of abusive drunkenness. It was after one of Brokaw's sadistic beatings that Boothe left him, taking their daughter with her; later she married *Time* founder Henry Luce.

Frances had come along soon after the divorce. She saw in Brokaw a way of recouping the fortunes of her branch of the Seymour family. Not waiting for him to make the first move, she went to Tiffany's when she felt the courtship had gone on long enough and bought an engagement ring. She tied it with a pink ribbon and presented it to him, saying, "George, don't you think it's about time?"

After the wedding in 1931, they moved into the Brokaw family's Fifth Avenue mansion, which was, ironically, catercorner to the 63rd Street apartment where Fonda and his undiscovered actor friends were starving. Frances and Brokaw had had a daughter, also named Frances but called Pan. Brokaw became increasingly violent as his alcoholism careened out of control. In 1934, after he beat her once too often, Frances had him committed to a New York sanatorium. After a few months there, Brokaw was found facedown in the institution's swimming pool, drowned as a result of scotch or a stroke. Frances was left a free woman with an estate of several million dollars.

Always the passive figure in his relationships with women, Henry allowed Frances Brokaw to sweep him off his feet. They were quite unlike each other: she was voluble and vivacious, a conservative Republican who liked the decorousness of traditional social occasions; he was comfortable in silence, a dyed-in-the-wool liberal who liked slightly raucous Hollywood parties because there was always someone else acting wild. His costar in *Wings of the Morning*,

Annabella, with whom he was carrying on a mild flirtation, later said, "Frances came on the set and suddenly I never really saw Hank again."

Frances had shipped her Buick to Europe so that she and Fay Keith could tour the continent after their visit to England; they wound up at the Summer Olympics in Berlin. After shooting was finished, Henry flew to meet them at Tempelhof Airport. They watched the Olympics from Frances's box, annoying patriotic Germans when Henry filmed Hitler's arrival with a movie camera instead of standing at respectful attention. After Fay had flown home alone, Henry and Frances drove from Germany to Hungary, a romantic passage from the Black Forest to the Blue Danube. After several days in Budapest, they drove on to Paris, where they checked in at the Ritz.

It was a swift courtship, given urgency both by the perilous situation into which Europe was falling and by Frances herself. As her capture of Brokaw had shown, she was not one to wait for things to happen. "When a woman wants a man," she was fond of saying, "she should be the one who pursues him and gets him. Let him know that you care for him. Lots of women are poor shrinking violets. . . ." Frances later told a friend that she was frustrated in Paris when it was time to return to the United States and Henry hadn't proposed yet. Shortly before the ship was to sail, she showed him a cable she had drafted to her mother: "Arriving New York soon and will announce my engagement to Henry Fonda." He looked at it for a moment and then said, "Sure, fine."

The wedding took place in mid-September. Sisters Harriet and Jayne, Henry's only remaining family, came from Omaha and filed into Christ Church on Park Avenue alongside the Biddles and Fishes and other New York aristocrats. Henry had not always felt comfortable with these people during the swift courtship, sometimes retreating to their libraries during the dinner parties to which he was invited, and sitting there alone thumbing through magazines ·

until Frances came to find him. But now he tricked himself out in a black coat with swallowtails, and high hat and ascot—he remarked to his best man, Josh Logan, that he felt as if he were on a set—and made his way to the altar. Henry's agent and friend Leland Hayward thought to get a contingent of police, who were useful in clearing a path through the large crowd that gathered as the ceremony was ending. When the bride and groom left the church, people threw rice. Henry, thinking of his poverty just a few years earlier, said that he had to restrain himself from picking it up and putting in the pockets of his rented coat.

After one night's honeymoon in the Sulgrave Hotel, they flew to Hollywood and checked into the Beverly Hills Hotel. Henry went back to work, and Frances looked for a house. She found a cozy furnished place in Pacific Palisades and leased it on the spot. Soon after they moved there, Leland Hayward and Maggie Sullavan, who had just gotten married, moved in about a block away. Henry started filming *Jezebel* with Bette Davis. The movie was directed by William Wyler, like Fonda an ex-husband of Sullavan's who was represented by Hayward. The two of them got Hayward on the set to mediate a faked quarrel and then had a picture taken with him; they said they would title it "The Maggie Sullavan Club."

Frances was not much interested in what she called Hollywood's "incest." While Henry talked about acting, she talked about money. She personally oversaw not only her own sizable investments but also Henry's income. When he left for the set in the morning, she was already on the phone to New York getting stock market quotes. When he returned in the evening she talked of her conquests in buying cheap and selling high.

Henry was an attractive man given to well-controlled flirtations, such as one with Barbara Stanwyck which began on the set of *The Lady Eve*. (Later, with his forefinger and thumb about half an inch apart, he would tell actor Michael Parks, "Jane came this close to being Barbara Stanwyck's daughter.") Yet he needed to be married and allowed Frances to organize his life. As one friend said, "He was as warm and faithful as a golden retriever."

They were something of an odd couple, but the ways in which Frances was different from other wives in the film colony reflected well on Fonda. With the understated elegance of her black dresses and single strand of pearls she easily outshone the other women in their gaudy gowns and large diamonds. As one friend said, "There was a group—Jack Benny's wife, Mary Livingstone; studio executive William Goetz's wife, Edie; Zeppo Marx's wife, Marian—who all competed over jewelry. But Frances bought the most beautiful aquamarines you've ever seen. She took them to Count Fulco Verdura, one of the top jewelers in the world, and he designed a setting with platinum. The ice blue of the aquamarines and the platinum of the necklace and bracelet were something that none of these Hollywood ladies could match."

But soon Frances was wearing maternity dresses. Before Henry started *Jezebel,* he'd inserted a clause into his contract that allowed him to go to New York, where Frances's physician practiced, when it came time for the birth of their child. A baby girl arrived on December 21, 1937. Because of a matrix of puns—Henry's middle name, after his mother, was Jaynes; Frances traced her lineage back to Edward Seymour, the sixteenth-century English noble whose sister, Lady Jane Seymour, was Henry VIII's third wife—they named the baby Jane and called her "Lady Jane." Eventually "Lady" stuck, and in her first clothes "Lady Fonda" was stenciled on the label.

Henry admired his daughter and photographed her, but he didn't pick her up very much. The nurse the Fondas hired was a strict behaviorist opposed to handling infants, and she browbeat Henry into submitting to her regimen.

·   ·   ·

It was the beginning of a golden period for Henry. He loved the baby, whom he sometimes surreptitiously held and played with. He loved his wife. He was happy with his career, having found a film personality unlike that of any other Hollywood star: he projected diffidence and honesty, unaffected restraint and quiet intensity. One director wondered about the intensity in the Fonda stare for years until he finally understood where it came from: Henry never blinked. There was an almost virginal quality about him. (Fonda later said that the only thing he hated in the movies were kisses: "They used to tell me that I should open my mouth for the kisses but this seemed too personal.") Most of all, there was never a sense that he was giving a performance. What he seemed to be showing on the screen was a slice of his own inner life.

Seeing the monumental quality in his face, Fox wanted him for *Young Mr. Lincoln*. Henry read the script and said, "I think it's absolutely beautiful, but I couldn't possibly play Mr. Lincoln. You know, it's like playing God or Jesus or something." The producer persuaded him to get into makeup and do a screen test. Henry had never recovered from the shock of seeing his face on the screen and hearing his voice, which he found grating. After viewing the test for Lincoln, he said, "Forget it."

Fox brought him to John Ford, already a legend not only for his directing but for his profanity. Later, in what was probably an expurgated version of the conversation, Henry recalled him saying, "What's all this shit about you thinking you're playing the Great Emancipator? For Christ's sake, he was just a young jackleg lawyer from Springfield." He allowed Ford to bully him into accepting the role, and it was the beginning of a long association. The movie they made went far toward establishing Fonda as the archetypal American hero. "Nature gave him long legs and arms, a strong and honest face and a slow smile . . ." the *New York Times* reviewer wrote.

"Mr. Fonda supplied the rest—the warmth and kindliness, the pleasant modesty, the courage, tenderness, shrewdness and resolution that Lincoln, even Young Mr. Lincoln, must have possessed."

At this point in his career, Fonda had fulfilled his contract to Wanger. Many of the actors of the day carped about the studio system but felt comfortable living within its constraints. (Jimmy Stewart liked being part of the MGM "family" so much that he sat in Louis Mayer's office crying when he came back from the war having decided not to renew his contract.) But Henry liked being an independent and did not want to sign with any of the studios. This intention to remain his own man brought him into conflict with the man he came to loathe above all other Hollywood figures, Darryl F. Zanuck, head of production at 20th Century–Fox.

One of their first run-ins came over Fox's *Jesse James*. Speaking to Nunnally Johnson, one of his producers, Zanuck suggested Tyrone Power for the title role.

"I know he's a great big sissy, but audiences don't think so. . . . In addition, there's a good part in the script for Jesse James's brother Frank. A very strong role."

"How about Henry Fonda?" Johnson suggested.

"Jesus," Zanuck responded. "I hate that arrogant bastard, and he's not even under contract to us and he'll cost a fortune."

Despite his feelings about Fonda, Zanuck finally authorized Johnson to offer him the role. Their relationship went downhill from there. At one point in the shooting, the script called for horses to be run off a cliff. Everyone on the set was aghast. The animals would break their legs. When the director, Henry King, relayed these concerns to Zanuck, he said everything would work out.

On the day the stunt was to be shot, the stars were standing a few yards from the cliff watching the doubles and their mounts. Fonda was glad to be on foot: he was scared to death when riding that the horse would fall on him. Tyrone Power watched in horror as the stunt horses were ridden over the cliff: "My God, it's murder!" Zanuck laughed at him, ran up to the cliff, and jumped off himself. As everyone exchanged perplexed looks, Henry muttered, "The bastard has a conscience after all. He's killed himself." Then they found out that Zanuck had ordered a platform built just below the cliff where man and animal could have a short jump and a soft landing.

Soon after *Jesse James,* Zanuck got ahold of something he knew Henry wanted and intended to make him pay for. It was the lead role in *The Grapes of Wrath.* Zanuck had bought the rights to the Steinbeck novel after Louis Mayer turned it down as "red propaganda." He hired John Ford to direct and Nunnally Johnson to adapt the book. After reading Johnson's script, Fonda was desperate to get the role. He had read and loved all of Steinbeck's work. He begged Leland Hayward to fix it for him. Hayward said he, Henry, would have to see Zanuck. Henry replied that he hated Zanuck because he was "a narrow bastard with only two interests in life, making movies and satisfying his cock." But Henry wanted the role of Tom Joad so much that he finally swallowed his pride and went to the Fox offices.

"I hear from Leland you like *Grapes of Wrath,*" Zanuck said after Fonda entered his office and sat down.

"You betcha."

"Like it well enough to sign a seven-year contract with me?"

"Hell no!" Fonda jumped to his feet. "I'm a free-lance actor and I intend to stay one!"

"Well," Zanuck said smiling, "I'm not going to give you Tom Joad and then let you go off and do some picture with MGM and Joan Crawford."

As Fonda sat down in defeat, Zanuck, a polo enthusiast, stood and began to swing a mallet he kept next to his desk. "I've got big plans for you, Fonda, and I want to be able to control you and keep you, and I've got to have a contract with you to do it."

Henry gave in and signed with Zanuck. It would cause him considerable grief over the next few years, help sour him on Hollywood and the film industry, and create a bitterness that cascaded over into his private life. But in return he got film immortality. Everyone connected with the movie when it was being shot knew that it would be a classic. At the top of his craft, John Ford handled the cast perfectly. In the final scene between Tom and Ma Joad, for instance, he let Henry and Jane Darwell wait until they were supercharged with emotion, then he shot their farewell in one continuous take.

Twenty-five years after *The Grapes of Wrath* first appeared, John Steinbeck would watch it once more for old time's sake and be amazed by Fonda all over again. He wrote: "Times pass and we change. . . . But I did thread this thing on my home projector and sat back to weather it out. Then a lean, stringy, dark faced piece of electricity walked out on the screen and he had me. I believed in my own story again." That image Steinbeck saw was probably the one Orson Welles had in mind when he said, "I look at Henry Fonda and I see the face of America."

After *The Grapes of Wrath,* Henry had become enough of a national figure that when a young woman overheard two men on a San Bernardino street corner saying something about kidnapping one or more of the Fondas, the FBI was immediately brought in on the case. It turned out to be a false alarm, and Henry left Pan and Jane behind with governesses and took Frances on a South American honeymoon which had been delayed for two years because of film commitments. From Ecuador, Frances sent friends postcards showing squat, grim-faced Indian women, with the message that this was not a place where she feared losing her better half to the competition. When she came back, she was pregnant again.

Frances gave birth in New York on February 23, 1940. It was her third cesarean, the last one she could have, and she was desperate for a son. (Later Jane said that her grandmother told her Frances was so anxious to have a boy that she had picked one out to adopt if the baby she had was a girl.) But she had a boy, named Peter Henry.

By this time, Lady Jane's authoritarian nurse had been fired, and Henry was able to be a hands-on father. As Frances wrote to a friend, "Hank is in fine form! He goes once a day to the hospital and feeds the baby and changes it. . . . Peter certainly is a cunning child!" But she herself was slow to recuperate from the birth and from the physical depression that followed. Finally, after several weeks, Henry brought the baby back to California on a plane with a nurse, and Frances followed by car. Once home, he showed Pan and Jane moving pictures he had taken of Peter in the hospital, and Jane ran screaming from the room.

That spring, the Fondas often went on picnics in the hills high above Sunset Boulevard. There was a knoll called Tigertail that they loved, a place with a panoramic view ranging from the ocean to the Santa Monica Mountains, where coyotes, bobcats, and rattlesnakes lived. Henry and Frances had come there since their marriage, hoping that the land would someday come on the market. When it did, Henry arranged to buy nine acres, and the two of them began to design a dream house.

He was characteristically precise, studying the movement of the sun and the wind currents in deciding where to build. Even before construction began, he had planted an orange grove, which he watered with fifty-gallon drums hauled up from below in his station wagon. When the contractor broke ground, Henry was there, a supervisor as well as a customer.

Finally, in 1942, the house was finished—a two-story Pennsylvania Dutch colonial faced in fieldstone with shake-and-shingle roof and siding. Inside, it was early American—pine walls, beamed ceilings, a massive brick walk-in fireplace. There was a tennis court, and a rock pool Henry had designed to resemble the Nebraska swimming holes of his youth. There was an outbuilding the size of a dormitory called "the Playhouse"; here Henry, thinking of every detail, had installed child-high sinks. At the entrance to the property, beside a split-rail fence splashed by a bed of geraniums, was a sign reading "Caution: Children and Animals."

In one of the first fan articles written about Fonda—shortly before his whirlwind courtship and marriage to Frances—the writer had said: "He wants, above everything else, to be part of an average American family with no fuss or publicity about it; he wants, if he married again, a wife and some kids and a good house."

Now, it seemed, he had everything he had ever wanted.

THREE

They would all look back at the years at Tigertail as the time of their lives. For Henry and Frances, there was a feeling of daily accomplishment; a sense that they were building a dream house and building their lives as well. They could see their relationship in the changes they made on their hilltop.

For Henry, the property allowed a return to the rootedness from which he had extracted himself when he left Nebraska. At Tigertail he became Farmer Fonda, clearing the nine acres, fencing in a growing area, and beginning to plant. He built a chicken coop and stocked it with chickens; he ritualistically collected the eggs and, more important, the manure. He had discovered the journal *Organic Farm and Garden* and rigorously followed its principles of composting.

For much of the time, Frances was a spectator. Peter's birth had left her with lingering fatigue, and also a nagging sense that something was amiss. Finally she went into the Scripps Clinic near San Diego for extensive tests and came out feeling better, ready to accept her share of the work at Tigertail.

She was in her little office by nine in the morning. Already having checked the stock market, she met with her secretary to go over the mail and pay bills; then she organized the day, touring the house and grounds and dictating a menu for the meals and a list of tasks for the cook, maid, and gardener. She continued to take care of the money and investments, Henry's and her own. As close friend Watson Webb says, "She loved the stock market and spent a great deal of time on it. She loved telling how she'd bought low and sold high. This sort of stuff just bored Hank to death."

Periodically during the day she looked in on the children. She had a special relationship with Pan, a quiet girl who looked just like her mother and seemed grateful to be part of the new family. The two of them communicated through meaningful looks and verbal short-hand that was like a code. Because the baby boy seemed so fragile, Frances devoted particular attention to "Little Petey," as she called him.

When Josh Logan made his first visit to Tigertail after Peter was born, Frances told him to go to the nursery for a look. He saw a child with the familiar blue eyes and whispered to him, "You can come out now, Hank. I know where you're hiding." In fact, Peter resembled his mother. It was Jane who looked like Henry. Jealous of the intensity of Frances's love for her brother, Jane remained aloof from her and tried to forge a bond with her father. Their behavior in the pool, where he taught her to swim at the age of two, was a metaphor for their relationship: she was secure when Henry held her, hysterical when he let her go.

Frances dressed Jane like a doll, picking out frocks from a local store specializing in Tyrolean clothes. But Jane was comfortable only when she looked like Henry. She chose jeans and flannel lumberjack shirts and put her blond hair in utilitarian pigtails. She imitated his distinctive posture—weight back on heels and hips thrust forward—and adopted his long-gaited walk. She followed him on his chores, chattering to compel his attention. A writer caught one exchange between them as Henry worked in the area they called "the North Forty."

"Dad. I sometimes think there's only one guy around here who is not a city slicker."

"Yeah?" answered Henry. "Who's that?"

"You." It was the highest compliment she could pay him.

It was hard for Henry to express his emotions, happiness even more than anger, but he told a friend he felt his family was like an artifact—the best thing he had ever made. He surrounded them with friends like John Wayne, Ward Bond, Jimmy Stewart, and John Ford, who came to the Playhouse occasionally dressed like cowboys and played a card game called pitch. With their noses pressed against the windows, the kids watched these western heroes dressed in ten-gallon hats and wearing six-shooters, which they took out of the holsters and set on the table beside them.

If he was happy in his life, however, Henry was increasingly miserable in his work. Zanuck was extracting full value from their contract, casting Henry in a series of films he hated—*Lillian Russell, Rings on Her Fingers, Tales of Manhattan,* and other banal vehicles which seemed to negate his achievement in *The Grapes of Wrath.* Even when the script he was given was not trash, as in *The Return of Frank James,* there was still a fly in the ointment—in this case, Zanuck's perverse choice of the great German director Fritz Lang to do a western action picture. Henry fumed while Lang, known for his meticulousness and countless retakes, spent hours personally arranging artificial cobwebs in a barn and reshooting chase scenes so many times that several horses died of heart failure.

Fonda said that he was learning to dislike Hollywood and bitterly blamed it all on Zanuck, whom he began referring to as "Fuck-It-All," for his middle initial. He pointed out that most of the good films he was doing—comic classics such as *The Lady Eve* and *The Male Animal*—came when he was on loan to other studios, or when a director managed to browbeat Zanuck into doing a project he didn't particularly like—as William Wellman had done with *The Ox-Bow Incident,* the brooding western that *The New Republic* termed "a significant moment in our culture."

The coming of the war offered Henry a respite from his difficulties at Fox. He had joined the Hollywood Anti-Nazi League, an industry group which forced Mussolini's son to cut short a visit in 1937 and the following year closed the studio gates to Hitler's favorite filmmaker Leni Riefenstahl. After Pearl Harbor, when many of his friends were entering the service—Tyrone Power in the Marines, Clark Gable and Jimmy Stewart in the Air Corps—Henry told Frances that he felt he had to go too. She pointed out that he was entitled to a deferment because of his age, thirty-seven, and because of the children. He told her he was stuck with the face of a younger man and couldn't bear the idea of people looking at him and thinking he was a slacker.

The day he finished *The Ox-Bow Incident,* he enlisted in the Navy. He came home for one last evening with the family and headed off to boot camp in San Diego the next morning. But when he got there, officers of the Shore Patrol put him in a car and returned him to Hollywood, where he found out that Zanuck had figured out a way to squeeze one more movie out of him, by convincing Washington that a potboiler called *The Immortal Sergeant* would help the mobilization. After spending a miserable summer filming near the California desert, Fonda finally headed off to war.

After boot camp, Henry was trained as a quartermaster. Before leaving for his billet with a new destroyer in Seattle, the *Satterlee,* he had a brief leave. Peter recalled sitting on his father's lap during this otherwise indistinct visit and listening to a nonsense rhyme:

My doggie's name is Guess,
My doggie's name is Guess,
He shakes his head for "No"
And wags his tail for "Yes."

Shortly after arriving in Seattle, Henry found that he had been reassigned to Officer Training School at Quonset Point, Rhode Island. He would have preferred to remain an enlisted man, but the orders were firm. As he had feared, at Quonset Point he was singled out not only as a potential officer but also as a film star. The men he served with treated him differently, and there were also civilians whose curiosity led to peculiar situations. After one brief leave in Providence, for instance, Henry was waiting for a bus to return to Quonset Point with his commanding officer, Rupert Allen, when a young woman who had been staring at him for a long time spoke up.

"Say, are you Henry Fonda's twin?"

"No, I'm not," he replied.

"Oh, sorry."

The girl sat in front of Fonda and Allen on the bus and overheard them talking about the theater. She turned around and asked again, "You're not Henry Fonda's twin?"

"No, I'm not," he repeated.

Finally, just as Fonda and Allen got up to leave the bus, the woman looked at him one last time. "Are you by any chance Henry Fonda?"

"Yes, I am."

"God damn," she called after him. "That's the meanest trick anybody ever played on me."

Frances came east to visit him in Rhode Island. They spent a weekend together in New York, and afterward Henry wrote to a friend on stationery of the Hotel Pierre that he was enjoying this last quick visit and that he had to leave for Quonset soon. "The School graduates the day before Xmas and then—nobody knows—I might be sent to ACI [Air Combat Intelligence] for an additional two months—or maybe to a navigational course in Florida—or maybe right to a billet." He added that he felt he was receiving the equivalent of a four-year Academy course in eight weeks and that the only advantage was that he didn't have a chance to get bored or homesick.

After graduation from OTS, Henry learned that Washington wanted him to narrate training films. He talked his way out of that assignment, and instead entered an intensive course in antisubmarine warfare, after which he was assigned to the battleship *Curtis* in the Gilbert Islands.

While on the *Curtis* he experienced short bursts of action and long hours of tedium. His family was always on his mind. As their anniversary approached, he wrote his friend Watson Webb and enclosed money for a present for Frances:

"Probably something like sweetheart roses unless you can think of something better. It's only to be a reminder that I remember." He asked that the gift be with her breakfast tray the morning of their anniversary and that she be kept guessing about how he had managed to arrange it from thousands of miles away, even if it meant "conniving with Ella, or Etta, or Emmy, or whatever the hell the maid's name is."

He also thought of the kids. All three were attending Brentwood Town and Country, a "progressive" school where they began the morning facing the east and reciting a "Salutation to the Dawn" and where infractions of school rules resulted in being "sent to Coventry."

Henry wrote Peter a letter that seemed calculated more than anything else to remind himself what he had left behind:

"I am living on a big ship. . . . I have a little room about as big as your bathroom that I share with another officer. . . . Most of the walls of the room are covered with pictures of you and Lady and Pan on the blue seat out by the pool—and if I look a little to the right, there you are when you were just a baby, sitting on Mummy's lap with your finger in your mouth and little Lady is standing behind Mummy playing with her hair."

There were moments of danger he didn't tell them about. Part of an island-hopping operation to root out enemy resistance, the *Curtis* was exposed to kamikaze attacks. Henry happened to be on leave in Guam when one such attack took place; the Japanese plane smashed into the area where he would have been working. Meanwhile, the children were hearing rumors of war; Japanese submarines were raising periscopes off the southern California coast. Peter's wartime memory was of sitting under a kitchen table during an air-raid drill, his mother stroking his hair to calm him as she read *Peter Rabbit* to her three children. During Henry's absence Peter often went to his closet and put on his shoes and clomped around the house. He opened his father's drawers and smelled the balled-up socks and handkerchiefs.

The children fantasized constantly about Henry. Like all warrior fathers, he became larger than life. What was different about him was that he existed as an epic figure not only in their imaginations but also on the screen. Jane had never seen one of his movies until he was gone; then she saw *Drums Along the Mohawk* and, during a long chase scene in which Indians almost capture Fonda, hid her head in fear, confusing the Indians and the Japanese.

At about the same time, Peter, then four, saw his first Fonda film. It was *Chad Hanna*, about a young man who joins the circus. At one point in the movie, when Henry has to get into a cage with a lion, Peter became terrified. He went up to the screen to touch his father as if to save him and, when he found that the image was something that could not be grasped, ran screaming out of the theater.

For Henry the war provided surreal moments too. During his leave on Guam, he hitched a ride to Iwo Jima in a C-46 loaded with fresh produce. The pilot veered off course and couldn't reorient the plane because the radio was being jammed. With fuel running low, he gave the order to jettison cargo to lighten the plane. The plane was flying over a Japanese outpost on a tiny island and so Fonda and other crew members wound up bombing the enemy with watermelons, cucumbers, and crates of tomatoes.

Henry's tour of duty ended just after the bombing of Hiroshima. He got back home on the day President Truman announced the Japanese surrender. Jane and Peter had been preparing for his arrival for days, carrying his picture around with them so that they would know what he looked like when they saw him. Still in uniform, he went to Brentwood Town and Country to pick them up.

Peter was coming out of a building. He saw Henry and did a double-take, then stared for a long time as he approached.

"Chad?" he finally asked.

"No," Henry said, "Dad."

He gave his son the Bronze Star he had won for helping to sink a Japanese submarine. Peter soon lost it somewhere at Tigertail playing war with his friends.

Serving in the Navy was a manhood ritual for Henry, an opportunity, after years in Hollywood, to ground himself in something "real" and to be with "real people." He was not a war hero like Jimmy Stewart, who had flown more than a hundred bombing missions over Germany. Yet he had done his part and he returned home feeling seasoned, with the conviction shared by most other veterans that life was a game played for keeps. It was hard to get back into the make-believe. Stewart, who left the service at about the same time as Fonda, didn't have anywhere to live because he had leased his house, and so he moved into the Playhouse at Tigertail. Every evening after Frances went to bed the two men sat around drinking and talking about their experiences. One of the experiences Henry didn't mention was not his but Frances's—a brief affair she'd admitted having while he was gone, because she was so lonely.

Everybody seemed to be talking and decompressing. There were frequent parties in the Playhouse. Jane and Peter watched as their father laughed with old friends Tyrone Power, Keenan Wynn, Fred MacMurray, and Watson Webb. Serving in the Navy had freed Henry's deadpan humor. During one game of charades he drew "'Tis a Pity She's a Whore" and convulsed the rest of the players with his hip-wagging and gum-smacking mime, and with the way he got down on the floor and simulated bored ecstasy. On another occasion he and Stewart, somewhat in their cups, were arguing about whether or not 78-rpm records were edible; Fonda grabbed one, took a large bite, and began to chew. But he was also the only father in their circle who was interested in high art, and he took Gary Cooper's daughter, Maria, and Jane to the ballet several times. When they both expressed the desire to be ballerinas, he told Cooper's wife, Rocky, "Maria has the face, but Jane has the body."

The Haywards were a crucial element in their social circle. Maggie had been intoxicated with fame but was not too keen on actually working, and so she was semi-retired, taking care of the children. Her first child, Brooke, was the same age as Jane and shared a nurse with her. The other two Hayward kids, Bill and Bridget, were closer to Peter. Henry and Maggie still had a bond from a time when life was young for them. Leland was not only Fonda's agent but one of his closest friends. The kids were like relatives, growing up in the shadow of their larger-than-life parents, aware that they were bonded if not knowing exactly how. But all of this somehow did not include Frances. The Haywards invited the Fondas to dinner, but she never reciprocated. She referred to Maggie archly as "Madame H" and, as one of her friends said, "always hated her."

Never particularly interested in the Hollywood crowd, Frances was even less so after being on her own during the war. Director Henry Hathaway's son Jack, a childhood friend of Peter's whose life Frances saved by jumping into the Fondas' pool to pull him to the edge when he was drowning, recalls, "She was very un-Hollywood. There was none of the pompousness and glitter. She was real—very uncondescending, and one of the few adults around you could really talk to."

But this very quality made her an outsider among Henry's friends. For them, she, the nonactor, was the one who wore the mask. Her interest in the world of high finance did not carry a conversation very far; they sensed that their world was not important to her. Thus they reacted to her as someone to be endured. As Josh Logan said dismissively, "She could talk on four subjects and on these she was great. Outside of these subjects, it was just a disaster. Money, babies, sex, and clothes. I never heard Hank's career mentioned by her."

One friend remarks of these postwar years, "Frances seemed lonely. It was like she was at a forty-five-degree angle with the rest of life." Bill Hayward's memory of her at Tigertail is of someone "always in another room working at a typewriter, and you never knew what she was typing."

Pan, a pretty teenager learning about boys and dating, was increasingly on her own. Relations between Frances and the other two children were difficult. Peter was hyperactive and thin, as if what he took in didn't nourish him. Never really well herself since his birth, Frances projected what some considered her hypochondria onto him. She nagged him about getting overheated in his play and insisted that he still take afternoon naps long after Bill and Bridget Hayward and other kids his age had stopped.

Jane was chubby; she seemed to need to consume everything— not just food but attention as well. Pan would sometimes find her little sister staring oddly at her when she put on makeup as she got ready to go out with a boy, and Jane spied on Pan's necking sessions.

She watched her parents too. With emotional seismic detectors sensitive to the shifts in their relationship, Jane understood that Henry was withdrawing from Frances, and she began to dissociate herself from her mother. Frances tried to finesse the conflict with her daughter, but she drew a line at Jane's aggressive tomboy act. She forced Jane occasionally to put on party dresses and go to birthday parties such as the one Joan Crawford staged for her daughter, Christina, where she wound up in a corner crying until her nurse brought her home.

The family may have resembled a typical Freudian quadrangle, the daughter connecting with her father and the son with the mother, but the geometry satisfied none of them. Henry knew there were problems, especially with the boy, whom he called "a sad youngster." But he decided that he "couldn't make up for what the war had taken away" from the two of them. In any case, he had what he considered to be bigger problems with his career.

While Henry gritted his teeth and went back to Fox, Frances focused on the stock market. The children fended for themselves. Peter was insecure— "quick to laugh," in the words of his friend Ned Wynn, "and quick to cry." Jane was overbearing. "Whenever she wanted something, she went after it," the mother of one of her playmates said, "and she had great stamina and staying power." She mothered and manipulated her brother. When they got their hands on some cigarettes, Jane only pretended to chain-smoke but got Peter earnestly to go through the remainder of the package so that he wound up deathly sick.

In addition to Peter and Jane and the three Haywards, the shifting membership of the gang that played at Tigertail included Keenan Wynn's son Ned, Fred MacMurray's daughter Susan, and Maria Cooper. Oversupervised, but rarely by their parents, they defied nurses and nannies by engaging in wild games. Jane and Maria pelted passing motorists with fruit from Henry's orange trees. Jane and her neighbor Sue Sally Hale dressed in buckskins and plaited their hair like Indians and threw avocados at unknown children who walked by. Neighbor Eve Johnson recalls, "Jane ruled over the others, saying whether and when they were allowed to swim. She was always in charge, and the game the others played, whether they knew it or not, was follow the leader."

Jane's introduction to sex came when she was riding Pedro, one of the two donkeys (the other was Pancho) Henry had brought home from Mexico after filming *The Fugitive*. Pedro was actually a female, and during the ride was mounted by Pancho. There was gender confusion in Jane's life too. As she said later, "I didn't want to be a girl, because I wanted to be like my father." She broke one arm in a fight with a boy who worked at the local stables, and the other staging a fall off a horse in emulation of the way her father overpowered villains on the screen. She chopped her hair off at her ears, and after a stranger asked whether she was a boy or a girl, she was so excited she couldn't sleep that night. But she also had what one male playmate calls an "instinct" about herself: "Jane pretended not to like it but she knew that she was pretty and that she had a power over boys. Once she pulled down her jeans and showed us her underpants."

Jane got into scrapes. Peter got into deep trouble. In one well-remembered incident, he and Bill Hayward were playing with matches on the North Forty and set a grass fire. For several minutes they raced back and forth between the pool and the fire with tennis ball cans filled with water, trying to put out the blaze. Eventually the fire department showed up, and Henry punished Peter not with a spanking but with one of his looks. Peter was the fall guy, the one who was never in control. He caused a scandal when he bit a governess in a fit of temper and drew blood. Looking back at those days, he said, "I was shy, difficult, and I lied a lot."

·   ·   ·

Group photographs taken of the Fondas during the days at Tigertail show a sunny, smiling family, so good-looking they resemble an experiment in eugenics. Examined more closely, however, these joint portraits give the sense of individuals who are subtly disconnected from each other and of one member, Frances, who always seems slightly out of focus. Henry had plunged back into his career and was frequently on location. Just as he refused to admit that he was unhappy when they were together, so she refused to admit that she was unhappy when they were apart. As one of her few friends from that period says, "She was finely tuned, like a rare instrument. She never had tantrums. She kept everything inside."

"Everything" for Frances included her dislike for the movie business and, most of all, what she believed was her continually deteriorating health. She spent whole days in bed and eventually moved her office into her bedroom so that she could continue to conduct business. Because her feeling of unwellness seemed so subjective, she stopped talking about it. Hidden within her, the fear of sickness became a powerful force, capable of erupting into sudden action. Once when Henry was off making a movie, Frances packed up on a whim and, without telling him, went to Baltimore to have a hysterectomy at Johns Hopkins, taking Peter with her so that he could be put through a series of tests to determine why he was unable to put on weight despite her cosseting diets.

Surrounded by the eternal youth of Hollywood as she approached her fortieth birthday, Frances worried about her fading beauty, especially since Henry, like so many middle-aged men, seemed to get better-looking as he got older. Frances once remarked that if she ever got fat she would cut off the excess flesh with a knife; this horrifying image was one of the few things she said that remained with her daughter. She wore taped "frownies" while sleeping to keep wrinkles from developing. She had her hair colored differently every few weeks, appearing by turns as redhead, blonde, and brunette, her appearance often so radically changed that some of her neighbors did not know who she was when they ran into her on the street.

Her concern with money, the one area of her life where she had always been in charge, became obsessive, as Frances entered what her mother, Sophie Seymour, referred to as her "dark period." When Clare Boothe Luce's daughter by George Brokaw died in an auto accident, Frances immediately went to court to get the dead girl's part of the Brokaw estate for Pan, saying of Luce, "George wouldn't have wanted *that* woman to get the money." In the middle of a discussion about finances, she took a neighbor to the master bedroom at Tigertail, where she whispered conspiratorially, "Now listen, if you want to keep your money, here's what you've got to do." Then she moved a desk, rolled back a rug, and pulled up the floorboards below to reveal a hidden safe. She opened it, showing off neatly wrapped bundles of cash, and said, "The IRS is not going to get me."

When Ned Wynn and other friends of the children came over to play, they would have to be quiet because Frances was "sick." Sometimes they were met at the front door by Henry, who made it clear that it was not a good time to visit and they should go home. Fiercely organizing things in her room, Frances was too high when she was high and too despondent when she was low. The unpredictability was what got to him, Henry said later.

He had always depended on a woman to draw him out. Now, as Frances's moods became erratic, instead of hearing a cry for help he felt only that something was being done to him. "He used to go for a week without talking when he was in a sulk," says Gary Cooper's widow, Rocky.

The impasse with his wife came at a time when he was back under Zanuck's thumb. He had done some good things after returning from the war, notably *My Darling Clementine,* John Ford's version of the gunfight at the O.K. Corral. (*New York Times* critic Bosley Crowther said of Henry's performance: "Through his quiet yet persuasive self-confidence, his delicious intonation of short words—he shows us an elemental character who is as real as the dirt on which he walks.") But most of the roles he was offered—opposite a faded Joan Crawford in *Daisy Kenyon,* for instance—were like those that had disillusioned him before he went into the Navy.

The situation in which he found himself made Henry focus on what he hated about Hollywood—the indifferent quality, the triviality of most projects, and most of all the constant devaluation of the actor's craft. For a film star, acting was sitting around and waiting, doing small takes over and over without seeing the results, and never having a chance to do a complex and extended characterization—that escape from the mundane self which had made him want to be an actor in the first place.

Blaming Hollywood for everything, including his failing marriage, Henry slowly changed. It was a reverse metamorphosis; a friend likened the change to a butterfly's entering the cocoon and becoming a caterpillar. The ramrod cavalry martinet he played in John Ford's *Fort Apache* was perhaps closest to his off-screen personality at this time.

Brooke Hayward found him "melancholy and saturnine," with volcanic forces within. Another of Jane's school friends who knew him at this time said, "We were all afraid of Jane's father." Sometimes a trivial annoyance would trigger a disproportionate rage and he would become "purple-faced, with veins sticking out in his temples." Pan learned to avoid him and stay in the background. Jane and Peter still followed him around Tigertail, but the outdoor chores were now therapy rather than pleasure, and he responded to their chatter with curt dismissals.

·   ·   ·

In September 1947, Henry was in New York trying to convince his old friend Josh Logan to come to Hollywood and direct a film version of John O'Hara's *Appointment in Samarra*. But Logan told him he had something else in the works. It was *Mister Roberts*, a play he and Thomas Heggen had adapted from the gifted twenty-eight-year-old Heggen's novel. Logan read it to Fonda knowing he already had a film commitment.

"Hank, I'm really sorry you can't play Roberts," he said after finishing.

"I'm going to play it," Fonda replied with a transfixed look on his face.

"But the picture. You've already made tests. Costumes have been fitted, and . . ."

"They can be unfitted. . . . I'm going to play Doug Roberts."

In *Mister Roberts* he saw a possibility of personal and professional regeneration. The stage had always offered something he needed from acting but didn't get in films—an escape from the heavy self-censorship and doubt, and access to feelings that otherwise were blocked. As he told an interviewer, "When I act I put on a mask and when I do that I'm not self-conscious or shy at all because I know that when I'm on stage I'm going to be funny or bright or brilliant. . . . I'm going to be another person who isn't me at all. You see, I'm not good on my own."

He left Hollywood in the fall of 1947 and started to rehearse, telling Frances that she could join him on the off chance that the play succeeded. He opened in *Mister Roberts* the following February, wearing the uniform he had brought home from the war. Opening night was exactly the sort of transforming experience Henry was looking for. He and the rest of the cast were summoned for so many curtain calls that he finally had to quiet the audience with a little speech: "This is all Tom and Josh wrote for us. If you want, we can start all over again." Soon tickets were sold out for two years into the future.

Frances had flown in for the opening and saw how happy Henry was. She thought that a great success onstage might help them renew their relationship. She agreed to relocate the family in the East. She put their hilltop on the market and, in a rare lapse of financial judgment, accepted an offer many who knew the value of the property regarded as too low. Peter would later compare leaving Tigertail to having been expelled from paradise. That it was an Eden only in comparison to the hell that followed never decreased its power as a metaphor.

FOUR

And so they settled in a big gloomy white house with red doors and black shutters on twenty-three acres with two small lakes and hidden glens. As a concession to Henry, Frances tried to establish a bucolic atmosphere by having chickens, but there was something eerie about the place. Brooke Hayward called it "Charles Addamsey."

The Haywards had already established a beachhead in Greenwich, when Maggie settled there two years earlier, after divorcing Leland. Brooke saw her mother and Henry as very much alike, "terrifying in their demands" on themselves and others, both "left-wingers in Republican Greenwich, idiosyncratic and unconcerned with what other people thought, fit for Greenwich Village but not Greenwich, Connecticut." There were a handful of country clubs featuring polite drinking and bridge. The Haywards and Fondas didn't join any of them, and so the kids felt even more conspicuous. After Hollywood, being in Greenwich had the feel of an object lesson, as if they were being made to experience what their parents regarded as "reality."

Frances swallowed her animosity toward "Madame H" for the sake of the kids, who immediately resumed their former status as something like an extended family, surviving a contretemps when

Brooke greeted her old friend as "Lady" and got a chilly response: "My name is Jane. J-A-N-E, if you don't mind." The children explored the new Fonda property, and did plays in which Jane was always the hero, Brooke the director, her younger sister Bridget the ingenue, Peter the villain, Bill his sidekick. Brooke felt that she was seeing her old friends for the first time: "Peter was gifted and fragile and creative. Jane was none of those things. There was an Amazonian quality about her, as if she was made of tempered steel. You never had the slightest doubt that she would adapt, however catastrophic the circumstances."

Frances sent Pan to a boarding school in the South. Peter was enrolled at Brunswick School, and Jane at Greenwich Academy, an all-girls school where the students wore green blazers, brown oxfords, and pleated skirts which had to touch the floor when one did a curtsey. As the daughter of Henry Fonda, Jane was quickly the most popular sixth-grader. She tried to consolidate this status by taking select kids to the shed on the school grounds and telling them dirty jokes about traveling salesmen; the teachers regarded her behavior as an example of decadent Hollywood morality. She and Brooke Hayward joined the Girl Scouts and were kicked out almost immediately because of their show-biz irreverence.

They came to accept Greenwich. But in contrast to the open society of Hollywood, it would always be a claustral world of pretense and prejudice. Henry didn't fit because of his politics and profession, Frances because she did not do the things expected of a mother—take the children to school and pick them up, supervise their recreational activities. It was a place where the word "Jewish" was spoken as if describing a foreigner. Peter always recalled how, shortly after they relocated there, movie mogul David O. Selznick arranged to pick them up on his immense yacht. There was plenty of room for the boat in Greenwich harbor, but the city fathers would not let him dock because he was a Jew.

It was not the external environment that was the problem. As the move east failed to achieve the objective of bringing their parents closer together, and as the family sank back into the grim patterns of the last days in California, the children suffered. Brooke Hayward could never square the brooding Henry Fonda she knew with the young man her mother spoke of as being lighthearted and enormously funny. When they all ate a meal together, Frances always seemed to be in another room, sculpting a head of Henry and making an angry slapping sound on the clay. Henry presided over dinner as father and mother. The children were so wary of him that they often failed to perceive his dark humor. But Bill Hayward always watched in case Henry did a favorite "bit" at the table. Pretending something was stuck in his teeth, he would struggle a long time with it and finally hold up to his mouth a napkin in which he had hidden, say, a chicken thigh bone, he would then pull the bone out slowly as if that were what had been irritating him. By this time everyone would be looking at him, but Henry would not acknowledge them. It was almost as if he had done the elaborate and quite funny piece of stage business all for himself.

Peter suffered racking stomach pains as a result of the silent tension. His governesses took his temperature and, because it was normal, told him he should be too. For Jane the fear had a name: divorce. Her animosity toward her mother was such that at times she wished it would happen. But she also feared it. "I imagined how they must have felt," she said of friends whose parents had divorced. "My only thought was, It must be like falling down a black hole. Who would love you? Who would take care of you? And then I'd think, Oh my God, maybe it's going to happen to *my* family, and it will be us who will fall between the cracks."

There was no one to reassure them. Their mother was trapped in a manic cycle: she felt either unreasonably optimistic or totally despondent. She had begun trading in real estate, and went so far as to buy a hideaway on the St. Lawrence River for the time when the marriage healed itself; she called it "Fonda Isle." The children could count on her for a neurasthenic concern but not much more. (In Brooke Hayward's view: "The children were aware that she was peculiar as hell, and withdrawn, and depressed.") Henry was the only one they could rely on for predictable behavior. When he turned his back on them, therefore, it was all the more devastating.

He was touchy on the set of *Mister Roberts*. (Gary Cooper and his wife came backstage after one performance and found Henry banging his head against his metal locker because he felt he had given a bad performance for them.) At home he was moody and hypercritical. His typical refrain with Peter was, "Jesus Christ, when are you going to straighten out?" He gave Jane lectures about her constant plays for attention and especially about her tendency to want something so obsessively that she would do everything in her power to get it. Certain of her mannerisms—such as nail-biting—infuriated him because of the message of neurosis they seemed to convey. Sometimes she was so terrified he would see her nails gnawed to the bloody quick that she sat on her hands at the dinner table.

He could be cold and cutting in his remarks and observations, but his silences were even more forbidding. As Jane said, "Even when I was with my father, he often didn't say a word. We'd drive somewhere and there was no communication."

Henry felt remorse over this behavior, but he was powerless to stop it. Things were falling apart with Frances, and their poisoned relationship leached into other areas of his life. He hated the idea of becoming divorced again because it represented such a defeat. Later he would say that at this time of his life he felt his own father speaking negatively through him, as if by ventriloquism from the next world.

In the spring of 1949, doctors discovered that Frances had a kidney condition, and in April they operated. She was left with a twelve-inch scar and five weeks of recuperation, yet she felt that perhaps at last she'd been cured of the malaise that had nagged at her for so long. "They just cut me in half!" she wrote to a friend on May 28 as she started to feel better. "I can't ever recall having suffered so much." She went on to say that she was slowly regaining her strength and that she was optimistic that doctors had figured out the basis of her problems.

But developments on the horizon would kill this tentative optimism. Pan had been scheduled to go to Europe with an art instructor before entering Briarcliff Junior College in the fall. Instead she suddenly married Charles "Bunny" Abry, a grandson of chain-store executive R. H. Kress, and like Pan seventeen years old. The newlyweds went to Europe, and Frances, concerned about her young daughter, went with them, traveling a few days behind, then catching up to check on them before letting them go ahead.

After the couple returned, Pan suffered a miscarriage. Frances wrote to a confidant in jagged sentences that mirrored her sadness: "Pan lost her baby last Friday—premature—a girl who lived two hours—a difficult time."

As Frances sank into deeper despair, everyone else grabbed at a lifeline. For Peter it was playwriting, an activity he chose, according to Bill Hayward, because "he was being told to shut up a lot at home and this gave him a way to say what he wanted." For Jane it was horses. She quickly went from western style to English and then to show, taking lessons three times a week and on weekends hitting the dressage circuit.

For Henry the lifeline was Susan Blanchard, stepdaughter of lyricist Oscar Hammerstein. Although Fonda said that the twenty-one-year-old beauty reminded him of Alice in Wonderland because of her long blond hair, her smooth feline features actually resembled Lauren Bacall's. It was said that they had met on the set of *Mister Roberts,* where Susan's brother Billy Hammerstein was working. In fact, Fonda had first known Susan in Hollywood when she was under contract to Zanuck as a stock girl playing typists, telephone operators, and other anonymous figures in Fox films. She'd had a schoolgirl crush on him then, and now, with Henry living a virtual bachelor's life in New York, it developed into a romance.

In an autobiography written more than three decades after the fact, Henry described the scene when he delivered the bad news to his wife. After putting an arm around her and telling her that he would always love her and the children, he said, "Frances, I want a divorce. I've met someone." According to his account, Frances reacted by looking calmly out the window at an empty birdbath in the yard, pausing, and then replying, "Well, all right, Hank. Good luck, Hank."

The next morning Jane was about to leave for school when her mother said abruptly, "If anyone mentions that your father and I are getting a divorce, tell them that you already know it." But a letter Frances wrote to a friend shortly after the talk with Henry indicates that calm acceptance was not her only response. She was shocked by her husband's calm announcement that he intended to remarry so soon after her serious operation. "Since he has told me he *hasn't been happy during our thirteen years of marriage,* all I can say is I wish him great happiness in this *new marriage.*" Frances added that she felt sorry for her children, whose plight was the only thing that kept her from telling Henry what she really thought of him.

She rewrote her will, excluding her estranged husband. Henry came up from New York on weekends to see the children. At first Peter and Jane looked forward to these excursions: at least he would be with them because he wanted to, not because it was his duty. But their fishing trips and other outings turned into grim exercises all three of them came to dread; Henry would bitterly criticize Peter's inadequacies and Jane would try to insert herself as a buffer between them. One friend saw the three of them at the circus and noted that not only did Henry fail to buy his children hot dogs or souvenirs but he didn't say anything during the entire performance. The Fondas got up wordlessly and left after the circus was over.

Frances made plans to go to Nevada to obtain a divorce. Jane and Peter were cared for by governesses and housekeepers and by their maternal grandmother, Sophie Seymour, although Jane succeeded in denying that anything was wrong. ("If I had been living in *that* house," says Brooke Hayward, "I would have been depressed as hell. But with Jane the more awful it became the more lighthearted she became.") Jane and Peter developed a unique bond—dependent on each other, while still struggling for advantage. Their family life was the basis for something approaching a private code they would use the rest of their lives when telling what they referred to as their "war stories."

Frances became an almost ghostly figure, victimized by wild mood swings. She would get into the car at odd hours and drive off by herself, looking desperately for relief. A friend who lived in New York gave her a key to her apartment and kept a couch made up in one room for her unpredictable visits. Once the friend awakened with a start in the middle of the night to find Frances looming over her, staring down at the pulse in her neck like a vampire, and murmuring in explanation, "I was just curious where the jugular vein is."

There were times when Frances would sit silently at the dinner table crying into her food while everyone else continued to eat pretending that nothing unusual was taking place. After a grim Christmas she began receiving intensive psychiatric treatment at the Austin Riggs Foundation in Stockbridge, Massachusetts. When her condition continued to deteriorate she and her mother decided she should go to Craig House in New York State for full-time observation. She checked in there early in February 1950.

At first her alternating moods of agitation and despondency deepened. But after a few weeks she seemed better. Her spirits brightened considerably after the visit to Greenwich when she got the razor blade that would be her death kit. She played bridge shrewdly with the other patients and had lucid discussions about her condition with Craig House doctors. There was a general agreement among the staff that she would soon be ready to return home. Then came the suicide, with a flurry of notes to her parents, her doctor, and the children, all of them containing the same sentiment: "This is the best way out."

Henry was in New York when he was informed of the death by his mother-in-law in Greenwich; he drove up at once. Before he arrived, Jane came home. Her grandmother said, "I don't want you to go out, your mother is sick." Jane ignored her and went off riding with a friend.

Henry arrived in Greenwich and took Sophie Seymour to the mortuary for a brief service at which they were the only mourners. Afterward, they took Frances's body to be cremated. While they were away, Peter came home and saw the housekeeper's ashen face; he asked what was wrong. She told him that his mother had "taken a turn for the worse."

When Jane returned from the stables, Henry was waiting for her. He said that her mother was dead—of a heart attack. Jane went to her room and sat on her bed thinking, "How weird. I'm never going to see her again and I can't cry." There was that last visit. What had her mother wanted? To tell her that she was going to die and to try one last time to bridge the gap between them? To call for help? In a way it was academic. "I knew from the beginning that she wouldn't last," Jane said later. "I knew she was too fragile to make it."

When Henry sat Peter on his lap and told him the same story, Peter did cry. It was partially out of guilt. For weeks he had been having premonitory dreams about his mother dying, and in his confusion he thought that perhaps these dreams had somehow contaminated her fate.

Henry, meanwhile, was guilt-stricken and asked friends what he should do. Leland Hayward told him he should return to New York

and do *Mister Roberts:* "A guy's got to keep going at a time like this."
And so Henry appeared in the 833rd consecutive performance of the
play that night. Eli Wallach, a member of the cast, says, "When he
was out there, it was as if he'd been spun around three or four times
until dizzy, then pushed out into the spotlight. He wasn't with it,
but he made it through to the end." It seemed unfeeling on his part,
but to theater people it made sense. He knew who he was onstage,
what character he was playing. Onstage there was certainty; offstage there was fear, doubt, and confusion.

Sophie Seymour stopped the magazines and newspapers. The
administrators of Greenwich Academy called an assembly and asked
the students to respect the official story of the heart attack and not
say anything to Jane. Bill Hayward was told what had happened but
strictly forbidden from saying anything to Peter until Henry figured
out how to tell him the truth.

Frances Fonda was dead and gone so quickly it seemed almost
that her life had been an illusion. Yet people continued to talk about
her in hushed tones. Margaret Sullavan, whose own life was beginning to go out of control, said, "If only I had been Jane's and Peter's
mother and Frances had been the mother of my kids, everything
would have been all right." Struck by the sheer horror of the death,
Rocky Cooper, who along with Ava Gardner and other stars had
shared a masseuse with Frances back in Hollywood, had a macabre
thought: "They say suicidal persons attack the things about themselves they like the best. Frances loved her neck. Our masseuse
used to work on her neck. She told Frances that she had a beautiful
throat."

It was a matter of things not just falling apart but falling into place
as well. As a widower Henry was burdened, but he was also free in a
way he would not have been as a divorced man. One day when Susan

was in jeans and sweatshirt cleaning the oven in his apartment he walked in with a small gift-wrapped box. He tossed it to her, saying, "Here, try this on for size." It was an engagement ring.

The kids shuttled between his New York apartment and the Greenwich house, where their grandmother Seymour was in charge on weekdays. Everyone tried very hard to pretend that nothing had happened. A few weeks after the fact, however, Brooke Hayward was with Jane in the back of a classroom at Greenwich Academy thumbing through movie magazines instead of doing schoolwork. Jane had given no evidence of being affected by her mother's death except for her compulsive eating every day after school, when she ran home and gorged on candy and cake while watching *Howdy Doody.* Now Brooke stumbled onto an article about Henry. When she saw the last sentence—which said that his second wife had recently committed suicide—she quickly turned the page. Jane flipped it back and read the article in its entirety without saying a word. It wasn't until years later that she indicated what she had felt: "It was dramatic. . . . It was a combination of horror and fascination. How much more interesting than a heart attack!"

At camp that summer she woke up screaming night after night from gory nightmares about her mother. It took the entire staff to calm her down.

Yet Jane was like Henry—able to deny. At first she denied the maternal bond: "I didn't like her near me. I didn't like her to touch me because I knew she really didn't love me." Then she handled the question of Frances by blanking out. "It probably had very profound effects on me," a typical answer about the impact of the suicide would go, "so profound that I don't even know what they are."

Peter was unable to distance the event. When he was an adult, his talk about the suicide and his use of it in constructing his legend would be calculated. When he was a child, however, it was all instinctive. He kept flashing on an image of his mother back in California, when they were still happy: she was treading water in their pool and holding out her arms to him as she called for him to jump. Unlike his sister, he was too young, too raw and dependent on his mother, to distance the event. And so it became his role for the next twenty years to talk about the hidden truths, often enlarging and fabulating, often rubbing salt into the wounds that his father and sister wanted to heal, and functioning as the Fonda family's memento mori.

After a period of sympathy, Peter was taunted by kids who skirted the edges of the secret truth. "Your mother was crazy," they chanted, or, "Your mother jumped out of a window." One day Peter picked up a water glass and struck one of his tormentors in the face, opening a jagged wound on his cheek. The episode was hushed up by school authorities.

It was Peter who orchestrated the event that was a delayed epilogue to Frances's death—the reminder that it was not possible simply to pretend that she had never happened. It came just after New Year's 1951, when Henry and Susan were honeymooning in a remote spot in the Virgin Islands; they had gotten married the week of Christmas. Henry received an ambiguous message that his son had been in a "shooting accident." He couldn't get any further information. Peter had shot someone? Someone had shot him? Communications with the United States were so poor that Henry had to go by sailboat to the airport and charter a plane to Puerto Rico, where he caught a Pan Am flight home. Sophie Seymour told him that Peter had conned her into letting him and two friends play with a .22 rifle by saying that they had no ammunition. In truth, the playmates did have bullets, and Peter arranged for the chauffeur to drive the three of them to a shooting range on the Kress estate belonging to a relative of Bunny Abry, Pan's husband.

Peter's two friends had a shotgun and an antique Civil War–era pistol, and the three of them had tossed objects in the air and shot at them. But there was no ammunition for the old pistol, and Peter held it against his stomach while trying to force a .22 shell into the barrel. The pistol had discharged, sending the bullet through his liver and one of his kidneys.

After being rushed by the chauffeur to a hospital nearly fifty miles away, Peter was wheeled into the operating room in a state of shock. The staff physicians had little experience with bullet wounds. Later Peter recalled looking down at the floor and seeing a pair of muddy boots suddenly appear. They belonged to the one doctor in the area who had worked with gunshot victims—the prison doctor at Sing Sing, who had been duck hunting when they called him.

Jane remembered later that at one point a physician came out of the operating room to tell the family it was possible Peter would die. It took a week for his condition to be regarded as stable, and another week for him to be out of danger.

For many years after, Peter would often lower his pants in the middle of some autobiographical rambling and describe the odd starburst shape beside his navel with a kind of pride. The result of either an accident or an unconscious move to join his mother, the puckered scar was a mark of his special relationship with her, an almost umbilical acknowledgment of how deeply her death had wounded him, a reminder that Frances Fonda had existed.

FIVE

A mild tug-of-war developed between Sophie Seymour and Henry over the children. There was still tension from events before the suicide and it had not been diminished by Peter's accident or by Henry's discovery that Frances had written him entirely out of her will and settled her estate primarily on Pan, with smaller trust funds for Jane and Peter. But father and grandparents agreed to split the children for the time being.

The Seymours were in charge through the first part of 1951, as Henry embarked on the national tour of *Mister Roberts.* It was one long triumph culminating in Los Angeles, where the play ran before packed houses which were, if anything, more enthusiastic than the original audiences in New York three years earlier.

Henry found the film industry wrapped in a frightened mood. Part of it was financial. The advent of television had resulted in the closing of thousands of theaters and in a slowdown of production. But the changes also had to do with the personality of Hollywood, a personality now embodied by such figures as Montgomery Clift, Marlon Brando, and James Dean, who were symbols of American neurosis just as Henry and Jimmy Stewart had embodied American innocence.

The big studios were losing their dictatorial hold over the stars and over the industry itself, as signaled by the recent retirement of Adolph Zukor, one of the first tycoons, and even more by the firing of Louis Mayer at MGM. The vacuum was being only partly filled by the development of large talent agencies such as Music Corporation of America (which had gotten into the business when the legendary Lew Wasserman bought Leland Hayward's gold-plated client list), and it was not clear what new power arrangements would emerge.

Another development had to do with politics, notably the case of the Hollywood Ten, a group of screenwriters who had refused to cooperate with House Un-American Activities Committee's investigations into communist infiltration of the film industry in 1947. The investigations had hit the industry hard, miring it in a crisis of confidence and identity that would take years to shake off. The atmosphere of fear set friend against friend and initiated feuds that would last for decades. The situation did not represent simply an outburst of groundless paranoia. The Communist Party had been influential in the industry at least since Upton Sinclair's campaign for governor of California. The Party had wrapped itself in respectability by Popular Frontism during the war, but it was well known, for instance, that John Howard Lawson, one of the Ten, still acted as the Party's commissar in the film community after the war was over. (In one instance he had ordered writer Budd Schulberg not to transform what became *What Makes Sammy Run?* from a short story into a novel, claiming that the piece was counterrevolutionary; Schulberg was so distraught that he left town.) F. Scott Fitzgerald, among other observers, had seen the Party as a genuinely malevolent presence long before the McCarthy era. "It is not that you should not disagree with them—" Fitzgerald had written shortly before his death. "The important thing is that you should not argue with them. . . . Whatever you [may] say, they have ways of twisting it into shapes which put you in some lower category of mankind

('Fascist,' 'Liberal,' 'Trotskyist') and disparage you both intellectually and personally in the process."

Fonda's own politics were those of the midwestern populist—he
had voted for socialist Norman Thomas against Hoover in 1928 and
against FDR in 1932—who had become a mainstream liberal.
(Peter later recalled: "I had never heard the words 'nigger' or 'kike'
until I moved to Greenwich. I heard the words at school and asked
my father what they meant, and he blew up.") He was fiercely
patriotic and disliked the machinations of the Communist Party,
but was unalterably opposed to HUAC and similar agencies. In
1947, Fonda, Gregory Peck, Paulette Goddard, Katharine Hepburn, and others had signed an advertisement that appeared in
Variety stating that they were "disgusted and outraged" by the
investigations of the Hollywood Ten. Now Fonda joined other liberals in protests and later claimed that he had been "graylisted" for a
time as a result of his actions. His friendship with staunchly
conservative Jimmy Stewart survived the ordeal only because the
two men agreed after a violent argument that they must never again
talk about politics. But he disgustedly terminated his relationship
with anticommunists such as Ward Bond and barely retained a
speaking relationship with John Wayne, men who had once joined
him in the Playhouse at Tigertail for poker parties during the old
days. What Henry saw in Hollywood in 1951 reinforced his distaste
for the film industry, and he left immediately after the tour of *Mister
Roberts* was finished.

Back in New York, where he signed on for another play, *Point of No
Return,* he and Susan established a routine at the townhouse Fonda
bought on East 74th Street. Jane and Peter began to spend more
time with him and less in Greenwich. They were initially suspicious of Susan, having been exposed to their grandmother's disap-

proving attitude. But as they got to know her, they discovered that she was actually quite like them: young and inexperienced and wholly under Henry Fonda's thumb. She was ready to devote herself to being the wife of a great man, even though she had caught a glimpse of his dark side during their honeymoon in the Virgin Islands. Susan had placed his expensive watch on a rock when they went for a swim and returned to find that the tide had swallowed it up. When she began to cry, Henry looked at her darkly and commanded, "Stop crying. Your crying disgusts me." Susan chose to overlook this and similar incidents, and tried to function as what she later called a "Japanese wife."

This meant, above all, ensuring that Henry had a peaceful habitat. He had been an avid hobbyist all his life, whether it was building model planes with Jimmy Stewart or making compost for his organic farming at Tigertail. It looked like puttering, but Susan realized that it was something more—a way to kill time which hung heavy on him when he was not acting, time which was a potential enemy because it might force him to face himself without a dramatic mask. ("Hank is really living when he is acting," one friend said, "just existing when he isn't.")

Now Fonda had discovered what for him would be the ultimate hobby—painting. He had become a fan of Andrew Wyeth, attracted by the smoothly realistic surfaces as well as the mysterious melancholy, and he began to emulate his style. (He eventually met his idol, after making an arrangement to drive to Wyeth's house. Fonda set out one of his own paintings alongside his car, and Wyeth squinted at it a moment and said a single word: "Harnett." What Fonda had done reminded him of the American still-life artist William Michael Harnett.)

He worked for hours in the third floor of the townhouse before his evening performances of the successful new play, barely saying hello when the kids came to visit. Symbols almost of a past life, his children weighed on his attempt at a new beginning. When he did speak to them, it was usually to say something critical.

With Peter (who, ironically, resembled one of the wistful, wounded boys in a Wyeth canvas) he was especially curt. The boy had been sent to the Fay School in Massachusetts, where he walked through life in a daze. Once, after mail call, Peter opened a letter that had been flung on his bed. The handwriting looked like his mother's and there were little pictures like those she had sometimes drawn. It was signed "Love, Mom," and in his confusion he thought for a moment that Frances might still be alive. But then he realized the letter was actually for the boy whose bed was next to his and had been put on his own bed by mistake.

Henry also had a fit when he heard about another incident involving guns — this time Peter was discovered by Maggie Sullavan holding a .22 rifle up to his eye so that he could check out the barrel. He was bothered not only by the neediness that called for a response he couldn't give but even by his son's genetic makeup. Peter had his mother's face but Henry's own skinny body. He ordered the boy to eat more and fill himself out, never acknowledging that his nagging had anything to do with his own thin arms and sunken chest, which had embarrassed him all his life.

With Jane the assault was more cerebral. Sometimes when she came to New York to stay with him, she stopped in a Presbyterian church near Henry's townhouse and sat for a few minutes of peace and serenity. He found out about it and, after getting her to admit that she was no more a believer than he was, taxed her with charges of being a hypocrite. Unlike Peter, however, Jane did not take it. Her friend Brooke Hayward remembers: "Jane's main thrust in life was to battle her father down. She would do it verbally — like a little mosquito buzzing around. She was defiant."

Yet it was not all negative. The children recognized Henry's deep fealty to them, his integrity and high standards, and this bonded them to him. They looked at him for hidden qualities and spent much of their time trying to understand him.

Peter learned about his father through the fierceness of his dedication to acting. When preparing for a role, Henry would sometimes offer Peter $2.50 an hour to run lines for him. Peter was astonished, saying later that Henry could have "memorized the phone book." Sometimes his father would hesitate and Peter would prompt him. "I know the *line*," Henry would grumble, and then Peter would realize that it was not the words but the character his father was trying to learn.

Jane not only saw the formidable presence who occasionally lashed out at them but also understood that her father was a fallible man perplexed and disappointed by the turns his life had taken. "There is a deep, deep sadness in him," she said. "If it weren't for the sadness, he would be cold, lifeless. But the sadness coming through creates an identifying thing. . . . It is finally like an animal that has been deeply wounded."

Seeing that Henry was unable to provide what his children needed, Susan tried to fill the gap. She did not mother them, although periodically she pulled her long hair back into a severe bun, put on a plain dress, and, hoping that she looked older than her years, went to see their teachers for parent conferences. She tried to be a friend. Recognizing the trauma they had suffered, but not treating them as fragile, she became one person they could rely on for predictable feelings and emotional stability.

A few months after getting to know Susan, in fact, Peter, who had resisted her strongly at the beginning of the marriage, was polling teachers at his school about whether or not he should call her Mom.

For Jane, Susan was even more important as a normalizing figure. Thirteen when the marriage took place, she had entered Emma Willard School in Troy, New York, in a kind of stupor. Attempting to deny that her mother's death had affected her led to disruptive behavior. She was fearful of Henry's censure and wrote one boy-friend imploring him to have patience with her and not to return her letters with corrections in red the way Henry did. But she always relied on her name to get her a safe passage out of the scrapes in which she found herself.

Now, however, her problems involved something more than pranks. In one incident that caused a small furor, she poured a trail of lighter fluid from her room to another girl's and then set it on fire, to let the girl know she didn't like her. She became a leader of a group of students calling itself the "Disorders," and wrote a friend that they had "at one time or another all been ostracized."

Never the ugly duckling she thought herself to be, Jane was now on the verge of becoming a swan, with agate eyes that looked permanently shocked and disconcertingly ripe lips. But she contin-ued to feel betrayed by her body—as if a different, more interesting self was imprisoned within her, as she phrased it, and unable to get out. She no longer had to worry about the pudginess or the squirrel-cheeked look she'd had as a little girl, but food—and the complex matters for which it was a metaphor—continued to be a problem. She had a recurrent dream in her first years at Willard about being in a large hall filled with mountains of food she was unable to reach. And after reading in a history class about how Romans adjourned to vomitoria after banquets, she began to binge and purge. She ate coffee ice cream by the gallon and pound cake by the pound, bagfuls of brownies, and peanut butter and bacon sandwiches. And then she retched them up. She sent for chewing gum advertised in pulp magazines that was said to contain tapeworm eggs, believing that they would hatch inside her and devour the food with which she stuffed herself.

Her difficult transition into young womanhood was something that, given their blocked communication, Frances probably could not have helped her with. But Susan was close enough in age not to condescend to her. She reassured and soothed Jane, more like a carefree young aunt than a mother. They went on shopping expeditions together; they tried on clothes and makeup. ("She began to show up in high heels, stockings, little black dresses, and circle pins," says Brooke Hayward, who did not go to Willard with her, "a clone of her stepmother who was very elegant.") Jane was intensely proud of Susan, and on Parents' Day at Willard she pointed out to her friends how lovely she was in comparison with the other mothers.

And so the patched-together family struggled back toward a tenuous normalcy. Susan desperately wanted a child but was unable to get pregnant, and in the spring of 1953 she and Henry adopted an eight-week-old girl. They picked her up at a foster home in a limousine, and named her Amy. Henry took pleasure in getting up for mid-morning feedings and changing diapers, and Jane and Peter were enthusiastic because the baby seemed confirmation that the Fondas were now involved with life instead of death.

That summer they all went to southern California for the first time since the move east and settled into a rented house. Brooke Hayward was there visiting her father, and she and Jane hooked up once again, becoming very visible young women around town. They talked about how Henry's strictness was exactly the same as Maggie Sullavan's: fervent and puritanical. They speculated about the past marriage between their two parents and imagined a passion continuing to smolder between them. They talked about their joint crush on Marlon Brando and drove around Hollywood in a convertible hoping to catch a glimpse of him. They never did see Brando, but once they ran into David O. Selznick, who, ignoring Jane, looked at sixteen-year-old Brooke and told her that she had the glamour and presence to be a star.

But if Selznick noticed Brooke, the boys were crazy for Jane. Peter's old friend Jack Hathaway hung out with them at the Sand

and Sea Club in Santa Monica. He remembers, "Jane was a beach wonder, so perfect, tan and shining with lotion, with this halo, untouchable and surrounded by older guys." Peter too had charisma: thin and gangly, the center of attention with a younger group, he showed off the scar low on his abdomen as if it were a badge of honor.

Hollywood was the place where they felt they belonged, but the East was where they lived. The summer over, the family returned so that Henry could take a starring role in another play that would become a classic, *The Caine Mutiny Court-Martial*. It was a tremendous hit and after six months the producers tried to convince him to stay through what would obviously be a long Broadway run. But Henry had gotten an offer that would make him end his long exile from the movies—to star in the film version of *Mister Roberts*.

Josh Logan and Leland Hayward, coproducers of the play, thought he was too old for the role. Logan wanted Marlon Brando, Hayward was for William Holden. But Warner Bros. selected John Ford to direct the movie and Ford insisted on Fonda. It was a gesture of loyalty to his friend and also perhaps a gesture of contempt for the work. Ford had seen the play on Broadway. When he came backstage to see Fonda afterward, he was asked his opinion and said he hadn't paid much attention. Asked why not, he growled, "Why should I look at a homosexual play?"

Always a heavy drinker, Ford was in an alcoholic daze throughout the first weeks of shooting. He was curt and abrasive toward the cast, and he cavalierly altered the plot and dialogue. When an alarmed Leland Hayward asked him for an explanation, he snarled, "Don't bother me, asshole."

Henry was horrified. He had deep respect for Ford, a man who not only had given him film immortality but also had been a carousing friend for years. But *Mister Roberts* was close to his heart—a professional triumph deeply involved with the decisive emotional experiences of his life. He hated what he saw as Ford's trivialization of the work, and as shooting progressed on Midway Island he became broodingly silent.

One night Fonda was in his cabin talking with a couple of the other cast members when Ford came to the door, his face flushed with drink, his legendary eyepatch awry.

"Well, Hank," he asked provocatively, "what do you think of the day's shooting?"

"I think it's shit," Fonda replied.

Ford stumbled unsteadily toward him and threw a looping punch. Fonda had to be restrained from knocking the old man down. After that, Henry was rigid and unforgiving, and Ford was drunk twenty-four hours a day. Jack Warner finally had to replace him with Mervyn LeRoy to get the film completed.

Despite the fact that it was pieced together, the film version of *Mister Roberts* was a popular success. For Henry, however, it was another reminder of why he disliked Hollywood. After he finished it, he looked for something to get the bad taste out of his mouth. There were many offers, but he took the one that seemed weightiest and furthest away, a proposal from Dino De Laurentiis that he star in *War and Peace*. He agreed to move his ménage to Rome for the summer of 1955.

That summer marked the fifth anniversary of Frances's death. In retrospect Jane and especially Peter would think of it as The Summer It Came Apart Once Again. But when they arrived in Rome, they were buoyed by the energy of the city. Rome was the center of the jet set and its *dolce vita*. It was also, as a result of the work of Rossellini, De Sica, Fellini, and others, the temporary capital of world film.

Henry's parents
William Brace and
Herberta Fonda set
a standard for
marriage that he
was never able to
match. (The Stuhr
Museum of the
Prairie Pioneer)

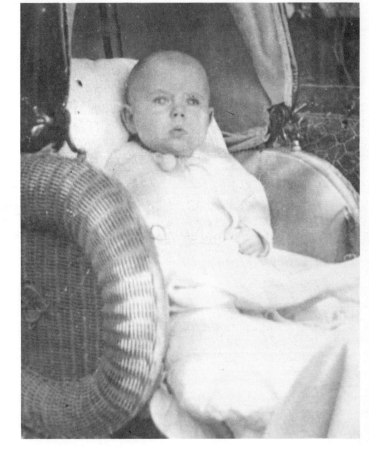

Henry Jaynes Fonda,
born May 16, 1905,
in Grand Island,
Nebraska, played
to the camera at an
early age. (The
Stuhr Museum of
the Prairie Pioneer)

When he arrived in Hollywood in the mid-thirties, Henry's enigmatic charms made him an instant hero in the new era of the talkies. His friend John Steinbeck called him "a lean, stringy, dark-faced piece of electricity." (Photofest)

Henry costarred with Margaret Sullavan in The Moon's Our Home *in 1936. "She had presence," Henry said of his first wife, "which is something you're born with, you don't acquire." (Photofest)*

In 1936, Henry tried marriage again, this time with a self-possessed socialite. "She was as good-looking as a model from Vogue *or any actress I'd met," he said of Frances Seymour Brokaw. (Photofest)*

Henry's two great roles, Tom Joad (above) and Wyatt Earp (right), established him, in Orson Welles's phrase, as "the face of America." (both Photofest)

Henry and Jane liked swimming in their backyard pool in the hills above Sunset Boulevard. She was completely relaxed when he held her and agitated when he let her go. (The Private Collection of J. Watson Webb, Jr.)

Frances, with Pan (her daughter from a previous marriage) and Jane, proudly showed off baby Peter on his christening day in 1940. (The Private Collection of J. Watson Webb, Jr.)

At four, Jane complied when Frances dressed her up in Tyrolean garb; later she became an incorrigible tomboy. (The Private Collection of J. Watson Webb, Jr.)

Home from the war in December 1943, Lieutenant Fonda posed for a family portrait with Frances, Jane, Pan, and Peter. (The Private Collection of J. Watson Webb, Jr.)

Henry was in his element in Mister Roberts *on Broadway. When the play opened in 1948, he said, "I've rehearsed forty-three years for this night, and it was sure as hell worth it."* (AP/Wide World Photos)

Heading off to Rome to film War and Peace *in 1955, Henry was accompanied by his third wife Susan Blanchard, their adopted daughter Amy, Peter, and Jane. Soon after, the family splintered.* (AP/Wide World Photos)

At fifty-one Henry embarked on a turbulent marriage with the fiery Afdera Franchetti, twenty-four (Photofest). Jane, here lounging by a pool with Afdera, was fascinated by the way her new stepmother manipulated her father. (The Private Collection of J. Watson Webb, Jr.)

In 1963, the Fondas rendezvoused outside Grand Central Terminal, where Jane was *filming* Sunday in New York. *(Photofest)*

Early in Jane's career, acting coach Andreas Voutsinas was her Svengali (AP/Wide World Photos); director Roger Vadim was her Pygmalion. (The Kobal Collection)

Jane (here with John Phillip Law and Anita Pallenberg) starred in Vadim's eroto-fantasy Barbarella *in 1968. Her role in* Klute, *in 1971, sparked a romance with costar Donald Sutherland. (both Photofest)*

532-8

Married at twenty-one to Susan Brewer, Peter embarked on a career as a clean-cut Hollywood actor. By 1969, when he and Dennis Hopper immortalized the biker cult in Easy Rider, *his persona had changed. (both Photofest)*

Henry had read *War and Peace* and was prepared to play the ursine Pierre as Tolstoy had written the character—halting but intelligent, an outsider because he was a bastard and an insider because of his connections with others. But the Italians demanded that Pierre be played as a traditional romantic hero. There was a running battle on the set when Henry began wearing wire-rimmed glasses to help in his characterization and De Laurentiis demanded that he remove them, with the result that Fonda had the glasses on in some scenes and not in others.

At one point he told director King Vidor, "You understand, don't you, that I can be a real son of a bitch." His anger had to do with things he found hard to define; it spilled over into his relationship with Susan, which became filled with long silences. His friend John Swope, married to Fonda's fellow Omaha actor Dorothy McGuire, said: "All the marriages ended the same way—beset with quiet. After a while, he just couldn't say anything to the woman. There was no communication. . . . He [could] cut someone right out of his life and not appear to have it affect him at all."

For Jane, who was so tuned in to her father's wavelength that she understood something was happening before he did, it was a time to watch and wait. As she described it later, this Roman holiday was the time she spent eating figs and gaining weight, and watching Gina Lollobrigida, who lived in a neighboring villa, through binoculars.

But for fifteen-year-old Peter, it was a time of discovery. For years he had tried to talk about his mother's death, but he was always rebuffed, as if it were a subject of guilt and shame. Early in the summer, he was in an Italian barbershop and picked up an American magazine. There was a story about the Fondas which mentioned that his mother had committed suicide. He went to his father for an explanation, but aside from agreeing that it was true, Henry was dismissive and refused to talk about it. Peter took one of the family's cars and drove off into the countryside. He stopped at a hotel in a tiny village, locked himself in a room, and began beating his head on the walls.

He spent the rest of the summer walking the streets of Rome alone, drinking cheap Italian wine by the liter. On one occasion he was standing drunk in front of St. Peter's when a young American Air Force attaché and his wife picked him up. They took him to their house and, as Peter told it later, the woman gave him his sexual initiation while the husband watched.

A teenager morbidly sensitive to hypocrisy, Peter was burdened by the growing realization of his father's imperfection. As he said, Henry had been "presented as perfect, the man who played Abe Lincoln and Mister Roberts and Tom Joad, the man who carried everybody's integrity on his shoulders, [but he] turned out to be a hollow man to me."

Susan was having a similar epiphany. Those qualities in her husband she had romanticized as American Gothic at the beginning of the relationship—staunch silence and withheld strength—she now realized were part of the scar tissue of psychic wounds that were beyond treatment. Within the emotional rigidity there was no chance for fun. She had outgrown the desire for a mentor and didn't want a husband mired in a crabbed middle age. Most of all she didn't want someone who treated her like another of his troublesome children and refused even to buy her an automobile of her own. As her mother, Dorothy Hammerstein, commented, "Her life was wretched." Henry had never physically hurt her but, she said later, she had always been afraid of him.

By the end of the summer, Susan had decided to leave Henry. She told Peter about her decision at the breakfast table one morning. As they were talking, Henry walked through the room, his face set in a mask of pained annoyance. He didn't stop to add anything to what Susan was saying, although his son had just broken into tears. Peter went to Jane's room and told her the disturbing news. "I've known that for a few days," she said with boredom. "They're too different, too incompatible." Later Peter told a friend that while his world was breaking up again in Rome, all Jane could talk about was the pleasure of sex, which she had recently discovered. She described in painstaking detail the sound of it, the smell of it, the feel of it.

Leaving Henry to finish his doomed film, Susan took the kids back home. She helped Jane enroll at Vassar and, after taking Peter to the family doctor, who said he should see a psychiatrist, enrolled him at Westminster School in Connecticut. She kept Amy with her. Henry called and begged her to come back. Susan refused. She had tried so hard to please Henry and be the perfect wife. But now, saddened and bewildered by what she perceived as failure, she had passed her breaking point. She met his sister Harriet by chance in New York and told her that Henry had made her miserable, that he was stingy and tough and she was going to be just as tough when it came to the divorce settlement.

Henry wandered around Rome early that autumn with the anguished look he displayed as Pierre watching Moscow go up in flames. He fell in with the jet set and, as a friend remarked, was "looked at hard" by every woman in town. He had a brief fling with Anita Ekberg, who would be Fellini's symbol of sex and decadence in *La Dolce Vita,* but she was not his type.

Early in autumn, with shooting almost finished on *War and Peace,* Henry's costar Audrey Hepburn took him to a dinner party where he captured the attention of the hostess's twenty-four-year-old sister, Afdera Franchetti. She compelled him to look at her by repeatedly asking him to pass things to her during dinner—salt, pepper, bread, salad. When he finally looked at her he saw a striking sloe-eyed woman with golden hair and a sleepy Venetian beauty. She asked him about the role he had just finished. "It would have been right for Peter Ustinov," said Fonda sadly, "but I'm no good at all."

Afdera came from an unusual family. Her father, Baron Raimondo Franchetti, resembled one of the Nietzschean heroes of his friend and contemporary, the writer Gabriele D'Annunzio. The six-foot-six explorer named his children with the places he had conquered in mind: the eldest daughter was Simba, "lion" in Swahili; her sister was Lorian, named after a swamp where elephants went to die; Nanucki, Franchetti's only son, was born after the Baron's conquest of the North Pole. Afdera was named for an active volcano he explored in Ethiopia not long before he was killed by a bomb that exploded on a plane he was taking from Cairo to Addis Ababa.

Afdera grew up in a Palladian villa in Treviso with a long winding drive lined by ruined Art Nouveau statues of naked women which Nanucki and his friend Ernest Hemingway had shot up with elephant guns. Afdera claimed to be the inspiration for the character of Renata, the young *baronessa* in *Across the River and Into the Trees*. She told reporters that Hemingway was desperately in love with her and that she had visited him at his *finca* in Cuba. Hemingway called these her "little girl fantasies," and said that it was "no sin to indulge them."

True to her name, Afdera had a volcanic temperament. She also had a calculated mysteriousness and a sure touch as a social climber. Henry had never met anyone quite like her. She accented her fractured English to amuse him. She bragged about being engaged to a duke's son, whom she held in reserve should nothing come of the flirtation that began that night at the dinner table.

Over the next few weeks, Henry and Afdera saw each other in nightclubs around Rome. Afdera trolled for him artfully, holding herself aloof, appearing regally unattainable in comparison with the other women who had thrown themselves at him that summer. But like the other women with whom he had become deeply involved, she subtly controlled the courtship. Finally, after a few weeks, they were close enough for her to take Henry to meet her mother. The *baronessa* was so excited about meeting Henry Fonda that, still dressed in black, she came out of her private quarters for the first time since going into mourning for her husband some twenty years earlier.

Upon returning to the United States in the fall of 1955, Henry began shooting *The Wrong Man* and working on *Twelve Angry Men,* the first and only movie he ever produced. But his heart was still in Italy. He spoke to Afdera almost daily by telephone. It was decided that she would come to New York for Christmas. She told her fiancé, the duke's son, that she needed to leave him for a while to make sure that their love was strong.

When she arrived in the United States, Afdera immediately made contact with the community of European expatriates. She played during the day while Henry was on the set, tantalizing him each evening with tales of the other admirers she had already found in New York. When she returned to Italy after the first of the year, she told her fiancé that the engagement was off.

With the exception of a brief interlude in London, the courtship progressed by telephone until the following summer, when Henry took a house at Cape Cod and doggedly reassembled the family. It turned out to be a sentimental moment. The manager of the playhouse where he'd started some twenty-five years earlier with Maggie Sullavan and the other University Players badgered him into agreeing to do a few performances of *The Male Animal* with Jane in a supporting role.

The two had acted together briefly the previous year when his sister Harriet had persuaded Henry to star with fellow Omahan Dorothy McGuire in a benefit performance of *The Country Girl* for the Omaha Community Playhouse. Harriet had asked Jane to play the ingenue. At that time, Henry had been amazed by his daughter, whose only experience had been a few bit parts in productions at

Willard. But she was, Henry realized, a natural. Required to enter crying in one scene in *The Country Girl,* she at first thought of asking a stagehand to bat her around, but then made the tears come by herself. Afterward she came up to Fonda dry-eyed and said brightly, "How'd I do?" He didn't tell her that she had accomplished something that many professionals spent a lifetime unable to bring off. Only later did she reveal how she'd cried on cue: "While Daddy was onstage, I'd look at him sentimentally and think, 'Daddy's going away and I'll never see him again, never, never again.'"

Henry was bowled over once more when he saw Jane in *The Male Animal.* He noticed that the audience imperceptibly sucked in its breath when she made her entrances, and sat a little straighter in the seats. He didn't tell her this reaction made him realize she could probably make it if she chose theater as a profession, but the three weeks they performed together were the happiest days he could remember between them since she was a little girl. It was as if acting was a substitute for the private language of the heart he spoke only haltingly.

The idyllic experience was interrupted when Afdera arrived from Italy at the end of the summer, blowing into the Fonda family like a sirocco. Only a few years younger than his father's new love, Jane was intrigued by her continental poise and the feminine wiles she employed on Henry. Peter, who was fighting harder than usual for a share of Henry's attention because of Jane's stage success, was suspicious. Afdera made no attempt to ingratiate herself with the children or to adopt a maternal attitude. She was there for a reason and the reason was Henry. They went on long moonlit walks along the seashore. Afdera was in a melancholy mood. Henry assumed this meant she was pining for a commitment, and so he proposed. Later she would say that her mood had been caused by something else: depression over meeting Henry's kids.

Proposing to Afdera was a punctuation mark in Henry's life. Before, it had seemed that life had dealt him a bad hand; now he had no choice but to see himself as one of those much-married celebrities people made jokes about. In the fall of 1956, while filming *The Tin Star* with Fonda, Anthony Perkins found him in a deeply reflective mood. The two men drove out to the Paramount ranch every day in the same car. Perkins had heard of the legendary Fonda reserve and was taken aback when Henry began telling him the story of his life. "It was one hour out and one hour back for three weeks," says Perkins. "He paced the story to last, picking it up every morning where he'd stopped the day before."

If he was unusually talkative, telling Perkins how much his new love meant to him, Henry's dark side was not warmed by this emotion, as producer-director Jed Harris discovered. Now down on his luck, Harris, who'd been the "other man" decades earlier when Fonda's marriage to Maggie Sullavan was coming apart, hoped to revive his career by directing *Our Town*. But Henry, who was to star in the production, vetoed him.

Afdera too was a punctuation mark in the life of his son, who heard the news of the engagement on the radio after he was back at Westminster. Peter took good-natured ribbing from school friends about Afdera's age and sensuous good looks. Then there was a minor disagreement with a teacher; it escalated into a shouting match in which the man yelled, "You're no good, like your father. Anyone who's been married as many times as he has and is getting married again is a son of a bitch." Peter uncoiled his gangly body and knocked the teacher down.

The wedding ceremony took place at Henry's townhouse on March 10, 1957. Jane, who had adopted a superior attitude toward it all, arrived by cab from Vassar and related that her driver, who didn't know who she was, had said, "I see that Henry Fonda's getting married again. . . . He's marrying some Italian broad." Peter, who had written Afdera sullen letters headed "Dear Stepmother," was best man, sulking through the entire proceedings. After the ceremony, he and Jane made snide jokes about how their father's wives were getting younger and younger. Jane said that the next one would be younger than she. Peter said that the one after that would be younger than he. The discussion then collapsed into black humor about how the great Henry Fonda would wind up changing the diapers of wife number ten.

Henry and Afdera went to Italy for a honeymoon. Peter went back to school and got into more trouble, fighting with schoolmates and rejecting discipline by teachers. He was gaunt, eating only when he had to, for fuel rather than pleasure. His eating disorder was the exact opposite of Jane's: she filled herself with everything, desperate for survival, while Peter deprived himself like someone punishing himself out of survivor's guilt.

He was taking large quantities of phenobarbital to combat his growing agitation at Westminster, but he became even more anxious and paranoid. One morning he called Jane at Vassar. He said he needed her help because he felt crazy. She borrowed a car and drove to his school and found him cowering with some stray dogs in the bushes outside a building. "Oh, wow!" she said, "I think you're Holden Caulfield!" Even in his agitated state this struck him as an odd comment, and for years after he sent her Christmas cards signed "Holden."

Jane called her aunt Harriet, who arranged for Peter to take the train to Omaha. Henry was informed and for the second time had to interrupt a honeymoon to deal with his son. He flew home and put Peter in an all-girls high school—the only private school in Omaha—and also enrolled him in classes at the local university because tests administered by a psychologist to check his emotional stability had shown that the boy had an unusually high IQ. He was sent to Nebraska because Henry believed it was a seedbed of midwestern values, a place where roots might be grafted onto Peter's unhappy alienation.

.   .   .

Henry and Afdera finished their honeymoon and took up married life in New York. They were two mismatched eccentrics. "He treated me the way he treated the world," Afdera said of Henry later: "with a sort of weary tolerance." Up at seven-thirty every morning, he stood on his head for five minutes and did yoga. He showered, then washed and tidied up the bathroom afterward so that it looked as though nobody had been there. He was extremely private, and for the first year of their marriage he didn't even let Afdera see him shave.

For her part, Afdera, who had been anemic as a child, was accustomed to drinking tumblers filled with bloody drippings from rare meat. She had an insatiable appetite and ate constantly, without appearing to gain weight. As Rupert Allen, Henry's former commanding officer who became a friend, observed, "She was mad for Henry and mad for his food. She cleaned out the refrigerator every night."

Afdera imported a pair of Italian servants and began to remodel Henry's townhouse in gaudy Venetian decor and then to throw expensive parties. They entertained celebrities such as Peter Ustinov and Richard Burton, just beginning to discover America, who came and sang Welsh songs until sunrise. But mostly there were Afdera's countrymen, who referred to her as "Baronessa" and occasionally called Henry "Barone."

Finding himself surrounded in his own house by people who spoke little English and whom he hardly knew, Henry adopted a bemused air. Leland Hayward later described the aftermath of one evening at East 74th Street: "For dinner they had ice cream and chocolate sauce. There was dancing, and all of a sudden these nutty Italians began throwing ice cream and sauce on the walls. I thought Fonda would commit murder. But he just stood there and smiled and enjoyed it."

In the summer of 1957 the whole family—Afdera sarcastically called it Fonda's "traveling circus"—went to Cap Ferrat on the

Riviera. They saw Garbo, their neighbor, swim naked in the ocean outside their door every morning. They went to Picasso's studio and watched him paint, as if attending a performance. They traveled to Pamplona for the running of the bulls and ran into Hemingway, whom Henry thought a pompous old man with a scaly beard who compared unfavorably with his friend Steinbeck.

Jane was visited by her boyfriend, fledgling actor James Franciscus. Afdera, by now an aficionado of Fonda foibles, predicted that the relationship would not last because Franciscus was too uncomplicated and Jane, she believed, had need of greater complexity in a man.

Peter was still looking for something from his father that Henry couldn't give. He fabulated self-aggrandizing and melodramatic stories to get attention, claiming, for instance, that he had been attacked by three hoodlums in New York who hung him on a Cyclone fence and threatened to drive nails through his hands. This only sharpened Henry's contempt. He ignored Peter that summer and Afdera subtly tortured him by asking him about his acne and other teenager embarrassments. As she said later, "I think he was always grateful. He simply loved to feel sorry for himself and I gave him good reason."

After they returned to the States, Jane decided to drop out of Vassar. It had never been clear to her why she had gone to college in the first place, especially a place like Vassar, whose main function, as one graduate said, was to prepare women for "marriage, motherhood, and menopause." She'd been there two years, and was involved less in academics than in perfecting her figure (she had added Dexedrine to bingeing and purging in her weight-loss repertory) and conquering men.

Brooke Hayward was at Vassar too, although Henry had insisted that the two girls not room together because of their episodes of adolescent wildness. Brooke watched Jane and was struck by the fact that she seldom attended class and that she engaged in casual sex, which made her "conspicuous" and led her to be called "the Anything-Goes Girl." The realization that men liked her may not have dispelled Jane's insecurity, but it did give her a power she never had before, a power she came to flaunt. "She had a reputation for being easy," says Brooke Hayward. "It was almost a joke."

Novelist Michael Thomas, who eventually married Brooke, says of Jane: "She was going out with two or three guys on the same night. She was this unbelievable-looking girl and it is easy to imagine the residential colleges at Yale vibrating with guys whacking off at the mere thought of her. She was promiscuous, which in those days was a way of expressing competitiveness." It was said that she'd broken the final taboo—having sex in the meeting place of the Yale secret society Skull and Bones.

She had found that it was possible to use her father as a built-in justification for her excesses. On one occasion, after spending a weekend AWOL with a boy, she readied a tearful plea for the administrator she knew she would have to face. But before she could even begin to spin out her elaborately contrived story, the man said that he understood that her father had just married for the fourth time and that she was emotionally upset.

Although Henry was preoccupied with his new marriage, he still "watched her like a hawk," says Michael Thomas. Jane often spun an elaborate web of falsehood when off for a weekend, calling home at various times to reassure her father that she was actually staying with the girlfriend whose name she had given. But she tired of all the intrigue and in the fall of 1957 told Henry that she wanted to go to France to study art. He reluctantly went along with her plan, arranging for her to live in a boardinghouse for girls run by an ancient contessa. Jane hated it because the woman tried to "finish" her charges, teaching them manners and the art of polite conversation. After a few weeks she abandoned the contessa and the art studies that were the ostensible reason for her being abroad, and dived into the Left Bank, where the Beats were trying to re-create the expatriate life of the 1920s. She hung out with people around *The Paris Review,* which gave her an entrée into the city's bohemian set.

Rumors of Jane's doings finally reached Henry. Enraged at the way she'd conned him, he ordered her home at Christmas. She returned to New York and settled sulkily into the townhouse and watched Afdera manipulate her father. After the first of the year, she began to take private lessons in art and music, but was frustrated by the idea that it required a lifetime's commitment to paint or compose a masterpiece.

It was a time of transition for the family. A generational changing of the guard was due, but it was unclear how Jane and Peter would ever accomplish it, given their father's towering presence. For his part, Henry felt uncertain about them and knew that the clock was running on his own career. *Twelve Angry Men* had been a critical success, but not a financial one. In 1958 he was doing *Two for the Seesaw* onstage, having put $20,000 of his own money into the production for a twenty-five-percent interest. It was another in his string of Broadway successes, but he hated it because, he felt, he was playing second fiddle to costar Anne Bancroft and because his character (a repressed Nebraska lawyer living in New York, "one of those fellows who short change those he says he loves") was a little too close to home. He had worked with William Gibson, the playwright, to modify and build up the role, but he had never been satisfied. He became so upset with Gibson that on opening night he screamed at him in his dressing room, "Get your ass out of here! I don't even want to see you again. Don't come into my dressing room to wish me good luck. You've been no help to me!"

The relationship with Afdera was occasionally exhilarating, but it could not reassure him during the difficult moments. She had such voracious energy that she climbed socially for them both. For a dinner party that the Duke and Duchess of Windsor would attend, she ordered an entire new living room of furniture, which she had a moving van return to the store the day after the party. She had long since moved beyond expatriate society into the New York smart set whose laureate-to-be was Truman Capote.

"How does it feel to be the new Mrs. Fonda?" he asked Afdera in one of their first meetings.

"It's all right," she replied. "He's a lovely man."

"Any woman who calls her husband a lovely man has got to have a mind of her own. Perhaps you're just what he needs."

"I didn't know he needed anything."

"We all need something," Capote drawled. "And Fonda needs to learn how to be generous."

"He is generous," Afdera protested.

"He's a mean bastard. And you look like the kind of woman who's going to take him for everything he's got."

It was a shrewd prophecy, whose exact terms would take a few more years to work out.

In the summer of 1958, Henry, who was trying to get film work once again, rented a house in Malibu. Jane joined him there. While Afdera explored southern California's version of high society, father and daughter reestablished connections with the film colony. The beach house next to theirs had been rented by Lee Strasberg, who as head of Actors Studio had strongly influenced American acting. His daughter, Susan, who had played the title role in the Broadway production of *The Diary of Anne Frank* and was about to shoot *Stage Struck* with Henry, was there too.

About the same age and similarly burdened by overpowering fathers, Jane and Susan became friendly. Jane talked about her dilemma—how she was getting desperate, at the age of twenty, for some sense of direction in her life; she had already exhausted all of the things she thought she wanted to do. The two were walking on the beach one day when Susan suddenly said, "Why aren't you an actress?" It was a question Jane had never dared ask herself before, always fearing that the answer would be that she wasn't pretty or talented enough. Now she thought to herself, What the hell? It was so obviously what she wanted to do, even if she had never admitted it.

She mentioned the conversation to Henry, who was bothered by the idea of a second-generation Fonda parlaying his Hollywood connections into a career. "Do you *really* want to play things like Jimmy Stewart's daughter in *The FBI Story*?" he asked. But Jane persisted, and got Susan to arrange a meeting with her father. Jane went to Strasberg's beach house and spent a long time talking to him. At the end of the conversation, Strasberg invited her to become a student. "The only thing that made me take her was her eyes," he remembered later. "There was such panic in her eyes."

II

Peter doesn't have a core of tension. Something in him is still asleep, and perhaps always will be.
— *Pauline Kael*

Jane is an actress always in search of a script for her life.
— *Gail Sheehy*

SIX

Over the next few years, Henry would continue to work on Broadway and in Hollywood as one of the most durable and appealing of actors. But his great roles were behind him and he knew it. Added to his burden was the fact that just as he felt himself being shunted toward the wings, his children were clamoring for center stage. The experience of the entertainment industry until now seemed to confirm Scott Fitzgerald's maxim about there being no second acts in American lives. The sons and daughters who had already tried to capitalize on their parents' fame—Edward G. Robinson, Jr., Gary Crosby, even Diana Barrymore—had been failures on their own and parodies of the originals as well. That's what Henry feared would happen to the Fondas. It didn't occur to him that if his children succeeded they would rejuvenate and extend his career, making him not only an actor but also the founder of an acting dynasty. He feared they would make fools of themselves and, worse yet, subtract from his own achievements.

Jane's friends were skeptical too. As Brooke Hayward notes, "I'd known her all my life and there was never the slightest indication that she would ever become an actress. Suddenly there it was—her life." Yet with Henry's proprietary feeling about acting, her decision to become involved with Actors Studio was almost inevitable. Acting had already proved to be a medium of communication between them. If she made it as an actress she would be able to enter what had always been in effect his other family.

Actors Studio would have a role in Jane's career similar to that of the University Players in Henry's. It was *the* place to be, a place where professional connections were made that might last a lifetime. The difference between the Cape in the 1930s and the West Side of Manhattan in the 1960s, however, was that there were no gurus when Henry started acting. Jane had the commanding figure of Strasberg to subordinate herself to. The uncommitted stare and flat voice with a suggestion of Yiddish skepticism (which he used in the Hyman Roth character he later created in *The Godfather, Part II*) made him seem almost oracular.

Strasberg had been a force in American acting for almost thirty years, a presence long before he was a guru. In the 1930s he had been part of the Group Theatre; the movement, which took its inspiration partly from socialist politics, had furthered the careers of Elia Kazan, Clifford Odets, John Garfield, and others who rose to positions of prominence in American stage and film. In 1948 Strasberg became the artistic director of Actors Studio, which was actually less a school than the site for a philosophy of theater to be put into practice. This philosophy was known as "the Method," a shorthand term for Strasberg's ideas, which drew on Freudianism and on the Russian stage theorist Stanislavsky's ideas about how great acting involves "the imagined truth which the actor can believe as sincerely [as] and with greater enthusiasm than he believes the practical truth."

Traditional actors such as Henry Fonda "played parts," which they discarded when their performances were over, reassuming their "real" identities every time they stepped offstage. In contrast, Method actors such as Brando and Dean, prodded by Strasberg, tried to locate and gain access to emotions buried within them as they prepared for a part. They absorbed and transformed the characters they played, making them a part of their own personality. And then they tried to *be themselves* onstage. The first principle of the Method—that its practitioners weren't just acting but also conveying *reality*—was tailor-made for people who wanted to discover what Strasberg called their "authenticity." Even Marilyn Monroe had done time at Actors Studio.

When Jane enrolled at the Studio in 1958, she was an instant celebrity because she was Henry Fonda's daughter. She was seen not as just another starlet, however, but rather as something of a deb, a bit like Grace Kelly, who studied for the stage out of noblesse oblige rather than sweaty ambition. She did not begin as a member of the Studio per se: that was in effect a postgraduate operation for actors on the verge of success. Instead she began where everyone else did, in the private classes Strasberg gave novices who had demonstrated enough talent to warrant his attention. The others who paid $35 to attend two "sessions" a week in the converted church where Actors Studio was headquartered buzzed about Jane. One of her contemporaries remembers, "If she'd been Jane Doe or Jane Schwartz nobody would have given her a second look. But because of her name, people sucked up to her, although they secretly hoped she would fail."

Like other new students, she was required to prepare an "exercise," which entailed acting out an intimate physical action (some students chose masturbation or defecation), and a "private moment," in which a personal emotion was expressed in mime. It was trial by ordeal, a demonstration of a student's willingness to be vulnerable in front of the master and the rest of the group. Jane passed the initiation ritual with flying colors. In his analysis of her performance, the laconic Strasberg showed slightly more animation than usual, and the other students, always looking for clues to his real feelings, decided that he thought Jane had special talent. They flocked around her with congratulations. She described the moment as if it were a conversion experience: "Before . . . I was one person.

And then after the exercise I was somebody else." She was still aglow months later and spoke of it as her beginning: "Nothing that happened to me before last fall counts."

She was not the only young actor for whom Strasberg was a father figure. But she was probably the only one whose real father was an actor deeply antagonistic to the Method for professional as well as personal reasons. Henry had first encountered the Method during rehearsals for *Two for the Seesaw,* when director Arthur Penn and costar Anne Bancroft had tried to get him to explore the "unstated content" of the characters' relationship in a session of improvisation. The idea was repugnant to him; the reason he had become an actor in the first place was to escape rather than locate a self that didn't particularly please him. In one of his few extended comments on his philosophy of acting, made around the time Jane began her studies, Henry showed exactly how far away from the Method he was: "Most of us instantly recognize truth and forthrightness, in the theater and out of it. This does not mean that an actor must always be himself. But he must not lose himself in his role. He must always be the master of his emotions. . . . Being onstage is no excuse for not behaving like a human being."

Jane came home quoting enthusiastically from the sayings of Lee Strasberg, and Henry pronounced it all "crap." Sick of Afdera in any case, Jane responded by moving out of the townhouse into an apartment she shared with Susan Stein, daughter of MCA head Jules Stein.

Jane threw herself into acting with a ferocity that surprised Henry and everyone else, living on cigarettes, coffee, Dexedrine, and strawberry yogurt. Actor George Peppard, who was at the Studio around the same time, says she was like someone "going underwater and never expecting to come up again." Still worried that her cheeks made her "look like a chipmunk," she began an escalating dependence on diuretics to lose weight and achieve gauntness. She got an agent and applied for modeling work to supplement her income. Photographs of her at the time show someone looking for a dark bohemian petulance. Her face was all angles, a geometry at whose center were the eyes in which Lee Strasberg had seen such intriguing panic. Combining the fright of a startled animal with an emerging sensuality, it was a face that signaled a whole range of conflicting emotions burning beneath the surface.

By early 1959, Jane was getting jobs through Eileen Ford's agency at close to the $50 hourly fee commanded by supermodel Suzy Parker. She began appearing in magazines and at one time was on four covers, including a commanding photo on *Vogue* that had her dressed in a gold sheath. After her sessions at Actors Studio, she often waited around newsstands to watch people's reactions when they picked up a magazine and saw her face.

The novelty of being the next Fonda soon wore off and Jane began to realize that her connection with her father might be a liability as well as an asset. After she auditioned in front of the great English director Tyrone Guthrie, for instance, he looked at her and asked, "What have you ever done besides be Henry Fonda's daughter?" Dan Petrie, who would later direct Jane in the television film *The Dollmaker,* saw her do her first screen test (opposite Warren Beatty for *Splendor in the Grass*) and was struck by how much she resembled her father—it was like watching a female impersonator—and this would be a mighty obstacle to overcome.

She obviously had talent, but there was an almost eerie emptiness at her center waiting to be filled. Fellow Strasberg student Henry Jaglom says: "I was into Salinger then and very interested in who was phony. I remember Jane doing a scene for Strasberg with a partner who was being very phony. And she was being just as phony back. Afterward I berated her for being a sponge. But then I realized she was just absorbing what she was given and that was the way she was. If somebody was intensely real with her, she'd be intensely real back; if someone was phony, she'd be phony too."

It became an acceptable cliché among her fellow students to say that Jane Fonda was looking for a father figure. She went through a number of young men in the acting community. As one of them recalls, "She was there to be seduced by men and vice versa. Yet it was a strange feeling. Having won her, at least temporarily, you got the sense that she was hopeful you'd control her life." Another young man who knew her during this period (but who was unaware of her history of eating disorders) says, "Jane was so insecure and hungry for love that she tried to swallow you whole."

Soon she settled into a long-term relationship with Alexander "Sandy" Whitelaw, who at twenty-seven was six years her senior. Son of a Scots army man, Whitelaw had gotten into the movie business after meeting David O. Selznick in Europe and coming to New York at his suggestion to work in production. He had met Jane when she was beginning at Actors Studio. After they were romantically involved, she told her father about him. Henry did some investigation and said that he disapproved of Whitelaw not only because of the age difference but also because of his reported affair with a married woman. "And of course Henry's disapproval," Whitelaw says, "made me irresistible to Jane."

Others might think of her as brash, but as he got to know Jane, Whitelaw found someone deeply conflicted and unsure of herself. She was almost fanatically committed to becoming an actress, but the alternative life of marriage and kids and a house in the suburbs was also attractive, especially since it was a route Brooke Hayward had chosen. Whitelaw asked her how, since she had been unable to housebreak her Yorkshire terrier, which left a trail of tiny feces around her apartment, could she ever hope to raise children? He told her she was too egotistical and immature even to think of marriage, and she agreed this was probably true.

In the middle of their affair, Henry's old friend Josh Logan screen-tested Jane and signed her to a seven-year contract at $10,000 a year. For her first role he cast her as a cheerleader opposite Anthony Perkins in a sophomoric comedy titled *Tall Story*. Whitelaw had already moved to Hollywood to take a job as an agent when Jane arrived to begin shooting. He noted that she had adopted in advance the neurotic behavior of a film star, descending from the plane and saying melodramatically, "You've *got* to drive me to the beach. I must go swimming *right now!*" After going to the beach, she made Whitelaw drive her to Tigertail, where she sat silent in the car for a long time, looking at the house where she'd grown up.

As *Tall Story* got started, Warner Bros. issued a press release about her: "Jane Fonda is a blonde, beautiful, and talented answer to Hollywood's search for new personalities." She was put on the gossip-column circuit and showed up carrying balloons that were color-coordinated with her girlish outfits. Hedda Hopper and Louella Parsons both asked the obligatory questions regarding marriage and both got the obligatory answer: "When I marry I want it to be for all time. I have grown up with divorce and I want to feel sure before I marry."

On the set, she was made over with winged eyebrows, false eyelashes, a huge smear of pink lipstick, and ironed-down hair. Jack Warner decided that she was too flat-chested and ordered falsies. One producer suggested that she have her back teeth pulled and her jaw broken and reset to accentuate her high-cheekboned look.

Sandy Whitelaw was intrigued by the conflicts between her desire for star treatment and her scorn for it. He was struck most of all by the innocence right below the surface of the worldliness she affected. One afternoon he was at her apartment when the phone rang. She answered and, saying that it was a photographer, asked Whitelaw to hang up after she had taken the call on the phone upstairs. When nearly half an hour had passed and she hadn't come down, Whitelaw went up. He saw that Jane had used an extension cord to take the phone into the bathroom and was standing there with her shirt off, dribbling cold water from the faucet onto one of her nipples. "I think it is getting a bit harder," she was saying. "Yes, it is definitely getting harder." Whitelaw, realizing that she was talking to a crank, grabbed the phone away and hung it up. Asking her what this was all about, he learned that the caller had claimed he needed to know if Jane's nipples got hard in cold water because he was considering some T-shirt shots on the beach for *Vogue*.

Jane continued to talk about marriage, but Whitelaw knew she was too self-absorbed for their romance to go anywhere. The realization sunk in one day when he left work earlier than usual and came to her apartment.

"Warren?" she called out when he knocked. "Warren, is that you?"

"No, it's not Warren," he answered. It's Sandy."

He went inside and they got into an argument about who it was she'd been expecting. Just when Whitelaw smashed a mirror with his fist out of frustration with her denials, Warren Beatty walked in the open door. The actor, who was about to crack Hollywood with *Splendor in the Grass,* defused a tense moment by taking Whitelaw aside and saying, "Listen, I know exactly what you're feeling. Once I threw a bed out of a window in Philadelphia in a similar situation. I'll just go take a walk while you guys get this thing settled."

Before going his separate way from Jane, Whitelaw decided to steal her diary to try to decipher the inner core of the personality he felt had eluded him during their months together. Thinking she was out, he broke into her apartment one night. She was actually home, and remained in bed feigning sleep, afraid he had come in a jealous rage to kill her. He got the diary and read the entries, inscribed in a backhanded scrawl. "Met Louella today . . ." one of them began. And: "Talked to Hedda . . ." There was nothing more personal than what she planned to say to people she wanted to impress. It was, Whitelaw decided, a "status anxiety" diary.

In *Tall Story,* Josh Logan tried to do a movie that would establish what he believed was Jane's star potential and stand as an homage to his long relationship with her father. As Anthony Perkins says, "In a way it was touching. Josh crouched over the camera, having her do take after take in the style he had developed when directing Marilyn Monroe in *Bus Stop*. He coaxed a performance out of her." But Jane was disturbed by the inane script and especially by the fact that she'd been prevented from visiting the lower depths she'd explored at Actors Studio. As soon as shooting for *Tall Story* was over, she returned immediately to Lee Strasberg and her art.

While Jane was in Hollywood, Peter was attending college in Omaha and feeling he had been sentenced to prison in the midsection of the country. It was not that he felt superior to the staid life and traditional values of the Midwest, but that the experiences he'd already had made such a life seem surreal. It was almost as if his experiences had so misshaped him that he could no longer fit into normalcy. There had been signs of this problem not long after he returned from the Roman holiday when he'd learned the truth about his mother's suicide and lost his virginity to a married woman ten years his senior. Meaning well, his aunt had arranged a date with a "nice" girl. Almost immediately Peter had gotten the girl pregnant and financed a secret abortion by selling a shotgun his father had given him.

Isolated personally and culturally, Peter had gone on to college. He had managed to make one good friend there—Eugene "Stormy" McDonald III, son of the founder of Zenith Radio Corporation, who had left a fortune of some $30 million. Shunted away to school by a family struggling over his money, Stormy was like Peter in that he felt orphaned. The two formed a bond based on common need and black humor and called each other "brother."

Friends of the Fonda family had not seen Peter for years. But then, early in 1960, he turned up unexpectedly at the wedding of Bill Hayward to a girl from Topeka, Kansas. He had not been invited; the Haywards weren't even sure where he was. He happened to read in the society page of an Omaha newspaper that Bill was getting married, and jumped on the first plane that would get him to Topeka in time.

Grown to six-two, an inch or so taller than his father, and even thinner, with Henry's loose-jointed walk and slow drawl, Peter looked like a familiar stranger to the Hayward clan. He circled around them happily in a way that reminded Brooke of a puppy, glad to be reunited with a piece of his past. He was awestruck by Bridget, younger sister of Brooke and Bill, whom he remembered only as a tag-along when they were growing up. Now she was a dazzling young woman with bisque skin and shivering blue eyes. Like him she was troubled; already she had been in and out of the Riggs sanitarium for treatment, although in her case the emotional problems were complicated by epilepsy.

Peter fell in love with Bridget during the brief time they were together in Topeka, and was saddened by the fact that she was scheduled to go to school in Switzerland. When she dropped her bridesmaid's white gloves, he picked them up and vowed like some medieval knight to keep them close to his heart. He reverted to his old persona as the antic muse of the Fonda–Hayward clan and, in one of his extravagant conceits, told Brooke that he felt like a comet traveling between two great solar systems—their families—which conjoined only when great events were taking place.

Peter returned to Omaha after the wedding more aware than ever that he didn't belong there. Like his father some thirty years earlier, he decided that the stage was his best chance for escape. He had already played Elwood P. Dowd in a university production of *Harvey,* and now he decided to make a serious effort to become an actor. In 1960, at the end of his junior year, he left Omaha, as Henry had at about the same age. With $300 in savings he traveled to do summer stock in Fishkill, New York, where he painted sets, ushered, and played bit parts. When the summer ended, he showed up at his father's townhouse. Henry said he could live there and reluctantly agreed to get him an agent, but he was not very enthusiastic about his son's desire to enter what seemingly was becoming a family business.

Henry was not really enthusiastic about anything. It had been a bad year from the beginning. On New Year's Day he heard that Maggie Sullavan was dead of an overdose of sleeping pills after failing in an attempted comeback. A piece of his past died with her, and he said to Brooke: "There was nobody like her before or since. Never will be. In every way. In talent, in looks, in temperament. Everything."

It was hard not to compare the vivacious Maggie with his present wife, from whom he had become more and more estranged. Afdera agreed that they had fallen out of love and likened them to a pair of strangers uncomfortably sharing a compartment on a train. In fact, he had never been much more than a passenger in a relationship she engineered. When she lost interest in making it go, the relationship fell apart and Henry retreated into the cold passivity that had been the end state of his other marriages.

People told him that male visitors showed up at the townhouse soon after he left for the theater to perform in his new play, *Silent Night, Lonely Night*. It wasn't the hints of infidelity that bothered him, however, but rather what he had come to see as Afdera's triviality. The problem was especially clear in their friendship with Senator John Kennedy and his wife, Jackie, who stayed at the nearby Carlyle Hotel when they were in town. Afdera was interested only in the cachet the bright couple might give her. Henry had stumped the nation in 1956 for Adlai Stevenson, giving speeches written by his friend John Steinbeck; he was genuinely interested in Kennedy's ideas and had pledged to help him in his run for the presidency.

In the fall of 1960 there was another suicide in his immediate circle. This time it was Bridget Hayward, the strange third child of Maggie and Leland. She was back from Switzerland, living alone in

New York, collecting porcelains and not leaving her apartment for long periods of time. Peter found out about her death and came to his father for solace. But Henry, who did not know of his son's secret love for the young woman, sat there murmuring "Poor Leland" while Peter felt that he himself was in an emotional free-fall.

A few weeks later at Christmas dinner Afdera tried to make conversation with Henry, Peter looking on silently. "You know, Hank," she said brightly, "we've been married three years now, almost four."

Henry put down his fork and said in a Fonda drawl, "Seems more like seventeen years to me."

A month later, Afdera attended Jack Kennedy's inaugural ball alone, Henry staying behind because he had to appear onstage. She never came back.

Peter thought the departure of the woman he regarded as the evil stepmother might bring him closer to his father. But it didn't work out that way. Having failed in marriage yet again, Henry retreated further into himself. He and his son ate silent meals in the dining room of the townhouse, which still bore signs of Afdera's Venetian remodeling.

Peter was working hard to prove that he too could be an actor. He shared his father's contempt for the Method, and believed that he could learn by doing, as Henry had, rather than by studying. He got some attention in little theater around New York because of his name, and like Jane, he demonstrated some talent for droll comedy; but he could not catch on. He became so frustrated by his slim prospects that he found himself pounding the walls of his bedroom until his knuckles bled. He borrowed $150 from his aunt and flew back to Omaha to get control of himself, then returned to New York when he was asked to read for a new play. He got the part.

Blood, Sweat and Stanley Poole, a lightweight drama about life in the Marine Corps, opened in the fall of 1961. Henry was there the first night. He slowly worked his way backstage and when he finally arrived gave Peter one of his blank looks. "Well," he said, shrugging, "I don't know what to say." But the critics were more enthusiastic, one of them writing, "This is no doubt the very last morning in which Peter Fonda will have to be identified as Henry Fonda's son." He received the New York Drama Critics award as the most promising young actor of the year.

Peter had met a Sarah Lawrence girl named Susan Brewer, stepdaughter of Howard Hughes's right-hand man Noah Dietrich. Short and thin, with a pretty, dusky-complexioned face, Susan had grown up in Los Angeles on the edge of the film colony, living in Benedict Canyon down the street from Robert Walker, Jr., one of Peter's childhood friends. She was an accomplished young woman who spoke several languages and aspired to become an archaeologist. Bill Hayward met her on his way overseas for an Army tour and was struck by her sweetness and inexperience and her obvious love for Peter.

During the run of *Stanley Poole,* Peter married her. Stormy McDonald was his best man; Henry was not there. As part of the honeymoon, Peter took his bride to Beacon, New York. They walked through the sanatorium where his mother had been and talked to the psychiatrists who treated her before she killed herself.

After his play closed, Peter decided to try his luck in Hollywood. Like Jane, one of the first things he did upon arriving in southern California was visit Tigertail. The nine acres were still charred from a fire that had swept through a month earlier. The only remnants of the house Henry and Frances built were two brick chimneys. Desperate to acquire the property, Peter went to the woman who'd bought Tigertail from his mother in 1948 and offered everything he had, including a $90,000 trust fund left by Frances. But a developer had already offered more than $1 million for the hilltop; soon it would be bulldozed and covered with a dozen homes.

SEVEN

Making *Tall Story* had been bad enough for Jane. Reading the condescension of critics was worse, especially the one who wrote: "I have a hunch that Jane Fonda will do okay in pictures for about four years. Then, as soon as she gets Hollywood out of her system, she'll settle down with a nice handsome husband, make babies, and that will be that. I think she'll be on the society pages more often than the entertainment pages."

Deciding that she needed to smash her image as an amateur and a deb once and for all, Jane began by looking for a male mentor. This didn't surprise an old classmate from Vassar: "Even if you hadn't seen her for a while, you could tell where Jane was by what kind of man she was with at any given moment." Her *Tall Story* costar Anthony Perkins, who had introduced her to a tormented young actor named Timothy Everett, remembers Jane being impressed by Everett's edgy theatricality and other "James Dean–like qualities." Blond, with open-faced good looks, Everett seemed to be on the edge of stardom; he had won good notices for his role in *The Dark at the Top of the Stairs* on Broadway and for his performance in the movie *Exodus*.

One of the rites of passage at Actors Studio involved presentations for Strasberg, and Everett asked Jane if she would like to join him in a scene adapted from Dylan Thomas's *Adventures in the Skin Trade*. She agreed, and they planned a rehearsal at her apartment. As Everett told it later, "We talked for a while, the lights were low, then all of a sudden we were looking at each other in this strange way. I just got consumed by this wave of tenderness and desire, and so did she. We ran upstairs to the bedroom, tore our clothes off, and stayed in bed for three days."

Recalling Everett, Anthony Perkins says, "Timmy was a troubled guy. He was aggressive, antagonistic, soulful. He didn't leave anything out." Everett was also, at this point in his life, bisexual; he would identify himself as gay by the time of his death from a drug overdose in the early 1980s. For Jane, what was most appealing about him was the fact that he was regarded as an actor's actor, one of the inner circle in New York's avant-garde theater community.

Much to Henry's dismay, Josh Logan had decided that the next role for Jane was in *There Was a Little Girl,* a play about a young woman who is raped and forced to deal with the guilt and the indifference that follow. Everett took it upon himself to coach her into a performance he believed would finally allow her to draw on her repressed "emotional memory." Jane's decision to put herself in his hands seemed validated when *There Was a Little Girl* opened in March 1960. The play itself was panned, but she got rave notices.

By this time Everett and Jane had become inseparable. He took jazz-dancing lessons and she joined the class too. Because Strasberg encouraged therapy as a way of contacting dark and murky emotions which could then be used onstage, they both began seeing psychiatrists and comparing notes about their sessions. Strasberg also encouraged his students to talk openly about their problems, and Jane did, telling Everett and other Actors Studio friends that she still had horrid nightmares, including a recurrent one in which she was alone in an ice-cold house from which there was no exit. Sometimes the nightmares became ambulatory. She slept in the raw and said that early one morning pedestrians had found her standing dazed and naked on the street; she had let herself out of her apartment in the middle of a dream.

Although he was hardly able to function himself at times, Timmy Everett became Jane's guide as they walked down the hall of mirrors of the unconscious together. Along with others who knew about her history, he was struck by the fact that Jane would intrepidly confront almost any subject except for that walled-off psychic space that contained the remains of her mother. She seemed to feel there was a menacing void within her that could lead to a fate similar to Frances's, and she tried to fill it by constant activity. Lists and schedules became the musculature of her emotional life; busywork was the life's blood. But once in a while her defenses failed her, as after she heard news of Bridget Hayward's death. Arthur Laurents, author and director of *Invitation to a March,* a play in which Jane was appearing, found her in her dressing room under sedation and crying hysterically. After looking at her for a moment, he said, "You're afraid you may kill yourself too, aren't you?" She turned to him and sobbed, "Yes."

Having bound and gagged his own demons so tightly all his life, Henry was outraged when Jane publicly displayed hers. He said that anyone who submitted to psychoanalysis "had a hole in his head." He blamed Timmy Everett for what he regarded as Jane's extravagant acting-out. Once, after she had appeared at a testimonial for Josh Logan and delivered a teary, overwrought speech that had everyone snickering, Henry came up to Everett and got him in a headlock, hissing in his ear, "What have you done to make my daughter act this way?"

Clumsily but sincerely Henry tried to save Jane from herself and keep others from taking advantage of her. When he found out that photographer Richard Avedon had done a partly frontal nude for *Vogue,* he tried to kill it, admitting that while she was of age and had the right to pose, the photograph would damage the family. He interfered again when photographer Peter Basch got an assignment from the new men's magazine *Cavalier* to do shots of Jane as she might be imagined by great directors. He shot her in Felliniesque high fashion, in frontier gingham as a John Ford heroine, and tastefully naked front-down on a bed in a Roger Vadim pose. This time Jane resisted her father and made sure that the photos were published. "I am still fighting being Henry Fonda's daughter," she said. "I think I have to fight it a little more." This became her balancing act: using the Fonda identity to her advantage at the same time that she struggled against its constraints.

This effort would intensify as she replaced Everett with another mentor who was surer of himself, more calculating in his use of her, and better able to give her rebellion an audacity it had lacked so far. It was Andreas Voutsinas, a fixture at Actors Studio whom Strasberg had mentioned as a possible successor. A Greek born in the Sudan, brought up in Ethiopia, and educated in London, Voutsinas was a short, somewhat sinister-looking figure who struck beatnik poses with his black beret, long cigarette holder, and raincoat draped over his shoulders like a cape. Originally called to Strasberg's attention by his countryman Elia Kazan, Voutsinas had made everyday life a stage for his ongoing self-dramatization. He had a manner one person described as "Transylvanian mysteriousness" and others simply termed "creepy." A director manqué, he supported himself with occasional jobs as an actor. Mel Brooks gave him the role of a leering homosexual in *The Producers,* which apparently involved a measure of typecasting according to some at Actors Studio at this time.

It seemed strange Jane would go for effeminate men when she was one of the most sought-after young women in town. But, Brooke Hayward says, "she went from extremely loose sexual behavior at Vassar to her 'gay period' with Timmy. She was always very experimental, perhaps in reaction to Henry's rigidity. It was a case of anything goes during this time."

But the attraction was less sexual than professional. Far more than Timmy Everett, Voutsinas was on the cutting edge of theater. As director Dan Petrie, himself an alumnus of Actors Studio, says: "Andreas was the guy who always raised his hand first. He was at the top of the class, totally confident. He knew everything about acting and could quote Stanislavsky chapter and verse." He was the sort of person who spent a long time every day deciding what clothes to wear and checking his appearance in the mirror. If his "expertise" attracted Jane, so did the fact that he was the first person she had met who consciously sculpted his image, deciding what he would be day by day.

Voutsinas had functioned as a sort of Svengali for other young actresses. He had been close to Anne Bancroft at about the time she was making her reputation opposite Henry in *Two for the Seesaw.* And now he grabbed onto Jane, arranging, in the summer of 1960, to direct her in *No Concern of Mine* in Connecticut summer stock.

Timmy Everett, who thought he and Jane were still a couple, understood the power of Voutsinas's spell when he went to Connecticut to see her. "We'd be lying around with no clothes on," he later told writer Thomas Kiernan, "and Voutsinas would walk in and take off his clothes. I had a pretty good body then—Jane used to say how much she loved my body—and Voutsinas had a really ugly body. . . . [But] he was directing her in some deep way, and the way he talked to her about herself made an impression on her." Everett's relationship with Jane ended not long after the Connecticut visit in a hysterical scene at her apartment. He became so overwrought that he hacked at his wrists with a carving knife and had to be rushed to the hospital.

In addition to private sessions with Strasberg, Actors Studio offered formal classes to the most promising students. To be invited to join a class was like being asked to become a fellow. Voutsinas promised Jane that he would get her in, and used a scene from *No Concern of*

Mine as her audition. And when a jury comprising figures such as Elia Kazan as well as Strasberg himself enthusiastically recommended her, Jane was even more in thrall to him.

Soon Voutsinas was living part-time at the cooperative apartment on West 55th Street that she'd bought with her own money. He seemed to take over her personality, affecting her thinking and even choosing her clothes. His reshaping of Jane was symbolized by what he did to her ankles, which she considered thick and referred to as her "piano legs." Every day Voutsinas would soak Ace bandages in brine and wrap her ankles. As the wrappings dried, they constricted, causing Jane to "writhe in pain," according to actress Shelley Winters, who witnessed the operation.

Voutsinas also probed her emotions as no one else had, and he too was struck by the compartments she had created. "When I became close to Jane," he said, "I waited and waited for a burst of emotion about her mother. But it was sidetracked. . . . It's like her life started from twelve years on."

Voutsinas's hold over Jane, many believed, came from the way he encouraged her to express herself without worrying about what people thought. In 1961, when she signed to do a role in the film version of Nelson Algren's *A Walk on the Wild Side,* Voutsinas went along and encouraged her to adopt a more provocative persona than the one she'd had during her previous sojourn in Hollywood.

There was a barrage of new publicity capitalizing on her new image. Hedda Hopper headlined her interview "Jane Fonda Thinks Marriage Is Obsolete!" and the studio leaked information to the press that she was not wearing undergarments while filming her new role. But it went further than hype. Jane told reporters that she was entering her third year of sit-up (as opposed to lie-down) analysis, and she could now talk about her family with "desperate honesty." Of Henry she said: "Daddy should have been analyzed forty years ago." And while Peter had "great charm," he was "not an actor yet." Sometimes she would manage to strike a glancing blow at father and brother in one comment: "[Being Henry's child] is much harder on Peter because he's a man. He looks like my father and his voice is like my father's. And when he gets insecure, he acts like him."

Egged on by Voutsinas, Jane continued to give interviews and take potshots at Henry. He usually gave back as good as he got. But the public struggle with Jane took a toll. In repose, Henry's face began to take on the downturned look of Emmett Kelly, the famous sad-faced clown, whom he had recently portrayed in a television drama. "Daughter?" he replied bitterly when a reporter asked him about Jane. "I don't have a daughter." When Shelley Winters asked her to come to a party, Jane said that she couldn't attend unless her father, who was also scheduled to attend, was disinvited first.

On the set of *Wild Side,* director Edward Dmytryk had issued an edict that no personal advisors would be allowed during filming. Jane countered by saying that Voutsinas was her secretary not her advisor, and insisted that he not be barred. Always whispering to her and touching her in ways that Dmytryk later said gave him the creeps, Voutsinas "prepared" Jane for every scene.

Adopting her mentor's hauteur, Jane talked loudly about how Hollywood was run by "morons." Nevertheless, immediately after finishing *Wild Side,* she began a new picture, *The Chapman Report,* from Irving Wallace's novel about a research group like that of sexologist Alfred Kinsey. Voutsinas had advised Jane to take on roles with heavier doses of sexuality, and so she told director George Cukor that she wanted to play the role of the nymphomaniac. Cukor laughed and said he actually wanted her for the part of the frigid widow. Because it was an opportunity to work with a great director, she accepted.

Next she went to Greece to film *In the Cool of the Day,* a soap opera with Peter Finch. It was a bad experience made worse for Jane because Voutsinas, who was fearful that he would be drafted into the Greek military, could not accompany her. But he did go with her to London for a week of shooting before the crew left for Greece. And John Houseman, producer of the film, was struck by the unusual relationship she had with the little man. "Under his tutelage, before each take of a scene, Jane emitted a chilling and ear-splitting primal scream. After each scene her first look was to him, over the heads of the director and a perplexed Peter Finch."

Happy to have this film behind her, Jane returned to New York to prepare for a new play Voutsinas was directing. *The Fun Couple* was about a young married couple trying to arrange their lives to avoid adult responsibility. It was Voutsinas's big chance to prove his talent and render homage to their relationship; he would do for her career what Jules Dassin had done for Melina Mercouri's in *Never on Sunday*.

During rehearsals, Voutsinas was tense and demanding, complaining once again that Jane could not unlock the substratum of emotions surrounding her mother's death and that this was affecting her performance. Sometimes he would scream at her, "You have no talent!" Bystanders were amazed by her submissiveness and talked about her "slave-girl mentality."

The Fun Couple was a disaster. Critic Walter Kerr went so far as to call it one of the five worst plays of all time. Even more embarrassing, virtually the entire Actors Studio crowd had come to see what was supposed to be the apotheosis of Jane and Voutsinas, and left the theater sniggering at the debacle.

Yet Jane was irrepressible, ready to go on to the next step. "That woman has *great hungers*," Timmy Everett said to a friend in a discussion of what made Jane tick. "I've never met someone so hungry, someone so unable to become satisfied." When film critic Stanley Kauffmann wrote the first serious appreciation of her work in an essay that overlooked the inferior quality of the first movies and concentrated on her potential ("A new talent is rising—Jane Fonda. . . . With good parts in good plays and films, she could develop into a first-rate artist"), Jane had her agent make copies of the piece and send one to every important producer and director on his list. She also had it sent to *The Harvard Lampoon*, which had just named her Worst Actress of the Year for *The Chapman Report*. Brooke Hayward, still amazed by her old friend's sudden metamorphosis, said, "I've never seen ambition as naked as Jane's."

In trying to unravel the mystery of this woman, Everett, Voutsinas, and others who engaged in metaphysical speculations about Jane missed a simple fact: a large part of her ambition was aimed at gaining leverage over her father, the dominant figure in her life. For the first time she had an advantage; he was in a particularly vulnerable position. Another marriage had failed. His career was in a holding pattern as a result of some bad choices. Edward Albee had imagined Henry as the lead for his new play *Who's Afraid of Virginia Woolf?*, but Henry's agent had sent the manuscript back without showing it to him, implying that his client had become a national resource and did not play neurotic cuckolds. Instead of doing what would become a pivotal Broadway play, Henry signed on for a third-rate film, *Spencer's Mountain*.

Henry's personal crises and faltering career sometimes plunged him into periods of depression. He confided to Jimmy Stewart his fears that he had reached the end of the road, and wondered if he would ever work again. Stewart nodded and said, "You too?"

On top of all this, there was the constant war against him in the press, waged by Peter and especially Jane. Henry struck back with occasional sarcasm. "It gets boring to hear them say they missed Daddy when they were young," he said. "So I should apologize because a world war came along and I had to go away, or because I had to work while the kids were in a beautiful farmhouse out in Brentwood?"

Yet Henry did attempt reconciliations. On a day when Voutsinas was gone, he came to Jane's apartment. They had a good talk in which Henry explained why he objected to her mentor. He thought they were coming to an understanding, but then Jane looked at her watch and said, "You'll have to go now, Dad. Andreas will be coming back soon." Fonda walked out disconsolately. From her second-story window Jane saw him stand on the sidewalk for a moment as if disoriented, and then sit down on the curb to gather himself together.

Jane also continued her ongoing competition with Peter, who was in Beverly Hills trying to make it as an actor. He was taking a route opposite hers, cultivating an image of responsibility just as Jane was flaunting her rebellion. Peter called himself conservative and said he was a Republican. He relished his role as family man when he and Susan had a child, a daughter named Bridget in honor of his lost love.

Jane could not resist taking occasional jabs at her brother, as when she said that he had "some talent" as an actor but needed training. He knew she was not trying to hurt him, but was still possessive, still the mother-sister she had been when they were children. He understood too, or at least he told friends so, that Jane and Henry, for all their differences, had an intimate bond based in large part on a common view of him as the "crazy little brother, always getting in trouble." Although he tried to ignore his sister's provocations, he wasn't always successful. When someone asked him if he too was trained in the Method, he replied, "You expect me to get up on a stage with a bunch of little faggots and pretend I'm a rock or a tree?"

Peter had tested for the lead in *PT-109* but didn't get it, although he possessed a young Jack Kennedy's stringy charm and sense of hidden potential. In 1963 he played the male lead in *Tammy and the Doctor,* which he immediately rechristened "Tammy and the Schmuckface." Then came *The Victors, Lilith,* and *The Young Lovers,* each of which he scorned as trivial, although acting filled him with such stress that he threw up every day he went before the camera.

Some critics, *Time*'s Richard Schickel for example, thought he showed raw talent, especially in *Lilith*. But Peter was like his sister in that he didn't want just to be *in* films. He too wanted the kind of apocalyptic success Henry had enjoyed, the sort he believed would confer a ready-made identity on him. He wanted a career that would fill in the gaps of his life.

All this seemed far away. While he waited for it to happen, he wallowed in the Hollywood life-style, buying a house with pool and tennis court in a Coldwater Canyon cul-de-sac and cars such as a Jaguar XKE, a 300SL gull-wing Mercedes, and a Facel-Vega. Yet he also cultivated what friends referred to as his "weird streak," which manifested itself in acts ranging from wearing cowboy boots with a tuxedo to carrying a loaded pistol when he showed up on the set for work.

At the same time he was trying to be an upstanding good citizen, husband, and father, the reckless side he had tried to suppress since his prep school days sometimes led him to an almost violent reaction against authority. Classified 1-Y for the draft—he was deferred but had to report to the draft board every year for reclassification—he sent his draft card in an envelope addressed personally to his father's friend the president, with a handwritten message: "Stuff this up your ass." Living in a world of sealed psychological compartments, Peter saw no contradiction between engaging in such an act and continuing to call himself a conservative.

His career too was tormenting him. Peter was disturbed by the second-rate films he'd done, and by the fact that he was known as "son of what's-his-name and brother of what's-her-face." When Jim Mitchum, son of another famous acting father, took Peter to his room in the Carlton Tower Hotel in London in 1962 and gave him his first marijuana cigarette, he found a source of future relief for his peculiar position as the third Fonda.

· · ·

Jane was different from her brother most of all in her belief that she could *force* things to come out right by sheer persistence. This was the way it had been with her desire to be a great stage actress. She had believed that by wanting it she could make it happen. But by 1962 she was having second thoughts. How far she had yet to travel came clear to her when she took a role in one of the rare Actors Studio productions intended for a commercial audience, Eugene O'Neill's *Strange Interlude*. The cast included Strasberg alumni Ben Gazzara, Pat Hingle, and Franchot Tone. The lead role was played by Geraldine Page, who, with Kim Stanley, was considered the finest actress on the American stage at that time. Page gave a bravura performance in *Strange Interlude* that *The New York Times* praised profusely. About Jane's supporting role, the reviewer said merely that she had "happily contributed her vivacity and beauty to the final two acts."

The experience demonstrated that the prize on which she had set her sights was, if not unattainable, at least something that would require a long pursuit. For now she simply didn't have the talent to inhabit a character and claim it as her own in the way Page had done.

At this point in her career, Jane was not only blocked on the stage but typecast on the screen. She went from playing O'Neill to filming the sex comedy *Sunday in New York*. Her most successful and polished performance to date, it nonetheless seemed to underscore her current alternatives: a long apprenticeship in hopes of someday acquiring the power of a Geraldine Page, or modest success as a film ingenue. In an interview, she indicated the new uncertainties she was feeling: "Just to get up in the Actors Studio and do a scene is so hard. Mainly because I know that there are people there who have far more talent than I do. I know that I do have something else. I have star quality, I have a personality, I have a presence. . . . What I have is obvious, it's like a commodity and it's in demand. But in terms of acting ability, they have more. That's why it's so hard."

Faced with this dilemma—which was compounded by being still umbilically connected to Henry and his celebrity—she began looking for other options. A possibility arose when MGM offered her a role in *Joy House*, a film to be directed by René Clément and costarring Alain Delon. Clément's films, including *The Damned* and *Forbidden Games*, had made him one of the fathers of the French New Wave, whose techniques and attitudes (hand-held cameras, slow-motion and freeze-frame shots, frankness about sexuality, improvised dialogue to increase the sense of a grainy cinéma vérité) had taken the world of film by storm.

Jane signed for the role and set out for France. At the time it seemed like a lark. But it was actually a daring maneuver, similar to the voyage from Europe to America that had made stars out of Greta Garbo, Ingrid Bergman, and others, except that Jane had decided to do it the other way around.

From the moment she landed in Paris, she knew she had made the right decision. She was regarded as a phenomenon by the French press, "a cyclone of femininity" and "a panther of desire." She fueled this fire with comments about her costar, who had a reputation not only as a ladies' man but also as a habitué of the French underworld. "I will undoubtedly fall in love with Delon," Jane announced, "I only play love scenes well when I am in love with my partner."

Soon she was on the cover of the prestigious journal of the New Wave, *Cahiers du Cinéma*. Her pose of casual sexuality galvanized the French imagination, as Jean Seberg's had when she appeared in Jean-Luc Godard's *Breathless*. French journalists competed for metaphors: "Tall, blonde, the perfect American, with long, flexible movements," wrote one; "She is sultry and dangerous, like a caged animal," said another. All agreed, however, about one thing—that she was the American Bardot—"*la BB americaine*." There was speculation in the press about what might happen if and when she met the man who had created Bardot, Roger Vadim.

Joy House was not that good a film. (Critic Judith Crist would write that Jane "was alternatively impersonating the Madwoman of Chaillot, Baby Doll, and her father.") But it didn't matter. What Jane experienced in Paris was better than greatness as an actress. She had become an icon, a cultural force. People not only paid attention to her looks but actually listened to what she had to say.

Her brush with celebrity loosened the hold Andreas Voutsinas had on her. He was disturbed by her newfound independence, and before the production of *Joy House* was over, he told Jane he was "physically sick" and left for New York, ending their affair. But she didn't care. Tired of being manipulated, Jane was ready to be sculpted. She was ready to trade a Svengali for a Pygmalion.

EICHT

<hr/>

 here was no more successful sculptor of women in Europe, although Roger Vadim didn't at all look the part. He was tall and stooped, a shambling sort of man with a sad equine face and soft eyes capable of such sudden intensity that Jane's former stepmother Afdera compared them to spotlights. The French believed they saw in Vadim something distinctively French, but he actually represented an exotic grafting. His real name was Roger Vladimir Plemiannikov. His father, a White Russian, had fled his homeland after the Bolshevik Revolution and settled in France, where he married, had a family, and died of a heart attack at the dinner table when Vadim—the name his son eventually took—was nine years old.

Vadim (the single name was used in the same way "Fonda" was for Henry, representing an idea as well as an individual) had grown up fascinated with film. At first he wanted to be an actor, but by 1950 his interests had turned to making films and even more to making the people who starred in them. That was the year he met Brigitte Bardot, then sixteen and looking for a break as an actress. Twenty-two at the time, Vadim wooed her strenuously; he eventually moved in with her at her parents' home and married her in 1952. He took provocative photographs of her which he passed around Paris, and got her bit parts in several movies. Then, in 1956, Vadim put together the backing for the notorious *And God Created Woman,* in which allegedly he demanded that his wife's costar Jean-Louis Trintignant actually perform instead of merely acting out the love scenes.

The storm of publicity generated by the film, one of the most sexually explicit up to that time, along with the fact that Vadim had taken up with teenaged Danish model Annette Stroyberg, who was carrying his child, broke up his marriage. But Bardot remained close to him and in fact stayed in the house with him and Stroyberg until the day before their daughter, Nathalie, was born. Even afterward she considered herself a part-time member of Vadim's ménage.

He tried to make a star of Stroyberg in *Les Liaisons Dangereuses,* but by the time this film was released he had a new mistress, Catherine Deneuve. The couple didn't marry, although Vadim wanted to, especially after their son, Christophe, was born.

Jane arrived in France at a time when Vadim was looking for his next Galatea. They had met briefly at the restaurant Maxim's a few years earlier when she had left Vassar for her holiday in Paris. She caught his eye not only because she was young but also because she seemed innocent and fresh in contrast to jaded *parisiennes.* Vadim had convinced a close friend and sexual hunting partner, Christian Marquand, to ask her to dance while he studied her. During a pause, he slipped Marquand a note that read: "Have you seen her ankles?" Jane coyly snatched the note out of Marquand's pocket and read it, and was insulted because Vadim had noticed the one part of her body she had not been able to alter by diet.

He had seen her a couple of years later in Beverly Hills when she was filming *The Chapman Report.* She was done up in Hollywood style, which, he said later, made her as insipid as Alfred de Musset roses. But he saw a spark of something underneath. Just as Lee Strasberg had been struck by the panic in Jane's eyes, so Vadim was intrigued by the amoral energy in her body. He tried to interest her in doing a movie with him. But she was put off by his reputation as a voluptuary and, perhaps still smarting from the comment about the size of her ankles, had her agent cable him: "Miss Fonda will never film with Roger Vadim."

Now that she was in Paris for *Joy House*, he decided to try once again. Hoping to convince her to work with him in *Circle of Love*, his planned remake of Max Ophüls's classic French sex comedy *La Ronde*, he arranged a meeting at the home of Olga Horstig, Jane's agent in France. During the dinner, Vadim was touched and amused by Jane's valiant struggle with the French language; it suggested something innocent behind the brassy manner. He could tell right away that she had lost many of the inhibitions that previously had made her suspicious of him.

As the meeting went on, Jane became animated, even flirtatious. Speaking with apparent frankness, she told him why she had decided to leave the United States: "I am always Henry Fonda's daughter, one of Hollywood's promising new faces." She said she hated Hollywood and the traditional persona of the movie star. "I ended up no longer liking who I really was. . . . So I decided to escape all that and get out from under my father's shadow. Perhaps I'll be able to discover a real identity in France." She also said that she had been warned that she was ruining her career, that she would suffer just as Ingrid Bergman had suffered when she went off to Italy to live with Roberto Rossellini. Then she paused for a moment, shrugged, and said, "We'll see."

Vadim, who was, after all, Europe's chief provider of identity to beautiful young actresses, caught the subtext in her words. After dinner Jane said she had an appointment and left. Twenty minutes later she called Olga Horstig and said that this was the best evening she had spent in Paris. Like a character from the Laclos novel he had recently filmed, Horstig then called Vadim and congratulated him: "You've seduced her."

After this it was a matter of not whether but when the two would get together. They met briefly a few days later at a fancy masquerade ball at which she was dressed as Charlie Chaplin and he as an officer in the Red army. Soon after, Vadim came to the studio where she was filming the final scenes of *Joy House*. When she found out he was there, Jane came running into the room where he was waiting to see her, chest heaving, hair limp with the prop man's rain, ready to confess melodramatically to an attraction she could no longer hide.

Vadim took her home. As he told it later, they had worked their way to the bed and he was langorously undressing her when she suddenly leaped up and ran into the bathroom; she returned a moment later completely naked and got under the covers in a businesslike way. The abrupt gesture rendered Vadim impotent not only that night but for the next three weeks, despite visits to the doctor, pills from the pharmacist, and a variety of home remedies. The morning after he finally did consummate the relationship, Jane left for Geneva; she had to sleep with a lover there, she told him, to test the feelings she had for him. When she returned to Paris forty-eight hours later, he asked her what she had decided. She replied simply, "I love you."

They moved into a small apartment in a seventeenth-century building on the Left Bank. Because their images were perfectly matched—the American sex kitten and the French rake—their romance became something of a national obsession for the Paris media. Yet in private Fonda and Vadim were rather different from their public personas.

Jane found that Vadim was not really a reckless, jaded sexual adventurer but was actually a good deal like her father—reserved and dignified, even somewhat passive; bourgeois in his belief in marriage and children, and constantly fighting a riptide of melancholy.

For his part, Vadim was struck by the demons under Jane's

relentlessly cheerful surface. He was fascinated by the way she tried frantically to control time, filling up her waking hours with minutiae. Like others who had studied her, he interpreted this as an effort to avoid confronting what she feared was personal emptiness. She had the iron discipline required of a great actress, he thought, but lacked spontaneity and the understanding that everything in life would not yield to a triumph of the will.

Seeing her as a rough diamond, Vadim began polishing Jane in *Circle of Love*. For the first time, she had a role in which she was an overtly sexual figure, rather than a tease, and Vadim tried to get her to act like a woman. But he felt that most of his direction had to take place off screen. She was unfinished and needed to be educated. He got her to read the great Russian authors of the nineteenth century as well as André Malraux's *Man's Fate* and other contemporary French classics. And he talked to her constantly, expounding on his anarchistic notion that social conventions suppress individual freedom, particularly in areas involving sexuality. For someone with Jane's inchoate sense of rebellion and self-doubt, it was like going back to college. Vadim's "philosophy" was appealing because it told her why she believed as she already did.

In late April 1964, after finishing *Circle,* he took her to the Soviet Union. It was the first trip behind the Iron Curtain for both. They took a room on the fifth floor of a hotel near Moscow's Red Square and, the first afternoon there, were awakened from a jet-lag nap by noise outside. Jane went to the window and saw huge numbers of troops. Frightened, she ran back to the bed and cowered under the covers until Vadim explained to her that it was a preparation for May Day not World War III.

Jane was initially suspicious of the Soviets. When she saw a banner reading "27 Million Russians Dead So That the Children of the World Can Live," she asked through an interpreter whether that figure included those killed by Stalin. Vadim reprimanded her for this American insularity, insisting that such provincial political thinking came from the same source as her sexual inhibitions. When they went out and mingled with the people of Moscow and it became known that she was a Fonda, they were given red-carpet treatment because of the popularity of Henry's films in the Soviet Union. By the end of the trip, Jane was telling journalists they met that she had been misled in her American education about the nature of the Soviet Union and that the real evil was anticommunism.

That summer they went to St.-Tropez, the Mediterranean fishing village that had become a fashionable watering spot for jet-set celebrities. Jane got used to sharing Vadim with his ex-wives and children, as well as his former mistresses. "He's known beautiful women," she said with her newly acquired continental air. "I would feel insecure with a man who had to prove himself, who was restless, who had things he hadn't done."

In the fall Jane bought a small farm in the village of St.-Ouen outside Paris. The stone and tile-roofed cottage had been built in 1830 and sat on three acres; it was a symbol of the permanence of her move to France. An American journalist who interviewed her there got a sense of how deeply in thrall Jane was to Vadim when he asked her if she thought she was an exhibitionist. Before she could answer, Vadim, who had been in the other room, stuck his head in and began to talk. Suddenly it was a dialogue between actress and director, with the interviewer only peripherally involved.

"Ah, yes," Vadim said. "Well, you exhibit yourself as a kind of experiment. You would not need to do this if you knew, really, who you are. But you do not quite, and so you make tests, as in chemistry, to find out."

Jane's eyes dilated as he completed the aperçu. "Yes! Wow! Yes, you're absolutely right! . . ."

People said that Vadim was inventing her. But the truth was that she was using Vadim to invent herself.

Someone asked if she would like to act with her father and brother. "Good God, no," Jane replied. "It would be awful. I couldn't stand it, and neither could they. First, Peter's still got to find himself as an actor, and it would hurt him to be subjected to both of us — Dad and me — at the same time."

The condescending remarks came at a bad time for Peter. His fourth film, *The Young Lovers,* had been a frivolous flop. He believed his sister's comments would help sink him deeper into the nether-world of B movies. He retaliated against Jane by accusing her of prostituting herself as an actress.

But she was not listening. Exhilarated by the thought that she was finally liberated from her family and the selves she had carried with her since childhood, she let it be known that she found France more congenial than her homeland, and ignored old friends as well as family. ("One did not visit her there," Brooke Hayward says. "She had become an *expatriate*.") In truth, however, everything she did was done with one eye on America. She was still getting film offers, some of them very appealing. David Lean had wanted her for what became Julie Christie's role in *Doctor Zhivago,* for instance, but Jane was unwilling to leave Vadim. She wanted to turn down *Cat Ballou* too, but Vadim told her that she would regret it and that in any case they needed the money to complete work on the farmhouse. He knew she was anxious to return to Hollywood and prove that her move to France had been an intelligent one.

Columbia had no faith in *Cat Ballou* and probably would have dropped it, had it not been for a provision in producer Harold Hecht's contract calling for him to be paid whether or not the movie was made. So they cast Jane because her price was low and Lee Marvin because his drinking problems had made him virtually unemployable.

Vadim accompanied Jane on location in Colorado. Sitting quietly on the set in his horn-rimmed reading glasses and devouring *Mad* magazine, he was more of a celebrity than she was. At one point during shooting, Marvin, who spent his time off screen almost as drunk as he acted in the Academy Award–winning role of Kid Shaheen, wavered up to Vadim and said, "I hate the French. But I like you because you're half Russian, even though I hate the Russians too." They began to talk and became friends.

After wrapping up *Cat Ballou,* Jane and Vadim stopped in New York on the way back to France. She took him to her father's townhouse one day while Henry was onstage in *Generation,* a play about a father's relationship with his headstrong daughter and undesirable son-in-law. While in the living room, Vadim fingered a slight tear in the fabric on the chair where he was sitting and saw that it had been re-covered four times. "Each wife has done the house in different styles," Jane noted cynically when he asked her about it. "These are just the covers from each marriage."

Back in France, Jane energetically remodeled the old farmhouse. At Vadim's request, a partition of clear glass was installed between the master bedroom and the bathroom. The land was recontoured by a bulldozer and fully grown trees were trucked in for transplanting. Jane bought farm animals. Even Vadim could see what she was trying to do: re-create Tigertail.

To finance the renovations, she signed to do *The Chase*. It was an opportunity finally to work with one of her idols, Marlon Brando, with a script by Lillian Hellman. Because it was a serious enterprise, Jane tried to rectify her image and present herself as moderate and responsible once she arrived in the States. Asked by one journalist if she had perhaps tried too hard to shock when she first went to Paris, she replied, "There was certainly a time when I tried, partly to rebel against my being my father's daughter. . . . But now I don't feel the need to strike out with wild remarks. I feel more relaxed and tranquil than I did two years ago."

Jane was concerned about how Brando would regard her, especially when, in the middle of shooting, *Cat Ballou* was released. *Time* said that she was "outclassed by everything on screen including Lee Marvin's horse," but most critics were impressed. The movie raised her from a supporting actress to a lead and increased the salary she could command to the level of her father's. She was doing so well in films that she and Vadim decided to spend the summer of 1965 in Malibu.

Largely because of Vadim, they became the center of attention in the film colony's beach outpost. Soon Jane was running what amounted to a salon. She was pleased to be with a man of such power, and she basked in the reflected glory of his worldliness. For his part, Vadim was amazed at the reach into the sacred places of the film world that her status as a Hollywood princess gave her. One night she invited David O. Selznick for dinner. Afterward Vadim took the Hollywood legend into the living room for a game of chess. In the middle of a move Vadim began to cry. Asked what was wrong, he said, "I can't believe I'm playing chess with David Selznick."

As it worked out, Henry was also living in Malibu that summer. Amy, now twelve, was with him, and so was the latest woman in his life, Shirlee Adams. A pretty dark-haired woman just a few years older than Jane, Shirlee was a stewardess with American Airlines whom Henry had met through one of his agents. Lonely and isolated, he had quickly become attached to her, and often showed up at the airport in Los Angeles to meet her flights. Part of Shirlee's attraction was that, in contrast to all the other women he had married, she was a commoner, not at all involved in the entertainment industry. When Jane was introduced to Shirlee she was impressed by her normalcy, but warned her father, "She's too young for you. She'll drop you." Henry replied with a serious look, "Nobody ever drops a Fonda," which caused Jane to chuckle.

One morning Henry came over to meet Vadim, who was about to go fishing as he did almost every day; he would bring the perch he caught back to the house, fillet them in the afternoon, and make a Provençal soup. Henry went out on the pier and fished with him, the two men looking out at the ocean and speaking in monosyllabic generalities. Afterward Henry admitted to Jane that Vadim seemed all right, but primarily in comparison with people like Timmy Everett and especially Andreas Voutsinas. Vadim was struck by Henry's awesome reserve. He was both amused and annoyed by his ongoing dilemma with his children, who he felt were too old to be engaging in an adolescent revolt. He suggested to Jane that it would be good for her to accept responsibility for shaping the relationship with her father instead of simply trying to explain it through Freudian clichés.

Henry was there several more times that summer, gaunt and impassive, a slight frown on his face as if he were listening for distant signals. He was relieved to have a truce in his struggle with Jane, but was still perplexed by the life she had chosen. An acquaintance who saw him at the July Fourth party Jane and Vadim threw was struck by how out of place he was. Everyone was eating and having fun, a new band called the Byrds was playing Bob Dylan songs. Henry was sitting by himself in a lanai clouded by others' marijuana smoke, grimacing at the percussive music and watching his daughter do the frug. He shook his head as if trying to rouse himself, then looked up and said to nobody in particular, "What is going *on?*"

Peter was also at the party. It was he, in fact, who had gotten the Byrds to play there. While his life had not undergone the public scrutiny of Jane's, he had been involved in dramas of his own over the past couple of years. He had another child now, a boy named Justin. But he had abandoned any pretense of living the conservative life he had first adopted. Now he had shoulder-length hair and was seen all over Hollywood on his motorcycle wearing military hats and a tuxedo. He had begun to play the guitar and sing songs he composed himself, going so far as to record his own rendition of "Blowin' in the Wind."

Peter's film career had stalled after *The Young Lovers*. He had tested for the second lead behind Steve McQueen in *The Sand Pebbles* but didn't get the role. He thought he would have one of the starring roles in *In Cold Blood* but lost out at the last minute to Robert Blake. As a close friend from that period says, "This turned him off Hollywood and caused him to drop out. He started 'making the scene,' hanging out on Sunset Strip and listening to Jim Morrison."

He remained caught in a web of personal tragedy, centering most recently on the suicide of his best friend, Stormy McDonald, who had slashed his wrists in the bathroom of a Tucson motel and then, when bleeding to death proved too slow, shot himself in the head. There was an inquest because a large stash of marijuana was found in the motel room, and some talk that Peter would be called upon to take a lie detector test as part of the investigation of Stormy's death, but nothing came of it.

Peter talked constantly about this death and others and used them to forge a legend of romantic damnation. After first smoking marijuana in 1962, he had stayed away from it for a couple of years because of the strong reaction he'd had; instead he began to drink heavily when he saw his film career dying in front of his eyes. But by 1965 he had given up alcohol in favor of pot, which he smoked every day. He devoted himself to killing time. He saw a lot of his friend Robert Walker, Jr. Although they didn't talk about it, Peter felt he had a common bond with Bobby Walker, whose father had died a tragic death after his wife, Jennifer Jones, left him for David O. Selznick. Peter and Bobby spent time hanging out and skateboarding on Peter's tennis court.

Peter was still embroiled in a quarrel with Henry, less public than Jane's but more pointed. Bill Hayward, who had turned up in Hollywood too, recalls that Peter was always "tweaking" Henry by doing such things as introducing him as "my brother Bill" in front of his father, knowing it would get a rise.

But usually their conflict was more serious. The level of Peter's anger could be inferred from the provocative nature of his comments to and about his father. When Henry criticized him for drug use, for instance, Peter argued tendentiously about which of them was more hypocritical: "Okay, I can understand you being opposed to it, but don't call me guilty. There are laws against oral copulation and you choose to break these laws without feeling guilty." Behind Henry's back he told his wife, Susan, that the night before she died, Frances had called his father for help and gotten a cold shoulder.

It was hard to know what was truth and what was fantasy, as Brooke Hayward said later, because Peter didn't seem to know himself.

The guerrilla war between father and son was characterized by sudden ambushes rather than pitched battles. Because the causes and antecedents were never discussed, there were always grounds for new misunderstandings. When Peter went to the Arizona location of *The Rounders* to visit the son of Henry's costar Glenn Ford, for instance, he discovered that the cast was planning a surprise birthday party for his father. When he was not invited, he sent Henry a nasty and illogical note of blame, and he would have left in a huff had the director, Burt Kennedy, not stopped him and pointed out the obvious: Since it was a surprise party, Henry could not have been the one who excluded him.

Jane, for her part, was feeling secure as a result of her relationship with Vadim. So she thought she could afford to pick up the relationship with Peter. She told him she was sympathetic with his attempt to cut their father down to life size, but she advised him to find freedom by pursuing his own destiny as she had. The attention she gave him was close to patronizing, but Peter was in a condition to be thankful for small favors. When he began spending time at his sister's Malibu home, he expected to dislike Vadim as much as he had Afdera, the other foreigner who had entered his life. But to his surprise, he found the Frenchman a decent and sympathetic person and called him "a better version of my father."

And so, with Jane the leg that closed their triangle, there was an air of tenuous reconciliation among the Fondas in the summer of 1965. On the occasions Henry showed up at Jane's house, Peter was usually there with Susan and their children, and with new friends, among them Brooke Hayward's second husband, Dennis Hopper (who, in the nasty phrase of a common acquaintance, joined Peter in "a confederation of losers"). On Sundays, Vadim's friend Christian Marquand would come by, joining writer Terry Southern, Jack Nicholson, and others. Jane tried to organize them all into a salon. As one of the guests said, "She made a great *crème brûlée*."

The time seemed to call for a commitment. And in August, Jane finally accepted Vadim's request to marry him. Partly to indicate that they were superior to the bourgeois ritual, they put together a small group and traveled to Las Vegas aboard a chartered plane, exchanging vows at the Dunes Hotel. Christian Marquand was best man; Brooke Hayward was bridesmaid. Peter sang folk songs, accompanying himself on guitar. Henry stayed at home.

After the ceremony, they all watched a bizarre floor show in which a naked woman was mock-guillotined as part of a striptease version of the French Revolution, which was accompanied by the erotic rhythms of Ravel's *Boléro*. They stayed up all night gambling and then, through a haze of marijuana smoke, watched the desert sunrise. Jane signed the marriage register in a way that summarized all her identities so far: Lady Jane Seymour Brokaw Fonda Plemiannikov.

NINE

The newlyweds returned to France in September to begin filming *The Game Is Over.* Vadim's adaptation of Zola's *La Curée* was the story of the egotistical young wife of a businessman who falls in love with her stepson, and the film was supposed to establish Vadim as a major director and Jane as a great actress.

Yet they had entered a collaboration that was more profound than the films they did. In their deepening relationship, Vadim took it as his job to continue leading Jane toward absolute sexual frankness and to convince her to shed her last inhibitions. He had affairs and told Jane about them. Going further, he confessed to an interest in sexual threesomes and brought his women into their home, into their bed. He told Jane he wanted her not just to tolerate what he was doing but to be an active "accomplice." She didn't resist, he noted later, but "went all out."

She told reporters that Vadim had given her "a new way to live, the European way . . . a life in which there can be no secrets between a man and a woman." Yet in some ways she was still quite conventional and American, so much so that it was the subject of jokes among their friends. Her old boyfriend Sandy Whitelaw passed through Paris not long after she was married, and was invited to dinner at the farm. Jane told him that since Warren

Beatty was also in Paris, she thought she would ask him too and, because of his growing reputation as a womanizer, watch what happened when he was introduced to the ultimate woman, Brigitte Bardot. Whitelaw arranged to travel to St.-Ouen with Beatty. On the way he found out that his old rival for Jane's affections was in fact already having an affair with Bardot; Beatty asked him not to mention it so they could have fun with their hostess.

As Whitelaw remembers the evening, Vadim was slightly drunk and there was plenty of pot around. After the first course of the elaborate haute cuisine dinner Jane had worked hard to prepare, Beatty looked up at her politely and cleared his throat. "Well, this is very good soup, Jane," he said, staging an elaborate pause before turning to Bardot. "But I must say, Brigitte, I'd rather be eating you." There was a brief silence and then everyone except Jane began to laugh. She became furious when Vadim said to Beatty, "Yes, I must agree with you. Brigitte tastes better."

When Vadim and others said that despite the distance she had traveled, Jane was still very much like her father, she felt insulted. Her father was so conventional. After a two-year courtship, which all along he claimed would never lead him back to the altar, Henry had married Shirlee Adams, going off to a New York judge in a limousine rented by his best man, George Peppard, who brought along his wife, Elizabeth Ashley, and a bottle of Dom Perignon. There were jokes and repeated citations of Samuel Johnson's maxim about remarriage being the triumph of hope over experience. But one of the former wives, Susan Blanchard, offered a different perspective: "Henry is a very moral man. If he were not, he wouldn't have married so many times."

Henry felt he had finally met the right woman, and he told friends that if he had met Shirlee earlier in his life he would have been married only once. Although happy now, he was embarrassed about his previous marital record. "Strange to think of a hick from Nebraska like me being married five times," he said. "I'm ashamed of myself for being married so many times. It makes me seem like a fool or a failure." Yet he had come to a point where he accepted the life he'd been given. When he was asked at a Hollywood party what it was like to have been married to so many women, two of whom had committed suicide, onlookers expected Henry to become angry. Instead he thought for a moment and replied evenly, "Well, I loved them all, and in a way I still do. I could not have saved [any] one of them, and they could not save me. Everyone has to save himself."

At the beginning of 1966 Jane and Vadim were back in the United States so that she could begin *Any Wednesday*. She was about to become a bankable star but was not yet a household name for Jack Warner, who said to the film's director, Robert Ellis Miller: "I got you a great girl for the picture, Joan Fonda."

"Her name is Jane," Miller answered.

Warner shrugged. "Joan, Jane, what does it matter? You know, Hank's kid."

Any Wednesday was another of the comedies Jane felt were marred by what Vadim had called her "robotlike seriousness."

"Was that funny?" she'd ask dubiously after completing a scene.

"It was funny," director Miller would try to reassure her.

"Are you sure?"

"I promise you, it was funny."

When he saw that she was still uncertain, Miller finally took her to see the dailies for proof. The film rolled, and she held onto him nervously. He felt her nails digging into his arm as the comic scene began. When it got a laugh from the sound technicians, Jane squealed, "I am funny! I am funny!"

Although she was never really comfortable with these comedies, Henry was delighted. He was still ambivalent about her being an actress, but if she had to be on the screen, these girlish roles were the least threatening to him. He became as proud of her conven-

tional successes as he was bothered by her unconventional esca-
pades. Miller was driving down La Cienega Boulevard after the film
was finished when he heard frantic honking. It was Henry, who
pulled up beside him at a stop sign, beaming with pleasure. "Listen," he shouted. "They've screened *Any Wednesday* and they loved
Jane!"

She went on immediately to film *Hurry Sundown,* about relations
between blacks and whites in the South. Directed by Otto Preminger and shot on location in Louisiana, it was supposed to give
Jane the opportunity for a breakthrough dramatic role. But the
script was poor, and Preminger, capitalizing on the sex-kitten persona, made her do a scene in which she performs symbolic fellatio
on a saxophone placed between costar Michael Caine's legs. Critic
Richard Schickel called this "one of the most embarrassing moments in American film."

But if *Hurry Sundown* was not an artistic success, it did offer a
revelation about the growing racial ferment in the United States,
something Jane had so far been able to ignore from her exile. When
it was discovered that the actors, black and white, would be living in
the same motel and swimming in the same pool during filming,
there were threats from the Ku Klux Klan. Instead of being mobbed
for autographs, as was customary, the cast was shunned. But the
French press was there in force covering the filming and the social
background of the civil rights movement. A Paris photographer saw
a black boy watching the action and asked Jane to walk over and pat
him on the head. She went one better and bent over to give the child
a kiss, whereupon a local sheriff in charge of providing security to
the film crew began to sputter, "You can't do that! You can't kiss a
nigger!"

That summer Jane went back to Hollywood, where Henry was
making *Welcome to Hard Times.* She got to know and like her new

stepmother, a low-keyed woman who was absolutely devoted to Henry in a way none of his other wives had been. Shirlee was willing to ride out his silences and try to jolly him out of his moodiness.

Peter was more suspicious of his father's wife. By getting married a fifth time, Henry had created more static between himself and his son. Peter resented having been displaced yet again. Henry, in turn, saw Peter as someone addicted in an infantile way to the tragedy of his past, of their joint past. Jane, Henry felt, at least was moving ahead, even if he might quarrel with the direction she'd chosen. But Peter seemed to be regressing, always talking about his "tragedies," writing poems filled with adolescent weltschmerz.

But actually things were changing for Peter. As he had felt himself sinking down, unable to escape the heavy gravity of his past, he'd looked desperately for relief. He got some LSD and, with two friends who were acting as "guides," a medical supervisor, and a St. Bernard named Basil, went to a house in the desert outside of Los Angeles to take it. The experience turned out to be a symbolic death and rebirth, and he described it in awed, almost religious tones to whoever would listen.

The first part of Peter's trip was terrible. His body ached and he felt alone. He went into a linen closet and compressed his lanky frame onto one of the shelves. He lay there scared, thinking of his mother, remembering himself in her womb, secure yet struggling to get out. Then he saw his own daughter, Bridget, popping out of his stomach. Looking at his baby, he stopped being scared. As he sank deeper into the drug, he thought more about his relationship with his father and mother. He was swept up into a blissful sense of transcendent understanding, which he later tried to put into words: "Suddenly I busted through the whole thing and related to everything. I had no further relationship with the past. I'd licked it."

The door Jane had opened led away from the United States. Now Peter had opened the doors of perception.

After that first experience with LSD, there were several more, each a deeper confirmation of his transfiguration, of the "ego death" he believed had made him a different person from the one so badly wounded by the past. Every trip, he told an interviewer, was equal to "four years at a good psychiatrist if it could be done in one session."

Peter entered a time of therapeutic narcosis. He and Bobby Walker were doing drugs one night at Escondido Beach and talking about how once when Dennis Hopper was on a trip he walked around barefoot reading the Gospel according to St. Matthew. They heard a whoosh as a car left the road up above them, and then a crash as it hit the hillside. In the middle of their trip there were fire engines and police cars and red lights. It was actor Franchot Tone on one of his benders. After the car had been pulled out by a road crew and the hubbub had subsided, the two, still feeling like "kings of the universe," got in a two-man rubber boat. They rowed out beyond the surf, anchored in the kelp, and floated around in circles talking about drugs, and finally came down at noon the next day.

Peter was now trying to live a life, he said, that was "like a movie"—filled with unexpected twists and unpredictable moments. He went with Walker and Hopper to La Paz in Baja California to look for a large tract of land where they could move their families into a commune (the term and concept had not yet entered the counterculture). Hopper and Walker were dressed in flowered shirts and blue jeans; Peter wore a three-piece suit and carried a silver metal attaché case, and let the people they spoke to believe he was an attorney for his two friends. The Mexican landowners they spoke with thought the three were crazy, and eventually Peter came home, leaving Walker and Hopper to wander through Baja by themselves for several more days.

Paradoxically, the new sense of personal conquest coming from LSD encouraged Peter to pick up his dormant film career. Because of his "ego death," he no longer cared what people in the industry thought, and could now seize opportunities he previously would

have scorned. Liberated from conventional expectations o
constituted a Hollywood career, he entered into an agreemen
low-budget American International Pictures in 1966 to do
films in exchange for some cash and a boat.

This was Peter's equivalent to Jane's going to France, an act that
was daring and unorthodox. As one film executive says, "AIP wasn't
exactly porno, but it was close. Nobody willingly did a movie for
them. The second-rate talent agencies would sometimes send starving actors to them, but nobody big."

The first AIP script was so bad Peter told the studio to forget the
deal; he'd give the boat back. But then he was offered a role in a
movie to be directed by Roger Corman, king of B movies. *The Wild
Angels* was about outlaw bikers raping and fighting and having
orgies. It didn't take much talent—in fact Peter later admitted that
he was stoned throughout the filming—but it did provide the begin-
nings of a new screen persona for him: in control, on the cutting
edge, nobody's fool or victim. He was the second Fonda of his
generation to have a face for the times—coolly immobile features,
flowing hair, tinted glasses. *The Wild Angels* was shown at the
Venice Film Festival and quickly acquired a cult following. Although Peter received only $10,000 for a film that made $10 million,
he found himself lionized as the Great American Biker; his poster
outsold those of motorcycle heroes such as Marlon Brando and Steve
McQueen.

For the first time in his life, Peter felt connected with things. He
was present at the countercultural "riots" on Sunset Strip and
claimed to have punched a club-swinging policeman. Not long after,
he was arrested with three friends for possession of eight pounds of
marijuana. His court appearance had some of the theatrical qualities of political trials later in the decade. Peter came to court in
shades and a flowered shirt, his father beside him. He wisecracked
his way through the first part of the proceedings, giving flippant
answers to the questions of the judge and the prosecutor. During a

recess Henry, seething with embarrassment and anger, took his son aside and gave him a bitter, finger-poking lecture about the impression he was creating. Peter behaved better during the rest of the trial and, largely because of his legendary father's presence, the charges were dropped and he managed to escape a jail term.

At about this time he saw a script Jack Nicholson had written. Titled "The Trip," it was for a film meant to give the viewer a vicarious experience of an acid trip through the eyes of the character Peter would play. When he read the script, Peter was so moved he began to cry, and he said to his wife, "I don't believe it. I don't believe that I'm really going to have a chance, that I get to be in this movie. This is going to be the greatest film ever made in America." He told Nicholson the script was brilliant; it reminded him of something Fellini might have done.

As promotion for the film, distributors handed out kaleidoscopes and flyers reading: "Listen to the Sound of Love. . . . Feel Purple. . . . Taste Green. . . . Touch the Scream that crawls up the Wall." The consensus of critics was that *The Trip* amounted to little more than an hour-and-a-half commercial for LSD. But it came out at a time when former Harvard professor Timothy Leary was preaching his chemical gospel and Ken Kesey and his Merry Pranksters were roaming the country on their endless acid test, and it solidified Peter's reputation as a prophet of the drug culture. He ingested every drug he could get his hands on, telling an interviewer in 1969 that he had taken twenty-five trips, some of them on "lighter and smoother" hallucinogens such as psilocybin.

For the first time in their careers, Peter's fame surpassed Jane's. It made her warily respectful and she talked to him about his experiences like someone doing fieldwork. Peter thought drugs had brought the two of them closer together, although it was Henry's respect he *really* wanted. "I really dig my sister," he said. "Probably a great deal more than she digs me, and she digs me. I dig my father too. I have a great deal of compassion for him. I wish he could open his eyes and dig me."

Back in France, Jane worked on the farm. She traveled to Paris daily for grueling ballet lessons; she had been taking lessons ever since she had joined Timmy Everett in his jazz class. Her career was still secondary to her relationship with Vadim. In 1967 she turned down lead roles in *Bonnie and Clyde* and *Rosemary's Baby* in order to remain in France and work with him on his next project, a film version of the soft-core science fiction comic strip *Barbarella*. In preparing for the role, she began speaking out about sex, posing as the urbane demi-European appalled by the uptightness of her repressed countrymen. "I think the whole obsession with sex, and with the size of a girl's breasts, is a perversion," she said. "It's a real comment on the state of manhood in America. The real homosexuals are the big tough guys who think they're so manly. All they're doing is hiding behind their fears. They all want to go back to their mothers' breasts, that's all."

The pontificating was not quite justified by the character she played in the film—a "sexual Alice in Wonderland of the future," in Vadim's description, going from galaxy to galaxy in pursuit of pleasure. As *New Yorker* critic Pauline Kael said, "Jane Fonda having sex on wilted feathers and rough, scroungy furs . . . is more charming and fresh and bouncy than ever—the American girl triumphing by her innocence over the lewd, comic-strip world of the future."

Jane had not come to Europe to be seen as fresh and bouncy, however. She admired women who had a greater gravity. *Barbarella* was filmed partly on location in Rome, and during shooting Jane's costar John Phillip Law was visited by his girlfriend, Joan Baez, for several days. The two couples had dinner. Vadim spent time explaining himself to the male lead of his film: "You know, John, I'm not a homosexual, but I do have a feminine side I work to my advantage." Jane was intrigued to meet the folksinger, who was by now a veteran of the civil rights and antiwar movements. "Jane was like a little child," Law recalls. "She looked at Joan the way I did when I met the astronauts—in awe, starstruck, I suppose you'd call it."

During shooting Jane discovered she was pregnant. Once, when she didn't realize he was watching, Vadim saw her shiver slightly. He asked what was wrong and she said that the idea of having a baby made her think of her mother. Soon afterward she got the mumps and doctors told her there was a small chance the child would be affected. They suggested an abortion, but Jane said no. She spent two weeks in bed recuperating.

After she had recovered, Jane plunged into domesticity with the same doggedness that characterized all her new enthusiasms. She looked after Vadim's children, Nathalie and Christophe, when they visited, along with the farm's eight dogs, ten cats, chickens, and a pony. She got up every morning and gave orders to the servants, made interminable lists, planned meals with guests. Friends from the States observed that not only had she reconstructed a Gallic version of Tigertail at St.-Ouen, but she seemed to be re-creating her mother from the days when she was a little girl. She had to have everything under control and ran such a tight ship that Vadim called her "a monster of efficiency."

But the pregnancy had stirred dragons that had been sleeping since Greenwich 1950. As the baby grew larger inside her, Jane became more frightened. She was finally changing into a woman, which, as she later admitted, was what she had feared since she was a little girl playing the tomboy. Occasionally she would look at Vadim and blurt out, "How can you respect me? I'm nothing." She had suffered from broken sleep most of her life, but now her recurring dreams acquired the imagery of dire portent. Night after night she dreamed of dogs run over by a car she was driving, their bodies oozing gore. As the birth approached, she panicked. Would she become like her mother, nothing but a mother? In mid-July 1968, she signed to play the lead in *They Shoot Horses, Don't They?* and agreed to begin shooting in November, two weeks after the baby was due.

She felt out of it and left behind. Peter may not have been doing much in terms of his film career, but he was connected to the apocalyptic rush of events at home. Jane felt remote from all that excitement, parochial and intellectually gawky. An interviewer who spoke to her right after the completion of *Barbarella* was surprised by the conventionality of her ideas. "They say that pot isn't habit-forming, but everybody knows it leads to harder drugs," she asserted. And: "All Mexicans are fascists."

She occasionally argued politics with Vadim, trying to defend U.S. involvement in Vietnam and distinguishing it from the French war against the Vietminh.

"Your war was a colonial war," she began one dialogue.

"What's the difference between that and a capitalist war?"

"We're not defending our economic interests like the French did," she responded. "We're there to tell the communists, 'Stop, that's enough.'"

She subscribed to American left-wing publications such as *Ramparts* and *The Village Voice* to try to get a proper perspective on the Tet offensive, the insurgent campaign of Eugene McCarthy, LBJ's decision not to run for reelection, the assassinations of Martin Luther King, Jr., and Robert Kennedy, and the other great events of 1968.

In May she was caught up in the insurgency that shook Paris, as students and workers engaged in street fighting with the police. The turmoil affected the film technicians' union of which Vadim was a member. Jane went with him to union meetings and on a couple of occasions gave speeches of shrill sincerity about the workers' cause. She began to have long discussions about politics with Roger Vailland, a French screenwriter who had collaborated with Vadim on the script of *Les Liaisons Dangereuses* and who, along with his wife, Elizabeth, had become a frequent visitor at the farm in St.-Ouen. Vailland had broken with the French Communist Party in the early fifties but had remained a leftist.

Around this time Peter came through Paris. He talked enthusiastically of doing a romantic film with Jane, which Vadim would direct. (Of his brother-in-law, Peter said, "He's got one of the greatest love cameras I've ever seen—a *phallus!*") Peter's idea was for him and Jane to play a brother and sister who make pornographic movies directed by the woman's husband. That didn't pan out, but the two of them signed to appear in the episode Vadim was directing of the anthology film *Spirits of the Dead*. Vadim's contribution turned out to be a tongue-in-cheek, slightly decadent segment featuring Jane as a medieval lady who carries on a relationship with her horse. The horse metamorphoses into a man, played by Peter.

Soon after, Peter began discussing a film he and Dennis Hopper were planning about two bikers going across America. The project did not interest Jane; in fact she doubted that he would get it made. But she was intrigued by Peter's tales of what was happening back home and by the way he, like other young Americans, seemed to be burning with dreams of a New Jerusalem. Peter told her he had been having arguments about the war in Vietnam with their father. Henry had volunteered to go to Saigon on a handshaking tour for the USO to strengthen servicemen's morale; he took a Polaroid camera and a knapsack full of film along so he could have photos taken with the GIs. On the fence about the war when he went, Henry had come back feeling that it was justified. "I discovered it was my morale and America's morale that needed strengthening, not the troops'," he'd said. "You can't be there and come away and not . . . feel. Well, obviously we should be there and the job is being done and it's a good job."

Peter told Jane how he had repeatedly challenged their father, accusing him of being ineffectual even in his support: "Politically, I can prove better than you why we should be in Vietnam. But there's only one thing I can't do. I can't find one realistic, logical, humane reason why we should be there." The conversation had escalated into an argument and eventually Peter had walked out. He had refused to talk to Henry until weeks later, when his father called to say that he had decided to campaign for Eugene McCarthy in his bid for the presidency.

After Peter returned to the United States, Jane continued to hear rumors of war. She and Vadim were friends of Sargent Shriver, then U.S. ambassador to France, and he invited them to join him in the salon of the ambassador's residence on the final night of the Democratic National Convention in Chicago. As they watched Hubert Humphrey's nomination amid bursts of violence between demonstrators and the Democratic power structure outside the convention hall, Shriver said sadly, "They just put Nixon in the White House."

For Jane and Vadim, the summer of '68 marked a peaceful time in their relationship. Vadim was affectionate and attentive as she entered the midpoint of her pregnancy. A reporter watched Vadim run his hand up Jane's caftan during an interview in their rented house in St.-Tropez and fondle her breast tenderly. The other women Vadim had loved wandered in and out of their house, along with his children. Everyone was excited about the new baby: Bardot said it would be a girl, Deneuve insisted it would be a boy. As the due date drew near, Susan Blanchard arrived to function as a stand-in mother for Jane. There was a moment of alarm when Jane's water broke and showed a trace of blood, reviving concerns over the early case of mumps. There was also a slapstick ride to the hospital, after which Vadim had to carry Jane the last fifty yards because his car ran out of gas. But the baby was healthy, a girl born on September 28, Bardot's birthday. They named her Vanessa, partly because of

Vanessa Redgrave, whose acting and political activism Jane admired, but primarily because it sounded good with "Vadim."

Henry was on Long Island rehearsing a play when he heard the news. His reaction was more animated than it had been when Peter had given him his first two grandchildren. He rushed out into the parking lot, where the rest of the cast was getting ready to drive back to Manhattan, and yelled, "Jane has a baby girl!" Then he added, "If you guys had found out before I did, I'd have killed myself."

TEN

Alluding to the joke that had been around since Jack Warner's critique of her body, Jane wrote her agent that motherhood had been a great career move because it had enlarged her breasts. In fact, however, having the baby caused her anxiety and ambivalence. For the first few weeks, she mothered Vanessa obsessively, consulting books, making lists, establishing feeding schedules. At the same time she began a crash diet so that she could get back to work. On her birthday, some two months after the baby was born, she said to Vadim, "I've reached the age of thirty-one and discovered that I've wasted thirty-one years of my life." He tried to dismiss the comment as a postpartum attack and told her that if she had been able to talk at her own birth, her first words probably would have been, "I've just wasted nine months of my life." But he knew it was a serious complaint on her part.

Obsessed as she was with Vanessa, Jane could not wait to start work again. *Barbarella* had been a camp success, so Jane was inundated with scripts. But she concentrated on *They Shoot Horses, Don't They?* The Horace McCoy novel from which the screenplay had been adapted had a cult following in France and Vadim's leftist friends told her that the subject—marathon dancing—was a perfect metaphor for the brutality of the capitalist system. The character of

Gloria, a defeated young woman who signs up for a dance marathon, resonated with Jane's internal state. She had "wasted" time for the last few years. And she feared that motherhood would "waste" her future, as she felt it had for Frances Fonda.

But there were other reasons to get busy. She and Vadim had accumulated such a volume of back taxes that French authorities were threatening to seize the St.-Ouen property and the workers doing the unending renovations there were threatening to strike. Richard Rosenthal, Jane's new legal advisor, was surprised by the extent of their debt. In a memo he pointed out to Jane that the $90,000 trust fund left to her by her mother was mortgaged to the hilt and she'd been forced to borrow $15,000 from her father to keep stocks pledged as security from being sold. She had already drawn $200,000 of her $300,000 salary for *Horses* as a loan. Nonetheless, she and Vadim remained some $400,000 in debt.

Undaunted, they arrived in Malibu early in 1969 and set up housekeeping in grand style, leaving Vanessa back in France with a nurse but bringing their two Italian greyhounds, Mao and Lilliput. Some of her friends were shocked that the baby should be left behind, but Jane, who was still dieting strenuously to lose weight gained during her pregnancy, explained that she had to return to work, and soon Vanessa was brought over to join them.

Their sojourn took on an eerie quality as Jane tried to create a little French colony in Malibu and use it to wall herself off from her father. Brooke Hayward recalls a dinner at which everyone present, with the exception of herself, Jane, Henry, and Shirlee, was French. Remote from Fonda since the time when she had seen his marriage with Frances coming apart in the gloomy Greenwich house, Hayward felt a sudden surge of sympathy because of the way Jane treated him. "He was just cast aside completely at this dinner, completely ignored by everyone else, including Jane, who refused to speak a word of English. Perhaps it was not conscious, what she did to him, but it was very obvious."

If Jane was ambivalent, Vadim was much taken with the changes that had come over the United States, and Hollywood in particular, in the few months they'd been gone—rock music and abrasive anarchy, the aggressive sexual liberation, and most of all the sense of a mighty effort to break through the last membrane of authority to reach the revolutionary utopia shimmering on the other side. The new ethic of personal fulfillment at whatever the cost seemed to be an implementation of the philosophy of life he had been preaching for years. "*This* is the way to live!" he said to Jane. "It is so *American!*"

Vadim and Jane continued to pursue the sexual freedom they had embraced in France. The number of his casual indiscretions increased, and Jane kept pace with him. At a party not long after their arrival in Malibu, Jane disappeared with a handsome young man. She returned a few minutes later with a flushed face to tell Vadim that someone had just disturbed them while they were in the bathroom together, and she added archly, "I hate it when something is half finished."

Brooke Hayward recalls visiting Jane and Vadim at this time with her husband, Dennis Hopper: "Their peculiar marital situation involved sex with a number of other people. It was very open. Jane was immensely pleased with it. She said it was the only civilized way to live. 'Thank God,' she would say, 'Vadim showed me the way to this.'"

Jane and Vadim spent time with two of the other chief explorers in the new frontier of sex and drugs, Roman Polanski and Sharon Tate, a couple whose relationship—as director and actress, mentor and learner, experienced European and American naif—was similar to their own. All the personalities of the new hip Hollywood scene moved in and out of the Polanski–Tate circle, including the new sensation, Andy Warhol, and his troupe of improvisatory, orgiastic filmmakers centered around the campy Viva Superstar, renowned for her willingness to copulate and masturbate on the screen.

Viva later wrote a novel, *Superstar,* which some critics saw as autobiographical, although the author coyly denied it. One character, Jean La Fonce, was thought to resemble Jane somewhat; she is probably a composite of the many Hollywood figures Viva knew. In one scene, the heroine comes to Jean's home and winds up in bed with her, soon to be joined by Jean's husband, Robert, in a threesome. Later, in a telephone conversation with the heroine, Jean La Fonce discusses the ins and outs of masturbation and intercourse, the virtues of various drugs, and questions of lesbianism. Jean confesses almost sheepishly that she is "too straight" to live up to the reputation in which she finds herself encapsulated.

As rumors began to circulate about her new life-style, Jane was at pains to deny she was doing anything out of the ordinary. "It doesn't matter what I say to writers. They always imply that we live in some kind of weird, perpetual orgy. Good God, we don't even go to Denise Minnelli's, much less to orgies." Yet other evidence continued to accumulate. John Phillips of the Mamas and the Papas later told about being approached by Vadim after a party at Polanski's. The Frenchman invited him and his wife, Michelle, to the Malibu house. When they got there, they found the ubiquitous Warren Beatty in the living room reading magazines.

"Where's Jane?" Phillips asked as Vadim poured him some wine.

"Upstairs in the bedroom reading," Vadim answered. "Why don't you go up and say hi?"

Phillips went up to the bedroom and found Jane in bed, naked under a sheet. As he lit a joint, he heard footsteps. It was Michelle, along with Beatty and Vadim. They all partied in the bedroom until dawn.

The boundaries defining morality were coming down, as were the lines between art and life. Vadim negotiated to direct a film version of *The Blue Guitar,* a novel about incest between a brother and a sister. He planned to use Jane and Peter as stars. Peter suggested half seriously that the two of them do a film of Beat dramatist Michael McClure's *The Beard,* whose central scene involved Billy the Kid ripping off Jean Harlow's panties and performing cunnilingus on her. Jane said it was disgusting, but Peter persisted, noting that they could charge $100 for admission as at big prizefights.

In their exploration of the outer edges of their worlds, they found a place occupied only by Fondas. Pursuing the most extreme versions of their selves, they ran into each other, the only people they knew who had shared a certain kind of life and could really understand.

Peter was in a position to be outrageous, because *Easy Rider* had been released. The film was instantly successful, earning him millions of dollars and making him the first real cult figure in American film since Brando and Dean. As suggested by its advertising slogan ("A man went looking for America and couldn't find it anywhere"), *Easy Rider* was a later film equivalent of Jack Kerouac's *On the Road,* portraying the seismic shifts in consciousness and the battering of authority of the sixties. Perhaps without knowing it, Peter had created a character, Captain America, who resonated as perfectly with the Great Revolution of the sixties as his father's Tom Joad had with the Great Depression of the thirties.

Peter had conceived *Easy Rider* while in Toronto promoting *The Trip.* After several grueling hours of interviews, he'd returned to his hotel room and relaxed with a couple of beers and some sleeping pills. Floating on a lazy high, he had glanced at a photograph someone had left for an autograph. It was a still from *The Wild Angels* showing him and Bruce Dern on a Harley. He thought about two guys, each on his own bike instead of together on one. Then he *saw* it: a modern western; two loners riding across the country; men

who have made a big score and are going to retire to their utopia on a
boat or maybe a farm, when a couple of duck poachers who don't like
their looks blow them away.

It came to him visually, as a summary of other films he'd seen.
The two men would be like John Wayne or Ward Bond or Montgomery Clift—wounded heroes, searchers. In the middle of his reverie,
he picked up his guitar. "Fat Angel" by Donovan was the song that
came to him. The opening lines seemed to synchronize with his
vision:

> He'll bring you happiness in a pipe
> Then he'll ride away on your silver bike
> And apart from that he'll be so kind
> In consenting to blow your mind. . . .

As he thought more about the project, the image persisted. It
would be a film about a heroic figure of silent strength named Wyatt
(perhaps an unconscious allusion to his father's character Wyatt
Earp) who turns people on to drugs and then rides off. Wyatt would
be the Lone Ranger of psychedelics. Like the Lone Ranger, he
would have a sidekick riding with him on his quest.

When he came out of his trance, Peter called Dennis Hopper,
whom he considered "the only guy crazy enough to know what I was
talking about." After hearing the excited summary of the idea,
Hopper thought for a moment and said: "Listen, man, the score—
we gotta make it a *cocaine* score." Peter was amazed: while he was
thinking about the larger picture, Hopper was already thinking
about the details.

Peter returned to Los Angeles and invited Hopper to his house to
collaborate on the script. It would not be detailed or binding; there
had to be room for improvisation. They put chairs out on the tennis
court and began to work as three-year-old Bridget snaked in be-

tween them on her tricycle. When one of them conceived of a scene, the other would stand up and walk over and slap his palm.

One night at a party at the house of Monkees guitarist Michael Nesmith, Peter was talking about having gone to see Samuel Z. Arkoff of American International Pictures, who'd refused to back *Easy Rider*. Arkoff's position was clear: Bikers, yes; bikers who sell drugs, no. Would-be producer Bert Schneider overheard the conversation and asked how much money was needed. Peter said $500,000. Later, after director Bob Rafelson took Peter to meet him, Schneider said he could put up the money. Everyone knew the offer was good—Schneider's father and brother were powers at Columbia.

The fact that *Easy Rider* could be financed at all was indicative of the changes coming over the film world. The Production Code, the self-censorship unit of the industry, had died, which meant that new talent was not bound by old rules. Furthermore, there was a youth culture filled with anger, idealism, and self-righteousness and anxious for films that spoke its language. Studio executives knew this audience was there, even if they hadn't yet figured out a way to take advantage of it.

Along the way there were problems. Originally the creative profits were to be split among Fonda, Hopper, and writer Terry Southern. When Southern dropped out because of what he regarded as the intellectual chaos of the project, Bill Hayward, who had been brought in to coproduce, got a piece of his share, and Peter put the rest into his own production company without telling Hopper. The rift thus created would grow as filming progressed and leave the two men barely speaking by the time it was finished.

The people at Columbia kept looking at the film during editing and asking what it meant. Every time he heard the question, Peter gave an answer filled with the zen of the acid generation: It means what you think it means. Columbia executives accompanied him to the premiere in Cannes. They were skeptical at first, but when the film got a wild standing ovation, they finally became believers. When *Easy Rider* opened in New York and immediately began breaking records, the executives stopped shaking their heads in incomprehension, as Peter once quipped, and began nodding in incomprehension.

Almost immediately, Wyatt and his sidekick, Billy, were regarded not just as characters in a film but as the representative figures of a generation. So much attention was paid to *Easy Rider* as social metaphor that a personal element obvious to those who knew the Fonda family was largely missed. At one point in the dialogue, which was often improvised, Captain America says—in words that were an homage to the haunted past Peter had never escaped— "I've always thought about suicide. I've popped pills and drove a car over a hundred miles an hour into a bridge." And in a critical scene late in the film, Peter's character, high on acid in a New Orleans cemetery, looks up at a statue of the Madonna and says, "You're such a fool, Mother. I hate you so much."

The scene was Hopper's idea. He had come to Peter with tears streaming down his cheeks as they were about to film in the cemetery: "Oh man, you gotta get up to the statue now. I want you to get up there and ask your old lady why she copped out on you."

"Come on, Hoppy," Peter had replied, "you're taking advantage. . . . I'm hip to Captain America having a mother complex, but you want to take Peter Fonda's complex and put it up there on the screen?"

"Nobody will know."

"Everybody's gonna know, man, they all know what happened. . . ."

But Peter began to do the scene, thinking only that he had to make himself very vulnerable, as he had on his acid trips. As the cameras were being positioned, he began moving his feet back and forth and rubbing them together—it was a habit left over from

176

childhood which occasionally returned when he found himself under pressure. The film began to roll, and Peter asked his mother why she had done it. He began to cry. It was, he said later, no longer a character in a movie speaking a line, but Peter Fonda asking his mother Frances a real question.

Once again, the past had rushed in, and the mother who had deprived him of a normal childhood had delivered an unexpected gift, providing a pivotal moment in Peter's grand film statement.

Peter later said that if he had not made *Easy Rider* he probably would have gone to Europe, made some "funky" movies, and used the money to buy a farm on Madagascar, where he would have sat around growing grass and getting high the rest of his life. Instead, he went to Maui to escape the pressures of his sudden celebrity and contemplate what new worlds to conquer in Hollywood.

With his recent success, Peter had inadvertently created problems for Jane and Henry, who, whatever their other differences, had always found unity in their view of him as a flake. The low-budget *Easy Rider,* which challenged the old rules of moviemaking in Hollywood, made him an estimated $5 million at a time when his father and sister were still lucky to get $300,000 per picture. Henry admitted that he was in awe, at least of the money his son was making. It was more, he pointed out, than he himself would have even if he were to sell everything he owned. But Henry couldn't surrender all of the Oedipal high ground; he told a *New York Times* reporter: "*Easy Rider* will not become a classic in the sense that *Grapes of Wrath* is a classic. But, of course, it is the beginning of a *type* of movie."

Henry's own career had flattened out at just the time Peter's was taking off. His life-style was not threatened, but however successful he had become, Henry could never forget being a starving actor. He was always fearful of being out of work and took what was offered him, even roles in films he recognized were beneath him, such as *Sex and the Single Girl* and *The Battle of the Bulge*. He explained how it happened: "When I read them, I would say, 'Are you out of your mind! It's terrible! It's crap!' My managers would set me down and say, 'Now look, Hank, you like the theater. You want to go back. You've got a play you want to go into rehearsal. But you've got to be in a box-office picture that's going to last awhile on the screen.'"

According to some, Henry's problem in the sixties was that he was too old to be the leading man and not old enough for character roles. But there was more to it than that. He was also imprisoned in that persona of frozen dignity and towering integrity he had created over the years, the persona that was so different from his off-screen personality that it had led Jane and Peter to accuse him of hypocrisy. His friend Jimmy Stewart had ventilated his dark side in a series of psychological westerns—*Winchester '73, The Naked Spur, The Man from Laramie*—and gained greater definition as an actor. But Henry was still the unspoiled hero. Even in his successful screen appearances during the sixties, he was one-dimensional—the archetypal liberal awash in moral ambiguity and conscience. Whether he was portraying a Stevensonian candidate for the presidency in *The Best Man* or a Kennedyesque president in *Fail-Safe*, the role was the same: "the Conscience of the Nation," as he dyspeptically described it.

It was a tribute to his talent that he could inhabit a persona so at odds with his real character. Reporters who did stories on him and felt the chill in his private personality came away with renewed appreciation for his acting ability, which blocked that quality from ever reaching the screen. Not until the end of the decade did Henry play against his grain, when spaghetti-western director Sergio Leone cast him as a pathological killer of children as well as adults in *Once Upon a Time in the West*. Henry liked the film, and the idea that audiences would say, as he put it, "Jesus Christ, that's Henry Fonda! He wouldn't massacre a farm family!"

Although *Once Upon a Time in the West* was not successful,

Henry did get his first fan letter from Jane. She was struck by the sadistic figure he played. It was as if she were seeing her father on the screen for the first time.

Jane was aware that she had slipped in the family batting averages, and it disturbed her. Brooke Hayward was with her one afternoon when she was reading an article about Peter. It ended by saying that in a family version of the tortoise and the hare story, he might fool everyone by emerging as the most talented Fonda. Hayward was surprised when Jane said bitterly, "What has he really done to deserve this?"

Peter's good fortune added to Jane's feeling of being unfinished as an actress, of being left behind, mired in the pleasurable but dead-end identity of Roger Vadim's wife. In an effort to catch up, she poured everything into the role of Gloria in *They Shoot Horses, Don't They?* Her first gesture was to cut her mane of golden Barbarella hair, part of her identity for all the years she had been with Vadim, into a severe thirties bob. Vadim himself understood that it was a symbolic severing of the ties that bound her to her recent past and knew that it was only a matter of time until they had a crisis.

Adopting the heavy despair of her character, Jane became despondent like Gloria. Unlike Henry, who saw acting as a way of keeping his demons at arm's length, she was convinced that the more of herself she poured into her character, the better she would be—as an actor and, reciprocally, as a person. She moved into a trailer near the set of *Horses* and sometimes stayed there rather than return to the family in Malibu every evening. She was moody and distracted as she worked herself into the cynicism of the part. She plastered the walls of her trailer with pictures cut out of a police training manual showing gunshot victims and people decapitated in automobile accidents.

Discussing the role later, Jane said, "I couldn't tell reality from illusion. Big black walls of darkness and depression fell over me." And in a particularly revealing comment, she compared playing Gloria to carrying a dead baby inside her: "I went around wondering why I couldn't give birth." It was clear to those close to her that Jane was having enormous difficulty with her own role as mother to Vanessa. She said that having a baby had made her feel "numb and shriveled," and the image with which she described herself—"a raisin of wrath"—suggested the implosive violence of all her confused feelings.

Vadim stayed home and took care of the baby. Jay Cocks, a reporter with *Time,* recalls knocking on the door of the Malibu house and being surprised when the famous French seducer opened the door, diaper pins in his mouth and the child in his arms. "The feminine and soft side of his nature was immediately apparent," Cocks says. "And Jane was in the background, brisk and efficient and doing her thing, and I thought to myself, 'We've got a pretty interesting role reversal here.'"

But Vadim was tiring of some aspects of this role reversal. He resented Jane's obsessive need to take all things equally seriously. For her part, she was beginning to realize not only the emptiness of his fixation with decadent pleasure, but the extent to which it was frivolously out of step with the somber realities of America, which seemed headed toward a civil war as a result of the chaos caused by Vietnam.

The role of Gloria, therefore, had the possibility not only of a breakthrough but of a breakout as well. Jane was involved on the set, making suggestions about the narrative, trying to get the opening slow-motion scene of a horse taken out because it was too romantic, fighting against the attempts on the part of the studio to find an alternative to Gloria's suicide at the end. She lost weight and became drawn and exhausted, and when filming was finally over in June 1969, she left to visit Peter in Hawaii.

Jane found her brother in a very different frame of mind. Before the success of *Easy Rider,* his wife said, being married to Peter had been "like living with a Martian." He had lectured Susan on how every living thing was holy, the vegetable world as well as the animal. He had said that eating a carrot was like being a racist. He had resisted walking on the lawn because he said that he could hear the blades of grass cry out in pain. But now, with his new success, he had gained enough emotional equilibrium to be able to provide a strong shoulder for Jane. For the first time either of them could remember, she was looking at his life for possible answers. They hiked at Maui's Seven Sacred Pools, where Jane fell and chipped a tooth. They smoked pot and Peter tried to teach her how to play the twelve-string guitar. He told her about the impact meeting the Indian philosopher Krishnamurti had had on him, and how he had seen the Truth.

Jane's trip home from Maui to Malibu was a step backward. She found herself once again sinking into the libertinism of the Hollywood sex-and-dope scene. By comparison the purposeful utopianism of Peter's thinking seemed a galaxy away. She told friends that she felt as if she were rousing herself after a long sleep; the comment prompted her father to speak disparagingly of her "Sleeping Beauty syndrome"—always awakening suddenly to some reality she had ignored.

In August she, Vadim, and Vanessa sailed for France from New York. In a final touch that summarized the surreal forces on the loose in America, Andy Warhol, who had come to see them off, spent all his time scurrying around the French liner picking up empty Coke bottles and putting them into a shopping cart. He explained that since Coca-Cola had stopped embossing the glass of its bottles in France, these empties would soon be worth a fortune.

Shortly after they arrived back at their farm, Jane heard that Sharon Tate and others had been carved up by the Manson family in a gruesome murder that seemed to have tangential reference to the life she and Vadim had been leading. As she later told a friend: "That could have been us."

Jane had gorged on Vadim's views and life-style for almost four years. Now she was ready to purge it all, emptying herself so that she would be ready to fill up with some other identity. That she was approaching—indeed, creating—a crisis was clear to Vadim and others from the agitated way in which she began to fuss over herself. She enrolled in an hypnosis class to stop her heavy smoking, and took up speed-reading to keep pace with the abundance of literature about the United States which had begun to arrive at the St.-Ouen farm. She read *Steppenwolf,* a book about, among other things, the replacement of purposeless sensuality with a higher goal.

In October she told Vadim she needed to get away to a wholly new environment to think about the future. Because of her recent discussions with Peter, she had decided to go to India.

Once in Bombay, however, she found poverty not peace. She was disturbed by the young Americans who had gone there as religious pilgrims and who ignored the squalor while claiming they were blissed out by Eastern mysticism. She told Vadim that being in India made her realize the degree to which she was an American.

Jane returned directly to the States in mid-November to do publicity for *Horses.* She stopped in New York at the home of her attorney, Richard Rosenthal, and sat up late in the night talking about her experiences in India. Asked what impact the trip had had on her, she told Rosenthal that it had made her want to do something big with her life, something that might have little or nothing to do with movies. It was just a matter of finding the right thing.

Vadim joined her a week later in the guest house at Henry's Bel Air villa. The nights were often tense, with Jane sitting at a desk underlining articles about Vietnam and finally snapping at Vadim to turn off the Rolling Stones record he was listening to. She told him that after her promotional tour she didn't want to return to France. They sent for Vanessa, whom Vadim, thinking their stay would be brief, had left behind with a nurse.

Beginning the publicity for *Horses,* Jane spent part of New Year's Eve talking to journalist Rex Reed for a *New York Times* article. The interview took place at her father's townhouse, where she began by taking the tobacco out of a Winston and replacing it with fine gray marijuana. "You don't mind if I turn on, do you?" she asked, and then, after lighting up, she began to free-associate: "I wonder if at ten P.M. on New Year's Eve in 1959 people looked back on the fifties and thought their decade was as productive as this one has been. I don't think so. It was the end of a time when people had been fed sleeping pills by Eisenhower. Things are more exciting now."

She indicated that she felt she'd wasted her life so far and wanted to make up for it. There was a sound of the valedictory in her words on Vadim: "He's taught me how to live, and if anything happens to our marriage, he'll always be my friend."

At the end of the interview, shortly after midnight, Henry and Shirlee came home. Hearing them downstairs, Jane leapt up and began opening windows and windmilling her arms to clear the marijuana haze out of the room. "This reminds me of the times I used to clean this place on my hands and knees after my parties before my father came home," she muttered. "If only he knew how many bodies have passed out on his floor."

Henry came in and made small talk, asking her if she'd seen Dennis Hopper, whom he despised. Jane said she'd heard from Brooke Hayward, from whom Hopper was now divorced, that he had been around to give their daughter a Christmas present. The child had opened the elaborately wrapped box with great anticipation and inside found coils of Hopper's hair, which he'd had cut recently. Jane and her father then decided to call Peter in California to wish him a Happy Decade. After hanging up, Jane rolled her eyes and said, "Boy, was *he* stoned!"

Shortly after the start of the new decade, the three Fondas were together in Hollywood for a *Time* cover story. The sixties had marked their arrival on center stage as the most potent family act the entertainment industry had ever seen. There was nothing else quite like them, and in this, their first joint journalistic portrait, they had an investment in minimizing the strife that had often characterized their public statements about each other during the last fractious ten years. "We're close now," Jane said, trying to set the tone for the article, "closer than we've ever been." Behind the scenes, however, the team of reporters assigned to cover the Fondas found something quite different.

Reporter John Larsen did the preliminary interviews with Jane and Peter at Peter's place in Maui. Jane was obsessively mothering, as if trying to prove her commitment to her young daughter, while Peter was in the background, "freaking out and saying, in effect, 'Interview me! Interview me!'"

Meanwhile, reporter Mary Cronin had been assigned to begin interviewing Henry. "He was in his bathrobe because he was fighting a cold," she recalls. "He talked about death quite a lot. As I interviewed him, it was as though he was trying to wrap up his life and wasn't especially pleased with what he saw. He was worried about his eyes being puffy and about no longer being good-looking. Digging around in his 'psyche' made him extremely unhappy. He gave off strong vibes of being jealous of his kids and of the fact that they were eclipsing him."

The three got together at Henry's Bel Air house for a final interview with Jay Cocks, who was in charge of putting the final story together. Something of a film buff, Cocks tried to break the ice with Henry by asking him where he got the idea, in *My Darling Clementine,* to have Wyatt Earp lean back in his chair while sitting outside the saloon and make his feet do a little dance on the railing.

Henry narrowed his eyes and growled, "Everybody asks me that goddamned question."

During the interview Peter kept going outside to smoke on a joint and returning in an increasingly combative mood. This made Henry angrier, and made Jane try harder to smooth things over. Peter further broke the continuity of the event by saying with increasing vehemence that *Time* did not have the capacity for objective journalism. Eventually Jane looked at him, shrugged, and said, "Well, if that's the way you feel, Peter, what are you doing here?" Peter ignored her and went back to the attack. Suddenly Henry turned on him and yelled, "Shut up!" Cocks felt that Peter "just shriveled up."

Most of the conflict was airbrushed out of the version of the story that finally appeared in the magazine. But all three *Time* writers came away thinking they had just seen something very strange—a dada version of the Barrymores, One Man's Family in film noir.

It was like a foreign world. I felt so
happy, like I had come home. I was
also very lost, because it was a weird
place for a movie star to be.
                              —Jane Fonda

ELEVEN

An observer watching the unusual activity in the front yard of Henry Fonda's Bel Air house on the morning of March 25, 1970, might have thought someone was preparing for a vacation. Shirlee was bustling in and out of the house carrying boxes. Vadim and his friend Christian Marquand were standing in the driveway speaking French with Elizabeth Vailland, an old friend and longtime member of the French left who had recently arrived from Paris. Vanessa, now eighteen months old, was scurrying around saying "Bye" to everyone in sight. Henry was hiding behind his movie camera, filming every move Jane made.

Her hair was cut short in a boyish shag and she had on tight jeans and a long-sleeved T-shirt—the look, she said later, of someone "ready for action." After she had finished loading her Mercury with food, blankets, clothes, and other supplies, there was a pause. Then she hugged everyone and, after making sure she had her tape recorder, got into the car with Vailland and drove off. Watching the Mercury disappear, Marquand remarked to the grim-faced Vadim that the world was truly upside down when the wife goes off to war while the husband stays home to change the diapers.

Jane was not going into battle, at least not yet. But she was going on a reconnaisance of an America that seemed on the verge of civil war. This was not the same place she had derided as empty and provincial during her French exile. Another America had grown up during her absence, an undiscovered country of dissidence and conflict, of impossibly high hopes and mundane despair; an America above all pulsing with energy and spirit. "It's happening here," Jane had said to Vailland. What "it" was couldn't be precisely defined, although the people in the radical movement who were marching on the Pentagon, setting up communes in New Mexico, and fighting the police in Berkeley's People's Park had a term for it: the revolution.

Like other explorers who learned about exotic places from the tales of those who had gone before them, so too had Jane begun to form a picture of this new America in the preceding weeks by eagerly interrogating New Left activists and radicals. She had always thought her own life choices to be somewhat daring, but in comparison with what she now heard they seemed empty and mediocre. What she discovered excited her but also caused a shiver of uncertainty. "I realized that I didn't believe in anything," she said later, "and I knew that people whom I might respect wouldn't respect me."

The first sign of her need for a new self had come after she finished *They Shoot Horses, Don't They?* She immediately went to Vadim's barber and told him to cut off her marcelled hair. He cut it so short that someone commented she looked like "a young Henry Fonda, only prettier." She wanted to be rid of what the hair symbolized: the doomed femininity she had adopted as the marathon dancer Gloria and also as the character she had been playing much longer in her real life, Lady Jane Seymour Brokaw Fonda Plemiannikov. As she said of her new look, "I always had a deep-rooted need to be a boy and now I am one."

The adoption of the unisex disguise signaled a metamorphosis similar to others in her life—when she joined Actors Studio, when she fled to France—a moment when she emptied herself of a previous identity and was waiting, in a state of heightened receptivity, to be filled by a new persona. But this time the drama of rebirth was projected onto the backdrop of a radical apocalypse which gave it the added weight and resonance of a historic event.

Just recently members of the Weathermen, a homegrown terrorist sect, had blown themselves up in a Manhattan townhouse with a bomb intended to spark a national uprising. (The two women survivors who stumbled out of the rubble had shown up in dazed condition at a neighboring brownstone owned by Susan Blanchard; they begged overcoats from her, then disappeared into the underground.) The Black Panthers were waging what amounted to a guerrilla struggle against the police forces of several major cities. There was a sense that a transcendent moment might be approaching, and Jane was desperate not to be left behind. *It was happening.*

Her attempt to climb aboard the revolution had begun on a foggy January morning when she went to Alcatraz. When she was in India, Jane had read a story in the radical magazine *Ramparts* about how the island in San Francisco Bay, until the 1950s site of a maximum-security prison, had been occupied by militant Indians from tribes across the United States. She had contacted the author of the story and asked him to take her to Alcatraz; she wanted to get involved in what she called the "new politics."

Jane had sailed to the island in one of the local yachts defying the Coast Guard blockade and resupplying the Indians, and had looked up in awe as she neared the weather-beaten rock cliffs on which some brave had painted the words "Indian Territory" in bleeding red letters. After meeting representatives of the various tribes, she realized that the Sioux, playing on their historical identity as a warrior elite, were the most radical group, and she spent the rest of her afternoon on the island smoking dope with them in their corner of the old prison exercise yard and making plans to tour Indian reservations across the United States to publicize the problems Indian people faced.

For Jane, Indian affairs was a safe entry point. Indians had been wronged by history in a way that could not be denied. They had also been supported by Marlon Brando, one of Jane's heroes and the only major star in Hollywood until that time to cultivate an identification with the New Left. But in the intellectually coercive atmosphere of 1970, it was impossible to be concerned with only one cause. Everything was interconnected. The plight of the Indians was indivisible from other issues—racism, sexism, and imperialism— and part of what radicals saw as America's epic guilt.

After her visit to Alcatraz, Jane learned about the Black Panthers at a party at the home of her Malibu neighbor Elliott Gould. There she met Shirley Sutherland, wife of actor Donald, and the Panthers' chief supporter in the film colony. At another Hollywood party, for Italian director Michelangelo Antonioni, she met an activist named Fred Gardner, who had contributed to the script for *Zabriskie Point,* Antonioni's film about American radicals. Gardner was also in- volved in the GI coffeehouse movement, setting up off-base meeting places to entertain servicemen bound for Vietnam while also trying to turn them against the war.

For the next few months, Gardner would function in somewhat the same way Andreas Voutsinas had earlier in Jane's life. (Some people even noted a slight physical resemblance between the two men.) A dogged footsoldier in the Movement, Gardner knew his way around the radical scene and was a repository of opinions and attitudes about the New Left.

Shortly after their meeting, Gardner put Jane in touch with Mark Lane, the radical lawyer who had gained notice a few years earlier with *Rush to Judgment,* a book on the Kennedy assassination, and who had since also become active in the GI movement. Shortly after the first of the year, Jane had arranged to meet Lane in Seattle, where he was spreading his antiwar message among soldiers. She gave a speech to some GIs about Vietnam in which she told them she

From the time they were married in 1965 until his death, Henry and the former Shirlee Adams were practically inseparable. "After stepping up to bat five times, I finally hit a home run," Henry once said of his marriage to Shirlee. (Photofest)

In his hippie phase after Easy Rider, *Peter played the family man to children Justin and Bridget and first wife Susan. (Photofest)*

Jane's visit to Vietnam in 1972 immortalized her in the American consciousness as "Hanoi Jane." (AP/Wide World Photos)

As one of five convicted in the Chicago Seven trial, Tom Hayden emerged as a hero of the New Left. After the trial, he fielded questions from the press, flanked by attorneys William Kunstler (left) and Leonard Weinglass (right). (UPI/Bettmann)

After her trip to Hanoi, Jane teamed up with fellow radical Tom in London. "Tom's the brilliant one; I'm only a chameleon," she said. (AP/Wide World Photos)

Henry's portrayal of Clarence Darrow on Broadway in 1974 marked a joyous moment in his career. "If Darrow was not like this," a New York Times *reviewer wrote, "he should have been." (Photofest)*

||||||||||||||||||||||||||||||||||||||||||||||||||||||||||||||||||

*While Jane was
achieving stardom in
films like* The China
Syndrome, *Peter was
directing and acting in
such B movies as*
Wanda Nevada.
(both Photofest)

During Henry's appearance in First Monday in October *on Broadway in 1978, his pal Jimmy Stewart paid him a backstage visit; their friendship spanned fifty years. (*AP/Wide World Photos*)

Putting his jeans aside, Peter squired his second wife Becky and his teenaged daughter Bridget on the town in London in 1982. (AP/Wide World Photos)

With nearly $2 million of her own money, Jane helped Tom launch a successful campaign in 1982 for a seat in the California legislature. (AP/Wide World Photos)

Shirlee, Peter, and Jane helped Henry celebrate his seventy-fifth birthday. "The years have come as fast as Halley's Comet," said Henry. "But I don't consider myself old." (UPI/Bettmann)

His role as the
curmudgeonly Norman
Thayer in On Golden
Pond (1981) won Henry
an Oscar (UPI/Bettmann);
too ill to accept, he ceded
the honor to his family:
(left to right) Tom, Jane,
Bridget, Vanessa, Amy,
and Troy (front).
(AP/Wide World Photos)

Jane dreamed that Tom
could be president someday
and constantly encouraged
his visibility; in 1986 the
Haydens, along with
Shirlee, participated in
Hands Across America, a
nationwide effort to raise
funds for the poor. (Janet
Gouch/Celebrity Photo)

Jane solicited Peter to
accompany her on a trip
around California in
support of a local
environmental law. (Scott
Downie/Celebrity Photo)

Whether supporting the Solidarity movement in Warsaw (AP/Wide World Photos) or attending society functions in California (Greg DeGuire/Celebrity Photo), Tom and Jane put on a united front; privately, their marriage was showing strains.

Proud father Peter, with wife Becky, showed up at a 1989 screening of Shag: The Movie, *which starred his daughter Bridget. (Jim Smeal/Ron Galella Ltd.)*

Arrested on drug
charges in 1989,
a somber Vanessa
Vadim was escorted
out of Manhattan
Criminal Court; the
charges were later
dropped. (AP/Wide
World Photos) Bridget
Fonda made headlines
that same year as
British call girl
Mandy Rice-Davies
in Scandal. (Photofest)

After Jane's separation from Hayden, son Troy and brother Peter escorted her to an awards ceremony. "I've never seen her so wounded," said studio executive Mike Medavoy about the split. (Scott Downie/Celebrity Photo)

The Academy Awards ceremony in March 1990 was an occasion for Jane to confront her peers, her past, and her future. (Scott Downie/Celebrity Photo)

was not one of those entertainers like Bob Hope who supported sending men to war. Soon after, she got a panicked call from her publicist reminding her that she was up for an Academy Award for *Horses* and that Bob Hope *was* the Academy. She responded by firing the man and replacing him with Steve Jaffe, a former journalist with the radical *LA Free Press,* who although he was now working in public relations retained his Movement connections.

Jane decided to enlist Elizabeth Vailland as a traveling companion on her cross-country trip. When she arrived in New York, Vailland, who had seen Jane struggling clumsily with political ideas in France, was stunned at the change that had come over her friend, transforming her from a hedonist and dilettante into someone incandescent with commitment.

Others who had known Jane only superficially were also taken aback by the change. But to Brooke Hayward it all made sense. "Jane is not deeply intelligent. But she's very smart and she can sense which way the wind is blowing in a way that many more gifted people cannot," said Hayward. "She has always had a nose for the prevailing winds. From the beginning, her radicalism was chic."

The relationship between them cooled. Jane tried to recruit her childhood friend to the cause of the Black Panthers and became annoyed when Brooke expressed doubts about the group. But one person Jane would not stop trying to convert to her new views was her father. She told him of her ideas about the fundamental evil in the American character. She even arranged a meeting with a friend of Fred Gardner's who had been in the Special Forces in Vietnam, who briefed Henry on massacres of civilians by the U.S. military. Henry listened to the pitch and then, with Jane looking at him expectantly, said, "I don't know what I can do besides what I'm already doing—that is, campaigning for peace candidates."

It was a reaction she could interpret as a rejection. This gave her upcoming odyssey an Oedipal dimension: along with whatever else she was doing, she was challenging Henry's liberalism as hypocritical, rebelling against his indifference, and most of all trying once again to capture his attention.

Leaving her father behind in his Bel Air mansion, Jane headed off on her pilgrimage to the Indian reservations. She expected sleek warriors like those on Alcatraz spouting Red Power slogans. But at every stop—from Pyramid Lake in Nevada to the Blackfoot reservation in Fort Hall, Idaho, she found conservative tribal leaders who were politically inarticulate as well as personally reserved and, worse yet from her point of view, overweight. She struggled to maintain her illusions but grew baffled by the gap between the Indians' plight and their quiescent reaction to it.

In early April, Jane interrupted her journey to return to Los Angeles for the Academy Awards. She flashed a clenched fist to admirers as she arrived at the Dorothy Chandler Pavilion and did not disagree with them afterward when they said she had lost out to Maggie Smith because of her new radicalism. Then she and Vailland headed back on the road. Zigzagging through the Southwest, they visited more reservations and, after pausing for demonstrations against the U.S. incursion into Cambodia, went with Peter, who was filming his western *The Hired Hand* near Santa Fe, on a tour of hippie communes resembling those in *Easy Rider*.

Jane called Henry often to keep him posted on what she was doing and what she thought so far about her experiences. He was puzzled, less by her words than by her tone. "You listen to her on the telephone," he said, "and she's like a fanatic!"

At the University of New Mexico, she addressed her first large crowd in a rally held right after four students at Kent State University were killed during a confrontation with Ohio National Guardsmen. Then she was off to Killeen, Texas, to visit an off-base GI coffeehouse Fred Gardner had established. She arrived on the East

Coast on May 9 to speak to a huge rally in Washington, D.C. From there she went to Fayetteville, North Carolina, for an "alternative" Armed Services Day observance set up by Mark Lane; she was detained briefly for passing out pamphlets inside an Army base.

Later Jane would say of her precipitous journey: "When I left the West Coast I was a liberal. When I landed in New York, I was a radical."

For many, this was exactly the problem: she had compressed into two hyperkinetic months a political journey others in the Movement had taken ten years to make. Moreover, she was not content to stay in the background behaving like an apprentice. She wanted to be visible, to display her feelings publicly, to confess and recant and bear witness, thus gaining the "authenticity" the Movement seemed to offer its dedicated adherents.

She was trying to give herself an existential pinch on the arm, to remind herself that her life was not merely acting. Yet ironically, she had entered the New Left at its most theatrical moment—a time of rhetorical recklessness; a time when acts, like words, were dominated by the proposition "The heavier the better." Jane immediately joined in, telling a reporter shortly after her cross-country trip, "I would think that if you understood what communism was, you would get down on your knees and pray that we would someday become communist."

How could she? That was the question for Americans who knew of her primarily as the daughter of that most American of figures, Henry Fonda.

Who was she? This was the question other radicals asked, glad to have a convert with such a famous and usable name, but suspicious of the overnight nature of the conversion. Yet the doubts she aroused only inspired Jane to try harder to prove herself and take ever more radical stands.

She flew back to Los Angeles, supposedly to spend time with Vanessa, although Vadim, who said he felt as if he'd been baby-sitting for Lenin, complained that once she got there she spent eighteen hours a day on the phone talking politics and the other six asleep. Jane deeply resented him for questioning her commitment, but she had to admit that there was truth in the nickname he had given her, "Jane d'Arc," because she *was* submitting herself to a radical fire which she hoped would burn away her past and reveal the pure essence of her new faith.

She systematically rid herself of what radicals termed her "ruling-class privileges." One of the few indulgences that remained was a weekly session at a pricey massage clinic in the San Fernando Valley. Jane went there to have her ankles massaged in the faint hope of reshaping what she regarded as her one significant defect. According to another regular customer who listened to her political monologues during the treatments, "She'd be talking about Indians, Vietnam, everything. One day I got fed up. I said, 'Jane, you go protest in front of the White House and then you come here to have your ankles reduced. If you want to change things, why don't you begin with yourself?' Jane answered, 'That's exactly what I plan to do. I'm going to change myself completely.'"

She was bright and enthusiastic, a quick study. But because of her inexperience, she had trouble discriminating between the approaches now offered to her. This sometimes made it seem that whoever talked to her last got her attention. After she agreed to help him set up a national office for the GI movement, for instance, Mark Lane arranged a meeting with a wealthy southern California businessman to try to raise money for the effort. A couple of days before the meeting was to take place, Dick Gregory happened to be in the middle of one of his fasts and with his well-developed spiel on the political as well as the physiological efficacy of abstinence, he quickly convinced Jane that the only moral course open to her was to join him. The problem was that the businessman Lane and Fonda would be asking for money was inordinately proud of his gourmet chef. When Lane suggested that she go off her fast for the evening, she replied, "I can't, Mark. It's a matter of principle." He thought she would come around, but when they sat down to eat, Jane said: "Just water for me, please. I'm not eating tonight." As Lane notes, "Needless to say, that was the end of fund-raising that night."

Even when she tripped over her ignorance and inexperience, she was not deterred. It was as if she was rehearsing for the role ahead, trying to discover the right costume, the right emotional pitch, the right way to hit her marks. Some said that she hoped to be an American Pasionaria. But if she was auditioning, the part she wanted was more like that of a postmodern Becky Sharp—someone making her way by her wits through the Vanity Fair of American radicalism, riding its updrafts, being charged by its energy, letting its picaresque movements take her where they would.

In fact, they soon took her to the top echelons of the New Left. In July 1970, when Black Panther cofounder Huey Newton was released from prison, where he'd done time for murdering an Oakland policeman, Lane arranged for Fonda to see him. She came away from their meeting extolling Newton as "a great, gentle man, the only man I've ever met who approaches sainthood," and began to hang around with the Panthers. Some of them called her a "rich white bitch" behind her back and bragged about having sex with her. But Jane was impervious, never addressing these rumors. She continued to champion the group as "guerrilla fighters" and adopted the maximalist views she thought would make them accept her.

Much of the time, in Mark Lane's discrete formulation, "her instincts might be good, but her knowledge was deficient." In one of several appearances she made on *The Dick Cavett Show* in her first year as a radical, Jane held forth on Vietnam, comparing it to the American Revolution and saying that the parties involved could settle the conflict without outside intervention. Asked if the American colonies hadn't had help in their struggle, she snapped, "Not that I know of." Whereupon Cavett said, "What about Lafayette?" Noting the blank look on her face, the studio audience hooted. "A lot of them were glad to see her make a mistake in third-grade history," says publicist Steve Jaffe. "It took us a long time to reverse that. For weeks people would come up to her with a grin on their faces and say, 'What about Lafayette?'"

Nonetheless, the summer of 1970 became Jane's moment of commitment, and showed the enduring power of Lee Strasberg's lesson that one gains access to emotions by displaying them; that one *becomes* how one *acts*. Finally she had something to do with her life that was worthy rather than "degrading," as she had begun to describe her experience with Vadim.

Richard Rosenthal, her attorney at the time, understood her new passion: "Here's a woman who grew up in the shadow of an enormously famous but not very attentive father, a woman whose brother had to shoot himself to get attention. First she was Henry Fonda's daughter, then Roger Vadim's wife. And then finally the Movement wanted her — not because she was part of someone else but wanted her for herself. Sure, everybody was using her. But Jane used them more than they used her."

Henry didn't see it this way. Still possessive about his daughter, although she was now entering her mid-thirties, he was bothered by people like Mark Lane and felt they were taking advantage of her. He was also bothered by the way her behavior reflected on him, and he noted sourly that for the first time in his life he was getting hate mail. While he shared her opposition to the war, he was disturbed by her scorn for the patriotism of the men serving there, especially because his old friend Jimmy Stewart had lost a son in Vietnam. Henry was exasperated that she was still capable of causing him such worry and embarrassment. On one occasion he was talking to a *New York Times* reporter when Jane interrupted with a telephone call. He left for several minutes and then returned to the interview with a grim look on his face: "Sorry, but I was on a long-distance call to Washington, talking with my—how should I say it?—with my erstwhile, my alleged daughter. . . ."

There was an emotional moment between them on the terrace outside his Bel Air home in which he asserted his prerogatives as father and tried to draw a bottom line for her: "Jane, if I ever discover for a fact that you're a communist or a true communist sympathizer, I, your father, will be the first to turn you in. I fought for this country and I love it."

After she tearfully denied she was a communist, he went on: "There are less human rights in Russia than in America. Maybe we do have inequalities, but it's worse over there."

Perhaps even more cuttingly, Henry said that he believed a good part of Jane's newfound radicalism was an attempt to confront the fact that Peter had become a symbol of the counterculture long before her own conversion. This recalled something he had previously said to a magazine interviewer: "My instinct is that after eight years abroad she came back to her country, America, and suddenly realized how aware Peter had become. It was almost as though she had to do it and had to do it better than he. Instant causes!"

Peter was indeed a reference point for Jane. She could no longer count on the fact that they would continue in the roles they had played since childhood—he the puppyish kid brother, she the older sister experiencing things first and bringing him along. For the time being, he had broken free. Henry saw it, and so did Peter himself. A rebel without a specific cause, Peter seemed sure of himself in a way she could not yet be. He would point to himself and say, "This is my authority. This is my constitution. There is no badge. There is no dictator, no president, no God."

Determined to recover her old position of superiority, Jane said that Peter "had no politics." For his part, Peter made it clear that he resented his sister's Janey-come-lately zeal, noting sarcastically that she would probably "teach revolution to Mao Tse-tung if she had a chance." Moreover, he implied that she was hypocritical—exactly the charge she was leveling against their father.

In a discussion with a reporter, Peter said: "I was going to send Jane to Cuba 'cause she was carrying on about how they got it together down there."

He claimed she had replied, "Well, what will happen when I come back? Won't they take my passport?"

"So what?"

"I got a film to do in New York in July. If they take away my passport maybe it'll hurt my career."

"Well, Jane, are you a communist or an actress?" Peter said he asked her. "I mean, what is your scene? Don't come on with all this shit about Cuba and then say you can't make it 'cause you got a film to do in July."

Jane shrewdly realized that the best way to talk to her brother—and father—was to speak to a larger audience. And so, in the period following her cross-country trip, she was everywhere, becoming an all-purpose resource for the left.

Jane's publicist had the heavy responsibility for giving order to all the commitments she made. "Once I got a call at six A.M.," Steve Jaffe recalls. "It was William X or some other Panther calling from Louisiana. He said, 'Tell Jane to send another Visa card.' I said, '*Another* card?' Then William X said, 'Yeah, we lost the card she gave us and we lost the car.' I said, '*The car?*' He said, 'Yeah, you know, the Hertz car we rented with the card. We lost the card and we lost the car and we need to get another one.' This really happened: she gave some Panthers her Visa card and they rented a car and lost it."

There were many rumors about her involvement with various radicals, leaders of the movement and followers too. In the words of a member of the Movement who kept an eye on her, "She was a queen bee spreading the royal jelly all around." Jaffe, who accompanied her on her travels, reflects, "Jane was very well organized.

She liked having things in order. This involved her personal needs too. When she met someone and decided to have a relationship, she scheduled it in."

A Berkeley woman recalls a tête-à-tête with Jane during which the discussion turned to the radical leaders each wished she'd had sex with. "My biggest regret," said Jane, "is that I never got to fuck Che Guevara."

In the midst of all this fervent activity, Jane decided to do *Klute*. Jaffe asked her why and she replied, "Because if I don't, I'll be completely broke." He knew she was telling the truth because he had seen her selling her jewelry to raise money.

Soon after agreeing to do the role, she got cold feet, fearful that playing a prostitute might hurt her image. But then she realized not only that the film was more daring than anything she'd done during her forbidden-games period with Vadim but also that it had a political subtext about the lives of women that was consistent with her new politics.

She prepared for the part of Bree Daniels by personally investigating New York's demimonde. It was almost as if she were looking for a piece of herself. There were rumors that she even turned tricks while hanging out with high-priced call girls; later, in a conversation with Andy Warhol's *Interview*, Jane herself said: "I came to New York to do my research. I spent a month with $1,000-a-night call girls, and madams and pimps, and I would go out with people to the after-hours clubs, and no one propositioned me. And they didn't know who I was, because I had cut my hair. And I thought, God, I'm just a failure as a whore, nobody cares."

The script of *Klute* had originally centered on the character of the detective, John Klute (played by Donald Sutherland), who is investigating a series of prostitute murders. But director Alan Pakula, struck by Jane's new intensity, expanded her role. She repaid him with moments she'd never attained before on the screen. In a celebrated scene in a psychiatrist's office, Jane expresses Bree's rage and grief with an astonishing display of real tears and mucus pouring from her eyes and nose.

That Jane should find new acting profundity at the time she was discovering radical politics made sense to director Henry Jaglom, who had known her since her Actors Studio days: "If you are absorbing a political message telling you that you've got to be real, that you have to be true to your basic feelings, then this political message can help you enormously as an actor. All the false concepts that get in the way of acting get stripped away. You start acting from a more human place. That scene in the psychiatrist's office, for instance, shows how struggling with profound issues made her a more profound actor."

By the time the film was finished, Jane was also beginning to play her off-screen role more plausibly. Mark Lane had gotten her involved with the Vietnam Veterans Against the War, and she was in on the planning stages for the Winter Soldier Investigation, an inquiry into atrocities allegedly committed in Vietnam by members of the U.S. military. On November 3, 1970, Jane flew to Cleveland from Canada to raise money for the Investigation. A customs agent opened her purse and found several vials of pills. Jane told him they were prescription diet and vitamin pills. (Actually, Dexedrine, Valium and Compazine were included in the mini-pharmacy she carried.) The customs agent detained her, and a melee ensued after Jane was denied permission to go to the bathroom, although she claimed she was beginning her period, and then tried to punch the officer blocking her way. Shrieking that she was being victimized by brutality on the part of "pig" police, she was handcuffed and locked up, and forced to spend the night in the women's section of the Cuyahoga city jail.

Lane arrived the next day to repeat publicly Jane's charge about female prisoners being beaten in the jail as part of a "Nixon–Agnew terror." When he went to court to get her release, he was amazed at her behavior: "She was so militant in court that she turned her chair around and had her back to the judge. I was trying to figure out a way to ask her not to do that, but it wasn't any use."

The charges were eventually dropped, but during the proceedings, Jane discovered that she was on a government list of radicals to be stopped by customs officers. Comparing herself to the defendants in the Chicago Seven trial and other "political prisoners," she could finally say she had arrived as a radical.

TWELVE

W̲hile Jane had been developing her persona as a radical, Vadim had whiled away the time halfheartedly romancing Hollywood starlets. After it became clear that she was not coming back to Bel Air, he returned to France to try to get a film project started. Late in 1970 Vadim was back in the United States, ready to talk to Jane about dissolving their marriage.

Their meeting took place in a room Vadim had rented at the Beverly Wilshire Hotel. He had retained an attorney but decided not to invite him, although he agreed that Richard Rosenthal should be present because he was a family friend besides being Jane's attorney. Jane asked for complete custody of Vanessa. Vadim had been both father and mother during the previous months, flying his daughter to Paris and back with him. (He liked to tell how he had once fallen asleep during a layover at Heathrow and Vanessa had hit an attendant who came to wake him up with her bottle, chirping, "You let my poppa sleep.") But he gallantly refused to mention Jane's lengthy absence from their child, saying only that he loved Vanessa as much as she did, and wanted joint custody.

After they agreed to share their daughter, there was not much to talk about. Vadim was perennially out of pocket and Jane was as broke as he was. Her salary from *Klute* was gone a few weeks after the final payment. She decided to sell the farm at St.-Ouen and flew to France to close the deal. There was no sense of sentimental loss. She had adopted the radical mindset of the left: there were no yesterdays, only limitless tomorrows. "I have no desire to live in France anymore," she said before leaving for Europe. "The fight is here, and this is where I belong."

In a mood to be as radical in her life as she was in her politics, Jane began to talk about leaving the movies altogether. She told Richard Rosenthal, "There are other things in life besides acting." She moved into a small house near the Hollywood Freeway and furnished it with a mattress on the bedroom floor and a Salvation Army sofa in the living room, and explained to a journalist, "All I need for my current life is a plane ticket, two pairs of jeans and two sweaters." It was a revolutionary uniform that ensured her a place on Blackwell's Worst-Dressed list, even though *Life* magazine noted that she carried her utilitarian wardrobe in a Louis Vuitton bag.

The ascetic life-style was therapeutic. It seemed "real" to her in the same way his spartan days in the Navy had to Henry twenty-five years earlier. William F. Buckley, Jr., was being ironic when he described Jane's "solemn Red Guard face," but folksinger Country Joe McDonald, who talked to her on an airplane at about this time, recalls how, in the middle of their conversation, she suddenly lowered her voice to a level of confidentiality: "What I'm trying to do is just become a good communist." McDonald, who had been a Red-diaper baby and watched his parents, real communists, deal with McCarthyism, knew by now that Jane had no intention of joining the Party; he wondered what she could possibly mean.

Working hard on the Winter Soldier Investigation, Jane tried to live up to an imagined standard of revolutionary purity. Mark Lane recalls being in Cleveland with her discussing which hotel they would stay in during their fund-raising efforts. He mentioned that when he was on the road he always tried to stay in a place that had a swimming pool, so that he could get some exercise.

"Mark!" Jane said reproachfully. "We're on a serious mission here!"

"Look, the Movement is a long-term thing," Lane explained. "On occasion you can go for a swim."

"That's a bourgeois attitude," she snapped.

It was easier for those who had known Jane as an actress than those who met her as an activist to understand what motivated her. "She was able to commit herself so completely to the radical mode that she really believed she was Rosa Luxemburg," Henry Jaglom observes. "She didn't want to hear any of the things that would dissuade her. Like an actor getting into a part, she wanted to become the character she was playing completely and not let in the contradictions."

During the filming of *Klute,* Jane entered into a relationship with costar Donald Sutherland, who had left his wife, Shirley, for her. Sutherland went along with Jane's radical politics, playing sidekick and straight man, a role that was more exciting than any he had played on screen. Convinced, for instance, that they were under surveillance, he and Jane spoke in code on the phone and set up a "supersecret" rendezvous—a house with an entrance facing one street and a connected garage facing the one behind it. Sutherland could drive into the garage and go directly up to the bedroom unobserved by someone watching the front door.

Sutherland's power as an actor and a person was the fey quality that undercut his hangdog face. He went along with Jane's increasingly "heavy" rhetoric but himself had a lighter, more self-deprecating touch. For Jane there was something riding on the game they played; for him it was only a game. He once got a note from a man asking for an autograph for his daughter, who had loved *Klute*. Under Jane's influence, Sutherland wrote back a long, heartfelt letter of refusal, explaining why giving autographs was acceding to reactionary elitism and thus perpetuating a society of inequality. He was amused when the man wrote back, "My wife and I would like to thank you for your letter. It was all bullshit, but we cut the signature off for our daughter."

The romance was unequal from the beginning, Sutherland functioning as something of a prince consort for Jane. As one friend says, "Donald was crazy about her. Because she was into left-wing politics, he was into left-wing politics too. Politics was the thing that elevated their relationship to a higher plane and made it something more than just another Hollywood affair."

Together they fantasized about radicalizing the entertainment industry, and Sutherland went so far as to declare his candidacy for presidency of the Screen Actors Guild. His campaign did not persuade many of his colleagues, however, and he was defeated by John Gavin, later Ronald Reagan's ambassador to Mexico.

Early in 1971, Jane and Donald founded Entertainment Industry for Peace and Justice, an organization intended to infuse the industry with left-wing politics. Close to five hundred people attended the first meeting, although many were there out of curiosity rather than commitment. (Steve Jaffe recalls trying to convince Ryan O'Neal, another of his clients, to come. "Well, maybe," O'Neal answered. "If Lauren Hutton is going to be there let me know.") After a few experiences with the inflated rhetoric and numbing ideology, membership dwindled to less than fifty.

It was also at this time that Fonda and Sutherland were forming FTA—Fuck (or, in polite company, Free) the Army. The antiwar troupe included, at various times, actors Peter Boyle, Ben Vereen, and Elliott Gould, comic Dick Gregory, and singers Holly Near and Country Joe McDonald. It would present an agitprop cabaret act, something like an anti–Bob Hope show; irreverent, pacifist entertainment for GIs, but without the sexy backdrop Ann-Margret and other women provided for Hope's troupe. (As Jane said, "We're not going to do that kind of chauvinist show with topless dancers and a lot of tits flying.")

Originally Mike Nichols was to direct the FTA show. But he had to back out at the last minute, and Alan Myerson, then a director of the Committee, a highly regarded San Francisco comedy revue, was conscripted as a replacement.

The first performance took place near Fort Bragg, North Carolina, in the spring of 1971. Soldiers wildly applauded Fonda in her saucy appearances, Sutherland's impish slapstick, and even some of the more "serious" moments, although one writer who covered FTA said these moments often sounded like extracts from the "Eighth Party Congress of Workers and Peasants."

Jane's appeal was in the dedication and brio she brought to all her activities. She was intellectually curious, devouring books and articles. Yet she continued to be susceptible to people with powerful messages. One of those who exerted significant influence on her during this time was Francine Parker, her guru in feminism. The feminist perspective brought everything else into sharp focus. ("It came suddenly," says Parker of Jane's evolution, "an 'Aha!' sort of thing.") All the embarrassments from her past could now be explained as episodes of victimization, whether it was enduring her father or "living in the world of Roger Vadim with my blond hair and falsies." Before, she had been sympathetic to feminism but assumed it was for other women. Now she saw it as something that involved her as well.

Her discovery of feminism had dire consequences for the men in FTA. Desperate to keep his relationship with her going, Donald Sutherland tried to accommodate, adopting an air one of the other male troupers characterized as "more feminist than thou." But some of the men who did not drop their "male privilege" quickly enough found themselves under siege. As Peter Boyle says, "Jane started surrounding herself with feminist revolutionaries. She let it be known that she thought the rest of us were liberals and sexists. She used these terms—'liberals' and 'sexists'—which were the worst terms for somebody on the left to use about another person at that time."

By that summer Jane was ready to make another movie, *Steelyard Blues,* which would be shot in the Bay Area with many FTA members. She was reluctant to play another prostitute, especially in light of her developing views about women, but she felt she owed a favor to Sutherland, who was executive producer of the film. Jane wanted to make up for the fact that the script of *Klute* had been changed in such a way that his role was diminished.

Almost from the onset the film was engulfed in bickering and bad feelings. Jane was unhappy not only because she was playing a prostitute again but also because the film was supposed to be a "socially significant comedy" (whose message she interpreted as "Stealing is not theft, property is theft") and she wasn't especially funny in it. As a result, she adopted a dour and forbidding attitude. "Jane was always off the set reading some revolutionary paper," costar Peter Boyle recalls. "She felt that we were all male chauvinists because we didn't laugh at her jokes. There was a moment when we were up in Santa Rosa and all these people from the Committee were there. Everybody was getting high, coming on, doing shtick, trying out bits, competing to see who was funnier, having a great time. Then all of a sudden Jane stood up and yelled at the top of her lungs, 'Doesn't anybody here ever listen?' That stopped the show."

The anxiety about not being funny, which had been almost as much a problem in her life as thick ankles, raised Jane's newly developed feminist hackles. A few weeks later, in a brief article she wrote for *The New York Times,* she noted: "Interestingly enough, with women I'm perceived as funny. And with men who are not oppressive I think I'm quite funny, but it's like a guy has his foot on your neck and he's shoving your face in the quicksand—if you don't laugh, you have no sense of humor."

The mood on the set became increasingly bleak. Alan Myerson, who directed the film, was struck by Fonda's dour anxiety, and by the fact that she seemed "haunted by time," and also by her naiveté. "She was into feminism and anti-elitism," he says, "but totally unaware of the contradictions in her own life. The best illustration I can remember came when she walked onto the set one morning and some flunky came up and said, 'Good morning, Miss Fonda.' Jane looked at her and said, '*Please,* call me Jane. There are no stars anymore, just equals.' And then, almost without missing a beat, she turned and yelled out, '*Where's my dresser?*'"

"There were all these factions and meetings and consciousness-raising sessions on the set and charges that people were thinking incorrectly," recalls Peter Boyle. "I'd never been around that sort of thing, and I hated it."

During some of the "struggle sessions," as Jane called them, the men were reduced to tears. In the middle of this strife, Jane made it clear to Sutherland that their romance was over. She was moving to a more radical stage in her life and did not feel he had the commitment to accompany her. The end of their relationship, in Myerson's view, "broke Donald's heart."

In addition to "empowering" her, feminism caused Jane to look back in anger. The subject of her mother, blocked for so long, was opened up, and she talked about Frances Fonda as someone killed by "bottled-up rage." But while publicly making her mother into a stock figure in the feminist psychodrama, privately she was as unforgiving as she had always been. A close associate remembers that "whenever you talked about her mother, Jane would give you this look and say, 'My mother was a hypochondriac. I don't like to be around illness. I don't like people who complain. I don't like my mother.'"

It was in her refusal to admit that she carried the weight of history that Jane was most unlike her brother. Although he no longer talked obsessively about the past, Peter still tried to function as the custodian of its truths and the righter of its wrongs. It made him both pugnacious and poignant. It was as if he were shadow-boxing with God.

Or with Henry. For his father continued to be Peter's problem. People had always claimed that Jane resembled Henry, and in terms of facial features this was true. But as he entered middle age it was Peter who called forth the Fonda essence, in the long-legged stride and flat midwestern intonations. And these signs of paternity came out in spite of Peter's obvious attempt to suppress them. Screenwriter Dennis Clark, who was on the edge of the Fonda circle, says, "I've seen Peter literally try to change the way he sits, while he's sitting, as if he is consciously aware that he's sitting like his father." He desperately wanted to be Henry's son, but he had learned that this desire always caused pain. This tension contributed to the impression Peter gave of being metaphysically ill at ease, someone, in the words of his friend Bobby Walker, who "seemed to be fighting gravity."

As Jane was finding her way into another world, the world of radical faith, the Fonda men continued to struggle. Peter saw his father as someone unable to give what he should and Henry regarded Peter as someone who wanted more than was reasonable. Even though they were in their early thirties and late sixties, respectively, they were still stuck in character as Wayward Son and Stern Father.

Actress Verna Bloom got a privileged look at this relationship when Peter interviewed her for a role in *The Hired Hand* at Henry's Manhattan townhouse. In the middle of their conversation, Henry walked into the room with a choleric look on his face and, ignoring Bloom, launched into a withering tirade against Peter, who had apparently put a small dent in the fender of his car the previous evening. Bloom's husband, Jay Cocks, then film critic for *Time,* said after hearing her account of the confrontation, "It was like watching a homicidal episode of *Leave it To Beaver."* As struck as she was by Henry's anger, Bloom was even more amazed at the way Peter buckled under the blast.

The Hired Hand was Peter's first film after *Easy Rider.* Paying oblique homage to his father, Peter had tried to do a classic western in the Fonda–Ford mold. The reviewers were generally positive, but somewhat perplexed by a few of Peter's directing and editing choices (which Alan Sharp, author of the screenplay, felt "reflected the influences of hallucinogens"). The film dropped from sight soon after being released. Verna Bloom, the female lead, was perplexed by the outcome. She concluded that Peter had some deep desire to fail, the artistic equivalent of a death wish: "The movie had everything—a fantastic script, Vilmos Zsigmond as cinematographer. Because of his great success with *Easy Rider,* Peter had the final cut, almost unheard of at that time. He could have made the great western, but he didn't."

People in the industry who had seen Peter as someone who could do no wrong now began to talk about how he was his own worst enemy. There was the preview of *The Hired Hand* for Universal executives, for instance. Peter was chronically late for appointments—it was part of his ongoing defiance of any authority; his friend and partner Bill Hayward emphasized to him that the screening had to begin precisely at ten in the morning. When Peter failed to show up, Hayward started the movie without him. Peter finally came in just before the end of the film; when the lights came on he rushed up to Ned Tanen, the Universal executive who was backing *The Hired Hand,* and angrily thrust a speeding ticket at him. "Here, this is your fault," he snapped. "*You* made me get it. Now *you* take care of it."

The sense of personal unity and calm purpose that Peter had felt after his first acid trips had now deserted him. Susan was happy staying home with the kids, but Peter, who seemed to have become addicted to a nomadic life after being shuffled from place to place as a child, felt at home apparently only when he was on the road. He tried to convince Susan to come with him on his aimless wanderings, and when she refused he went alone. Wherever he went there were other women. He was always honest with them, saying that he was happily married. He was frank with Susan too, never denying what he was doing, although he talked to her about his private life in the cosmic language of Krishnamurti, his favorite yogi. "You'd hear him doing his oracular talk with Susan," says one of Peter's closest friends, "and you'd think to yourself, This is not communication on any basis I know."

Living separate from Susan and the kids for long periods, Peter set sail on the eighty-one-foot ketch he'd bought from a Boeing executive. *Tatoosh* ("breast" in an Indian language) soon became almost as notorious a Hollywood craft as the sleek black yacht Errol Flynn had used in the fifties to pursue his amours with teenaged girls. In one much-discussed incident, Peter pulled the *Tatoosh* up alongside a smartly dressed sailing committee for a big race. When he appeared on the main deck, according to one report, race officials were shocked to see that he was completely naked.

He made frequent trips to Hawaii, and every time there were rumors that he carried drugs from the mainland. Once he and his crew rowed ashore in a rubber dinghy after anchoring in Maui. Peter walked ostentatiously onto the dock, where he dropped a large paper bag on which he had scrawled "The Shipment." The people who cautiously opened the bag as he was rowing back to his boat found that it was filled with beer cans.

Sometimes he would get word to Bobby Walker that he planned to appear in front of the beachfront home of Walker's mother, Jennifer Jones, at a certain hour. When Walker saw the running lights of the *Tatoosh* he would undress, seal his clothes in a plastic bag, and swim out several hundred yards to be hoisted aboard. The boat was always well supplied with booze, drugs, and women. They would sail off to the windward side of Catalina for a lost weekend.

The boat was Peter's ark. He was as drawn as Jane to the notion of an apocalypse and predicted a complete environmental collapse within a few years. In wild ecobabble meant to compete with his sister's radical jargon, he once said: "There'll be a mass panic. I don't intend to stay around for that. The day the smog clouds settle down and don't lift again, the day they come after us with guns, the men from Sphincter Control, I'll be gone. . . ."

A friend of Susan's said, "Peter felt that he had an obligation to be bold and original. I remember having conversations with him for an hour or two during which I didn't have the slightest idea what he was going on about."

As Peter talked, often in terms that stretched credulity, it was as if he was still reacting to the primal lie he had been told so many years earlier. If words had no value, why not throw them to the winds?

THIRTEEN

At the beginning of 1972, Jane went to Paris to film *Tout Va Bien* with the French director Jean-Luc Godard. It seemed like an opportunity for a marriage of true minds. With his Maoist politics (on full display in films such as *La Chinoise*), Godard, best known for the classic New Wave movie *Breathless,* represented the pinnacle of left-wing art. *Tout Va Bien* costarred Yves Montand, at that time still a committed leftist himself, and the politics of the film, in which Jane was to play a young woman journalist "radicalized" by a factory strike, were impeccable. She moved into a Left Bank commune with five French women and as filming began commented, "Godard is the only person I've met who's truly revolutionary."

Tout Va Bien turned out to be another fiasco for Jane. The film was only semi-coherent. Even worse, Jane fought almost constantly with the director. "Godard really hates people, especially women," she told film critic Molly Haskell after the experience was over, adding somewhat implausibly that she had wanted to leave the film but Godard had threatened to rough her up if she did.

The experience was painful, but not wholly in vain. Godard's formula for the movie—a young naif is changed by exposure to hidden political realities she discovers—would become useful to Jane in a few years when she was producing her own films. And while she was in Paris, Jane met secretly with representatives of the North Vietnamese government, who discussed with her the possibility of a trip to Hanoi.

Plans for the trip were under way when Jane returned to the United States for the Academy Award ceremonies. Until now she had been casual about the Golden Globe and other awards she had received for *Klute*. But the Oscar was something else. To appease her radical friends, Jane cobbled together an explanation for why she intended to go to the ceremonies: "The Oscar is what the working class relates to. . . . It is important for those of us who speak out for social change to get that kind of acclaim."

She was the odds-on favorite to win as Best Actress, and the film world was abuzz with rumors of what Jane would do. Would she spit in the face of the Hollywood establishment? Would there be a nasty five-minute rant against American imperialism? Henry implored her not to do anything undignified. But she was afraid of losing face with her radical comrades.

Before the ceremonies, Jane went to a Chinese restaurant near the Dorothy Chandler Pavilion with Richard Rosenthal. Her attorney had written down the speech he thought she should give: "There are a lot of things to say . . . but now is not the time to say them." With the pause between the clauses, Rosenthal's line was calculated to mollify Hollywood's establishment without diminishing Jane as a political person. When Jane was announced as winner of the Oscar, she nervously rushed the words, forgetting the pause. Later she whispered to Rosenthal, "I'm sorry I blew the line. I'm a lousy actress."

Jane was also nervous that the audience would give her an unenthusiastic response. But the applause was thunderous. She might have wounded Hollywood in some of her more extreme moments, but at heart she was still one of them, Henry Fonda's daughter and a star, part of the family.

. . .

Jane was the first Fonda to win an Oscar. But the award came at a moment of uncertainty and seemed something of an obituary for her career. There were no movies in her future and she still told people she was considering giving up acting and making radical politics her life. But the New Left was beginning to lose momentum, and in any case it was not clear that she had a place in it. She talked of undying commitment and of her willingness to go all the way for the cause. Yet however much she wanted to be just another radical, she could never quite shed her identity as the star, the princess of the Fonda dynasty. Country Joe McDonald saw this one afternoon at his house when he was designing a cover for a new album and Jane was helping him color it. When they finished he asked her to sign her work; she refused. This led him to conclude that she believed her name had a commercial value and she didn't want to be exploited.

Berkeley activist Robin Mencken saw another example of the same syndrome when she went to a bookstore with Jane. The actress, who always said she hated to be recognized, paid for the books by credit card, and when the clerk failed to recognize her and asked for another piece of identification, Jane started hauling out credit cards from her purse and slapping them hard one after another on the counter, furious at the clerk for not knowing who she was.

One of her friends from those days says, "By the spring of 1972, Jane had reached something of a dead end. She'd tried everything in the Movement and she hadn't found a foothold. She was in a sort of free-fall. People laughed at her behind her back. She was out of synch. It doesn't sound very flattering, but those of us who knew her well realized that she needed a man to follow."

But it had to be someone worthy of her, someone at the top of the radical heap. Even though they were physically mismatched—a fact

that would be commented on for the next seventeen years—there
was really only one man who fit the bill. It was Tom Hayden, as close
to superstar and everyman as the Movement had produced.

She had first met Hayden briefly in the spring of 1971 at a Howard
Johnson's in Detroit. He had been speaking about Vietnam at the
University of Michigan at Ann Arbor, the campus from which he
had launched the Students for a Democratic Society a decade
earlier, and she had been in Detroit organizing the Winter Soldier
Investigation. On that first day nothing clicked. Still "in a relationship" with Donald Sutherland, Fonda was stiff and silent as Hayden
tried to talk to her. He interpreted it as standoffishness. Later she
told him she simply had been intimidated by his presence, feeling
trivial in comparison with him and his achievements.

It was the same flustered feeling she'd had when she met Vadim.
Like the Frenchman, Hayden was not particularly prepossessing
physically, but his features—a bulbous nose, close-set eyes, glinting
darkly out of a moonscape of pockmarks—suggested a complex
presence.

Hayden was one of the few figures of the New Left to have
acquired a specific gravity during the sixties. After he finished his
term as president of SDS in 1963, he had gone south for the
Mississippi Summer and made an appearance in wire-service
photos as a young man on the ground in fetal curl being kicked by
local rednecks. A few years later, as the action switched to the
North, Hayden became a central figure in the ghetto insurrection
that torched Newark in 1967. He had been at Columbia University
for its violent student strike in 1968, and later the same year helped
plan the riots during the Democratic National Convention in Chicago which led to his arrest and trial as one of the Chicago Seven.

More than any other American radical, Hayden had become
associated with the gradual transition of the New Left from antiwar

to pro-Hanoi. He had gone to Vietnam in 1965 and had come back rhapsodizing about the "rice-roots democracy" he had seen there. What he said then and three years later, when he brought out the first American POWs, made him Hanoi's leading spokesman in this country.

Hayden was different from other New Leftists—not just a street radical but also an intellectual who put an emphasis on "authenticity" and the politics of selfhood in a way that distinguished this New Left from the Old Left it displaced. Yet he had also masterfully hedged his bets during his rise. If he had one foot in the camp of Hanoi, he had the other in the camp of Bobby Kennedy, at whose funeral he was seen weeping in 1968.

Anne Weills, a Berkeley radical who became Hayden's lover, said that after the experience in Chicago, he was "obsessed with making history." Some of his comrades decided that he had developed a Bonapartist streak as a result of his growing celebrity. According to Weills, his talk during the late sixties was filled with phrases like "When we govern . . ." After they saw the film *Wild in the Streets,* he told her that he wanted to be president someday. As she later observed: "That was sort of crazy, considering that we were trying to smash the state."

Hayden settled in Berkeley after the Chicago Seven trial, joining Weills and other radicals in an exclusive Berkeley collective that called itself the Red Family. They had target practice in the California foothills under the supervision of their "Minister of Defense." They talked revolution and affirmed the regime of North Korea's Kim Il Sung as a model for the new society they envisioned. Yet they were loath to become "tools of necessity" like members of the Weathermen terrorist sect who had destroyed themselves in their bomb factory in the basement of the Manhattan townhouse in late 1969, or like the Black Panthers who had been killed in shootouts with the police in 1969 and 1970.

Despairing finally of helping mold the revolution, the Red Family turned inward in lacerating "criticism/self-criticism" sessions on the Communist Chinese model. For the women of the Red Family, these sessions were an opportunity for angry attacks on the men. Hayden tried to ride out the sexual politics by doing his share of housework and by serving a stint as a "nurturing male" at the collective's Blue Fairyland nursery school. But because of his visibility and his persistence in thinking of himself as "an agent of history," he was held particularly accountable for past crimes against women.

One day early in 1971, Hayden came back from a speaking trip in the East and was confronted by the grim-faced members of the collective when he walked in the door. Ruthlessly using the private facts of their two-year relationship, Anne Weills bitterly denounced Tom in front of the rest of the group for his "sexually manipulative behavior" and repeated things he had told her about others in the collective during their intimate moments. Hayden tried to defend himself but was unable to deal with the angry accusations. He was not only purged from the Red Family but also ordered, in one last knife-twist of revolutionary discipline, to get out of town. That afternoon he got into his battered VW and left Berkeley; he drove almost randomly down the coast to southern California, a world away.

He settled in Venice, renting a seedy one-room apartment at $110 a month and identifying himself as "Emmett Garity" (the name of his Irish grandfather), although the FBI knew his real identity and whereabouts within days. After licking his wounds for a few months, Hayden decided he still wanted to "make a mark on his times." He believed the vehicle was the war in Vietnam, and told his remaining friends that whatever his old comrades might think of him, he had a responsibility to help Hanoi.

.　.　.

In the spring of 1972, Jane was as rudderless as Hayden. Although she had just won the Academy Award, she was unable to imagine resuming her career in film after the heady experience of the last two years. Yet the New Left was self-destructing in impotent theatrics and becoming critical of figures like Jane who were public and visible. She had disbanded FTA, and her attempts to organize Hollywood through Entertainment Industry for Peace and Justice had come to nothing. She wondered if she had a future as a radical.

Jane recalled this as her "lowest period." She was tired all the time. Her face had taken on a drawn, bleak look. If she hadn't gotten together with Hayden, she said later, she didn't know what she would have done.

They met for the second time in late April when she was narrating a slide show on Vietnam at the Embassy Theatre in downtown Los Angeles. Hayden was in the audience and after the show he came onstage to talk to her.

Jane was surprised at how he had changed in the year since she had last seen him. He had tried to distance himself from the dark Leninist persona he had cultivated during the sixties, adopting instead a more colorful Indian look, his braided shoulder-length hair secured by a beaded headband. He wore bright shirts along with baggy trousers and sandals. Sitting down next to her, he looked "weird but kind of neat," Jane later told a friend. In the course of their conversation about the slide show he accidentally brushed her knee with his hand. She remembered that touch: "I felt a current of electricity, real sharp, and I went home and . . . said to a girlfriend, 'I've just met a man I think I might spend the rest of my life with.'"

For his part, Hayden saw in Jane someone at the end of her tether. Her hyperkinetic tour of the New Left had exposed her to its ideas and jargon. But now that world view was crumbling and she was as isolated as he. Tom saw her as someone who had been drained by the Movement. He had seen others who gave all they could in hopes of achieving radical salvation but were always found wanting for not giving everything. "Their real solution," he later said of the leftists who had been influencing Jane, "was for her to give everything to them and then commit suicide. And she was headed in that direction."

He knew she had been seeing other men of the left, but thought she was being used as a mark on their scorecard and was not getting what she needed from her affairs. He also realized that she had stretched herself across too many political commitments, from feminism to black revolution. It seemed that his own solution—to draw away from the intramural fighting of the left and return to the single issue of Vietnam—might work for her too. He got Jane to agree to look at the slide show on Indochina he had put together.

The slides he brought to her rented house in Laurel Canyon and projected onto a living room wall were different from her own harshly propagandistic ones. His pictures tried to evoke what he saw as the subtle tragedies behind the long war. In the middle of a series of shots of South Vietnam, for instance, was one of a huge billboard in Saigon showing an Asian woman in a Playboy Bunny pose. It was an advertisement for a plastic surgeon whose specialties included changing the eyes of Vietnamese women from their natural almond shape to a rounder Caucasian look and, for a little more money, enlarging Asian breasts to an American woman's size. When she saw the image, Jane began to cry. Hayden asked what was wrong. She said she was thinking of the role she might have played in spreading such stereotypes, and it made her feel terribly guilty.

Emotions that had been building during her two years as a radical had finally come to the surface. Not long after the slide show, she and Tom made love for the first time. Physically they were in southern California, but emotionally they were in North Vietnam, the country and cause Jane too was now willing to embrace. That first night, three-year-old Vanessa walked into the bedroom, and stood and watched Hayden like an inspector.

. . .

When Jane later said, "Tom saved my life," it was not an idle comment. Emotionally, she had been at the bottom. Having found a man who might be a dependable mentor as well as lover, she began to be optimistic once again.

Among other things, Hayden had far better contacts in Hanoi than any diplomat, and he helped Jane complete plans for her trip there, now scheduled for early July. The day before she left, she stopped in New York at Richard Rosenthal's office to update her will. Steve Jaffe, who was present for the meeting, was struck by the fact that she was not sure she was coming back. After the will was updated, he and Rosenthal spent fifteen minutes trying to teach Jane how to use a thirty-five-millimeter camera.

When she arrived in Hanoi, Jane was as malleable as she had been when she returned to the United States after her Paris exile two years earlier—ready to find her relevance in the use others could make of her. On July 11, after meetings with high government officials, she was taken to visit the hamlet of Hong Phong. In a news release, the North Vietnamese said that the previous day American war planes had bombed the village, killing two elderly people, and that "Jane Fonda felt great indignation at the U.S. attack on civilian populations."

Then she was taken to see dikes allegedly destroyed the day before. "In her assessment," read the Hanoi news release, "the U.S. had made deliberate attacks on dikes to jeopardize life and terrorize the people." At a press conference she said that every evidence of bombing that she had seen was directed at a nonmilitary target. She also said, in words put into her mouth by her hosts, that she had visited "seven U.S. aggressor pilots" in prison and found them all healthy and fervently hopeful that the war would end.

In a weeklong series of broadcasts that would later be compared to those of Tokyo Rose in World War II, Jane read propaganda scripts prepared for delivery to U.S. servicemen within reach of Radio Hanoi.

"I'm sure if you knew what was inside the shells you're dropping," she said in remarks directed at American airmen, "you would ask yourself as I have been doing for the last few days since I have seen the victims: What do the men who work for Honeywell and the other companies in the United States that invent and make these weapons—what do they think in the morning at breakfast? What do they dream about when they sleep at night?"

A few days later she again addressed U.S. pilots: "This is Jane Fonda in Hanoi. I'm speaking to the men in the cockpits of the Phantoms, in the B-52s, in the F-4s; those of you who are still fighting the war, in the air, on the ground; the guys on the Seventh Fleet, the *Constellation*, the *Coral Sea*, the *Ticonderoga*, the *Kitty Hawk*, the *Enterprise*. . . . You know that when Nixon says the war is winding down he's lying. . . . All of you in your heart of hearts know the lies. You know the cheating on the body counts, the fictionalized battle reports, and the number of planes that are shot down and what the targets really are. Knowing who [is] doing the lying, should you allow these same people and these same liars to define for you who the enemy is?"

People in the States never heard these broadcasts in their entirety, although broken echoes would slowly make their way back home in the months to come. But they did have a chance to see silent slow-motion footage of Jane in a helmet climbing up into a North Vietnamese antiaircraft gun, sighting imaginary U.S. warplanes, and laughing. The news clip was only a few seconds long, but it fixed an image indelibly in the mind of the public in a way none of her movies had been able to do. It became her classic film moment, Jane's equivalent of her father's Tom Joad and her brother's Captain America. She had finally found the enduring role for which she would always be remembered: Hanoi Jane.

226

. . .

En route to the United States, she called Steve Jaffe from Paris and told him to get some reporters together in New York so that she could talk about the details of the trip. As Jaffe was beginning to make calls, Hayden showed up. "I'll be handling the press conference," he said peremptorily. "Don't you try to tell Jane what to say."

When she appeared before journalists, she was a different woman from the one who had been mouthing radical sentences for the past two years. She was trembling with rage over what she had seen in Vietnam, stammering with passion. One reporter saw the press conference as a "great performance." If so, it was because it was so thoroughly internalized; because, as if in obedience to the principles of Lee Strasberg, Jane had allowed the emotions to *possess* her. And if it was a performance, it was done primarily for the benefit of Hayden, whom she now acknowledged as the great director who would guide her through the political role she had to play. Roger Vadim, who was now watching his ex-wife from afar with a fan's appreciation, says: "It was like a movie but she was living it. She was acting the part of Jane Fonda in a big adventure. And Tom was the hero of her movie."

How Hayden felt about her was suggested by a conversation he had with his onetime lover Anne Weills. He told her that Jane loved him and when Weills asked if he loved her in return, Hayden replied, "I like her very much." The choice of words was more than a matter of semantics; it was an indication that by encouraging Jane's passions and keeping his own under control, he could wield the power in their relationship.

In the next few weeks, Hayden became something more than Jane's mentor and lover. He was also a buffer. Those around Jane soon learned that Tom had taken over. The Panthers, the dissident GIs, the radical feminists, and others to whom she had pledged herself became secondary. Fred Gardner, Donald Sutherland, and others who had remained close, if not intimate, were shut off. Steve Jaffe was shunted into the background.

Even Mark Lane, who'd had a special relationship with Jane, could no longer get her ear. At the time of her return from Hanoi, he was running what he called an underground railroad for cadets of the South Vietnamese air force who had been brought to Texas for flight training but didn't want to return to their homeland to go against Hanoi's MiGs. Lane was smuggling them singly and in pairs to a Canadian sanctuary. He had already helped nearly thirty out, paying the considerable expenses largely out of his own pocket. Broke, he told Jane about his activities and asked her to contribute $1,000 for air tickets for the next three men he had lined up for desertion.

"I appreciate what you're doing," she told him after listening to his request, "but I'm going to pass. I've decided that all my political contributions and activities in the future will go through Tom."

Peter recognized immediately that Hayden was not just another of Jane's passing fancies. "He hated Hayden," says a friend. "Pretty much from the beginning. He couldn't believe Jane could go for someone so ugly—he kept going on about that—but at a deeper level he felt Jane had been bamboozled. He felt that Tom was worse than the other men she'd known because he was using her and was too devious to cop to it, as most of the others had."

But Jane was scornful of her brother's opinions. Her love for Hayden had been forged in a revolutionary fire. She believed they could be one of those great couples whose impact as a unit is far greater than that either of the individuals could have alone.

In any case, there was work to do. When Jane returned from Hanoi, American politicians charged her with treason and she received death threats from anonymous callers and correspondents. She would later exaggerate the danger she had faced ("If it had been the fifties, I probably would have been electrocuted"), but she was in fact courageous in the way she defied her antagonists, including the FBI. Interested in Jane since 1970, FBI chief J. Edgar Hoover ordered agents to obtain some of her bank records surreptitiously and to establish a mail cover not only on Jane's house but on Henry's two homes as well.

None of this would have deterred her even if she had known about it. Jane had made an implicit bargain with Hayden. He would give her security and a long-term goal; she would make him visible again after a period of eclipse. By late summer 1972 they were both fired with enthusiasm about how they could "influence history." They went to Miami to demonstrate at the Republican National Convention, which nominated Richard Nixon for four more years. Then, having founded the Indochina Peace Campaign, they went on the road for a nine-week, ninety-city electoral tour that fall to try to rekindle outrage about the war.

After the election they took a break to go to Norway so that Jane could begin filming Ibsen's *A Doll's House*. Once again, she had a chance to work with a political director, in this case Joseph Losey, who had expatriated to England during the McCarthy period. As with Godard, however, the experience quickly turned sour. Losey accused Jane of spending her time "working on political speeches instead of learning her lines, and making innumerable phone calls about her political activities." Jane, who had brought along her own scriptwriter, Nancy Dowd, responded by accusing Losey of paring down the women's roles and building up the men's.

She constantly "consulted" with Dowd on the script, which Jane, invoking the blessing of Ibsen's ghost, wanted to make more overtly into a drama of women's liberation. Losey insisted on maintaining fidelity to the original. A heavy atmosphere of stalemate soon enveloped the set. Jane ran to Hayden between takes, much as she had once run to Voutsinas, and eventually refused to talk to any other male on the set. In a conversation with Vadim during the ordeal,

Losey said, "Sometimes I just want to leave the set, go out into the snow and walk until I drop from exhaustion and die there."

While they were in Norway Jane found out she was pregnant. In Oslo, she and Tom announced their intention to get married. Some reporters at their press conference were struck by the fact that they didn't kiss or hold hands, but Jane made it clear that their union was cemented by a higher purpose: "We are campaigning for peace together. That is what we are interested in. Our relationship is a very private thing and we don't intend to let it interfere with our activities in the Movement."

FOURTEEN

On January 23, 1973, the Reverend Richard York, formerly of the Berkeley Free Church, looked out at the forty or so people gathered in the backyard of Jane's Laurel Canyon home and intoned, "Will you, Jane, marry Tom, and will you try in the marriage to grow together, to be honest, to share responsibility for your children, and to maintain a sense of humor?"

Jane had inserted this last line into the marriage vows because she, like Tom, was so often accused of being humorless. And as she said she would marry him, she smiled broadly, as if to show that she had what it took to fulfill the vow. Yet the marriage itself had never been seen as a laughing matter. Rather, it was the culmination of a serious courtship, played out against a dramatic backdrop of war, commitment, and personal sacrifice.

Publicist Steve Jaffe, who had been around Jane during the first part of her radical experiment, thought at first that Tom was just another of the passing affairs she'd organized with the same brisk efficiency she brought to every other activity. He considered Hayden another of those Movement men Jane had gone to for information and insight and with whom she had wound up mixing some pleasure with business. He was surprised when the relationship proved more durable than that: "I guess one of the things that made it improbable was the fact that she was physically beautiful and he was not. But Tom also seemed so calculating and manipulative. You expected her to see through it."

Instead, Jane saw Hayden as an exemplar of a great cause to which she could attach herself unconditionally, a man like Vadim or her father, with a public reality so well defined she could sink down into it, but someone also with a compelling moral vision that would uplift her. She told Hayden that during her trip to North Vietnam she had been introduced to women who were in labor during U.S. air strikes. As the bombs were falling they had sung, "Nixon, we will fight you with all the joys of a woman in childbirth." She said she wanted to transplant that sense of dedication and commitment to her life in America. And so, shortly after returning from Hanoi, she came up to Hayden from behind in their New York hotel room and said, "Let's have a baby." It was a way to seal their love and also to show solidarity with their brothers and sisters in Vietnam.

Dressed in an Indochinese peasant blouse at the wedding reception, Jane was three months pregnant. She walked through the crowd smiling at the musicians who played Indochinese folk songs and the dancers who did Irish jigs in honor of Tom's roots. When it came time to cut the wedding cake, which was inscribed only with the Vietnamese word for "peace," she gave a little speech to the guests, a mixture of people from the entertainment industry along with a few of Tom's old radical friends. Jane said that North Vietnamese family ties were the closest she had ever seen and that she and Tom had married primarily to start a revolutionary family of their own.

As Jane said the word "family," some guests glanced involuntarily at Henry and Peter. The Fondas were not a revolutionary family, at least not in the way Jane was using the word. But they had never been a typical "nuclear" family either. They had always been sui generis, one of those families Tolstoy had in mind when he said that all unhappy families were unhappy in their own distinctive ways. Yet despite their noisy squabbles over the years, the bonds among them had proved to be surprisingly durable, if always imperfect.

Henry was now approaching seventy. His hair had thinned and his skin was liver-spotted, but he had come to wear his age easily after having fought against it for so long. It was hard to say he had mellowed, for he was still snappish when crossed, but he was happier than he had been in a long time. In Shirlee he finally had the perfect wife—someone who understood his limitations and did not try to extract emotions from him that he was incapable of giving. Another part of her appeal was the fact that she treated show-business people as amusing eccentrics rather than gods. When actress Verna Bloom met her at Henry's Manhattan townhouse, she asked Shirlee in the middle of their small talk why Henry had decided to do TV commercials for GAF film. Shirlee shrugged: "Because he's always afraid that he's never going to get another job." Bloom was incredulous. "*Henry Fonda* is afraid of not working?" Shirlee smiled and said, "All you actors are alike."

Shirlee seemed to have helped release Henry from the constricting anxiety he had felt all of his life; she made him less lonely and not so severe on himself. "One of the things I wish," he told an interviewer who asked him about growing old, "is that I hadn't spent so much time worrying about things. The worrying never did me any good."

There had been some losses along the way. But there had been unexpected gains too, especially with Jane. Although she still occasionally pushed him past the limit of his endurance, he respected and even envied her zeal and passion. He hadn't defended her Hanoi trip, but he refused to join the attack on her. In fact, he said he resented people who expected him to denounce his daughter: "Hers is not my way of life and hers is not too often my exact way of thinking. But I love her. I respect her right to say what she says."

This seemed a definitive statement, as if some final bargain had been struck between father and daughter.

When it came to Peter, Henry hadn't reached the same angle of repose. Their relationship was a perpetual bruise, always tender and never quite healed before the next trauma injured it all over again. Unlike Jane, who shared Henry's willingness to deny painful moments, Peter provoked his father with tales that might or might not be true, such as the anecdote he continued to tell about being "crucified" when he was a teenager by young hoods who pinned him on a Cyclone fence in New York. "Fucking lie!" Henry finally shouted to one interviewer who asked him about it. "He's got the goddamnedest imagination and he's a compulsive liar!"

Whenever Peter tried to analyze his relationship with Henry, he sounded eminently sane: "I have the feeling he thinks that in order to tell me the truth, he'd have to confess the past, which could be terribly difficult for him. We've made so much noise, Jane and I, about his past and our past, that he probably feels we would demand that he confess all his sins of omission. That isn't the case."

But on another level, Peter continued to try to get under his father's skin, irritating him by picking at his vulnerabilities. Bill Hayward says, "Henry wasn't the sort to say to Peter, 'Son, I love you.' It just wasn't his way. Peter knew this and so he would use the words to drive his father crazy. He'd say, 'Dad, I love you. Dad, I love you. I love you, Dad,' every five minutes, not only because he really did love Henry, but also because he knew it forced Henry to confront the fact that he wasn't the sort of man who felt comfortable saying the words back."

Henry appreciated achievement and in comparison with Jane, who had built such momentum into her life, Peter seemed to be stagnating. He was still a strong symbol, and whenever he was in public someone was sure to come up to him as if he *were* Captain America and ask him for drugs. But despite the huge success of *Easy Rider,* he could not parlay it into greater gain. After *The Hired Hand,* he had directed *Idaho Transfer,* an ecological fantasy in which the characters wind up using each other as fuel for their cars. He thought his magic touch would bring the film alive, but it sank without a trace.

Peter seemed indifferent. "Cyrano's restaurant was a big gathering place from midnight to three in the morning," says screenwriter Dennis Clark. "Peter was always there. We had great times. But the film business was passing us by and we were too stoned to notice it."

Peter's friends felt that he *wanted* to court failure; it was almost as if his tortured adolescence had left him addicted to adversity. "For Peter things aren't right unless they're wrong," says Robert Walker, Jr. "There has to be a problem for him to be happy. He's always resisting."

One of the things that had withered was his marriage. Susan had always been someone he could count on. She had family of her own in southern California who had nothing to do with the film business. She was not interested in drugs or the fast lane. She was a little like Peter's stepmother Shirlee—a sane voice, a normalizing influence.

Pursuing photography and other hobbies, Susan had tried to ignore her husband's philandering. Peter invited a writer he had commissioned to do a script to stay at the house while he completed his work. The script was about brother-sister incest and Peter hoped eventually to star in the film with Jane. The movie never came to pass, but something else developed. Lonely during Peter's long absences, Susan began a relationship with the scriptwriter. To her friends, the surprise was not that she had done such a thing, but that it had taken her so long. As one man close to both Peter and Susan says, "Imagine if you're married at eighteen and then at thirty you wake up and the only relationship you have is with an actor who is always gone carrying on with other women. Eventually you'd either have to find someone to validate you, or commit suicide."

Bobby Walker's wife, Ellie, had separated from him and was

living a hippie existence with her children in a tent in Trancas Canyon, California. Susan came to visit and told her about the new man in her life. Watching for rattlesnakes as they talked, Susan said that Peter felt jealous and betrayed and that he wanted a divorce. After a long hiatus in the conversation, she looked up sadly and said, "Can this really be happening to me?" Ellie Walker sympathized but felt that it was inevitable: "The guys we chose hadn't been brought up with any kind of love. They were kind of lost and didn't know how to love themselves or anyone else."

While Peter's marriage was ending, Jane was making hers into a political cause. One evening shortly after their wedding, Jane and Tom were strolling in the backyard of her rented house in Laurel Canyon. She asked him if he thought the garden was pretty. "Yes," he answered, eyeing the tiny swimming pool, "but it isn't right." After a Vietnamese student visiting them commented on how opulent the house seemed in comparison with the structures of his own country, Jane guiltily agreed to move to a run-down two-story clapboard house in a working-class neighborhood in Santa Monica.

The exterior was salt-corroded. From the kitchen there was a view of sand dunes and rusting patio furniture. They did the inside in "Movement *moderne*," with batik wall hangings and a mattress on the floor of their bedroom. The Oscar for *Klute,* spared in a burglary that cost them their stereo not long after they moved in, was used as a bookend. Henry called the house a "shack" but, as a friend says, "Jane loved it. This was *reality.*"

It was also a command post. Four days after their wedding, a peace accord was signed in Paris. A few weeks later, the first POWS began to come home. Irritated by the sympathy they received, Jane immediately attacked them as "liars, hypocrites, and pawns." She was livid at their claim that the North Vietnamese had tortured them: "Tortured men do not march smartly off planes, salute the flag, and kiss their wives. They are liars. I also want to say that these men are not heroes."

However, two of those who returned had been among the seven POWs North Vietnamese officials had arranged for her to speak with on her trip a year earlier. One of them, Lieutenant Commander David Hoffman, said that he had met with her only because he had been tortured: "I had a broken arm. It was in a cast. I was hung by that broken arm several hours and allowed to drop at the end of a rope from a table which was kicked out from under me." Unable to dispute what Hoffman said, Jane tried clumsily to close off the issue: "Nobody's perfect, not even the Vietnamese."

In the middle of this furor, the baby arrived. Jane and Tom had hoped that it would be born on July 4, but it came three days later. It was a boy, and his name was a symbol of their faith and commitment: Troi, after Nguyen Van Troi, the Viet Cong martyr who had tried to kill then Secretary of Defense Robert McNamara when he visited South Vietnam in 1966.

When Jane had set out to discover America three years earlier, she had left Vanessa behind. This time, though, as she and Tom fought Nixon's efforts to "Vietnamize" the war, they took Troi with them on their campaign. (Jane claimed that he spent his babyhood sleeping in converted dresser drawers). Describing South Vietnam as "the biggest police state in the world," Tom said that the Thieu government would not honor that part of the peace agreement calling for democratic liberties and free elections; this fact demanded one last effort by the depleted antiwar movement to end U.S. support.

Not everyone had such a rosy picture of the North Vietnamese. Peter too had met with their representatives in Paris. Perhaps thinking they could enlist him in their cause as they had his sister, the men from Hanoi laid out their case. But Peter was a different, less predictable Fonda.

"I've heard the whole story and I know what you're up to," he told them. "And I think you're right. But let me ask you a question: What interest do you have in the oil that is surrounding the whole Indochina peninsula?"

"We don't have any interest in oil," a Vietnamese diplomat said.

"You're a fucking liar," Peter said, and got up and walked out of the meeting.

There would be no such behavior by Jane. Throughout late 1973 and early 1974, she and Hayden pulled out all the stops for Hanoi. Under other circumstances, the efforts of their Indochina Peace Campaign might have had a marginal impact. But as Nixon became ever more deeply implicated in scandal, Hayden saw a "Watergate opportunity"—a time when Congress might feel confident enough to reassert its prerogatives in foreign policy against a wounded presidency. He and Jane went to Washington for weeks of intense lobbying to convince legislators to cut off support for the South Vietnamese government.

On April Fools' Day 1974, the two of them arrived in North Vietnam along with cinematographer Haskell Wexler to make a film, to be called *Introduction to the Enemy*. They left their nine-month-old son with a Vietnamese woman in Hanoi, and went into the liberated zone of Quang Tri Province with a film crew to capture the features of the faceless peasants the United States had been opposing for so many years.

The color footage shot over the next two weeks was shimmering and pure. And so were the men and women of North Vietnam who became the characters in the documentary. Tom and Jane hoped the images of these North Vietnamese would disarm folks back home who still believed such people would be capable of a bloodbath when they finally took over South Vietnam.

On the way back to home, Jane and Tom stopped at Vadim's house in Paris to pick up Vanessa and to visit with him and his new wife, Catherine Schneider. Vadim put together a party with guests ranging from Regis Debray, the onetime Guevarist who would later take a job in the Mitterrand government, to President Valéry Giscard d'Estaing himself. Giscard watched Tom sit down on the new and expensive carpet Vadim and Schneider had just bought and eat a greasy chicken thigh. After Tom and Jane had gone to bed, the French president observed, "These young American politicians are completely relaxed." Then, with a slight note of concern in his voice, he asked Vadim, "Do you think he'll be president of the United States someday?"

While Jane and Tom relentlessly pursued the cause of Hanoi and Peter drifted contentedly in a haze of drugs, women, and aborted attempts at filmmaking, Henry had managed to revalidate himself, achieving stardom once again on Broadway. In the one-man show *Clarence Darrow* he had astonished critics with his powerful portrait of the brilliant, acerbic lawyer. Fonda was in his element again and as happy as he was capable of being; he was excited by the play because it offered him an opportunity to portray a character who was better than he imagined himself to be. "He was a man with a tremendous heart," Fonda said of Darrow. "I wish I was a man like that. Now I'm able to be that man every night."

Darrow was directed by John Houseman, who realized that outfitting Fonda with a pad to simulate the famed lawyer's paunch and plastering a forelock on his forehead could not hide the physical disparity between the actor and Darrow. Nonetheless, he saw a "miracle" in Fonda's acting that accomplished the transformation. *New York Times* drama critic Walter Kerr agreed: "Mr. Fonda has never been much of an impersonator. He has looked like himself, talked like himself. . . . [But in this play] a subliminal Darrow usurps the Fonda personality and the game is won, not by charm or easy skill but by intellectual metamorphosis."

One night not long after the triumphant opening, the playwright, David Rintels, noticed Henry suddenly go pale in the middle of the play. Trying to get through the performance, Fonda rested by leaning against a chair or a table in a way that was not part of the stage directions but was consistent with the character. He left out an anecdote here and there, shortening the play somewhat but not noticeably for the audience. After the final curtain, Rintels went backstage and found Henry in a clammy sweat, gasping for air and panting, his pulse racing. Afraid he was dying, Rintels helped Henry into a cab for Lenox Hill Hospital.

It was the first time Shirlee had seen her husband sick. More frightened, as she later said, than she had ever been in her life, she phoned Peter in Europe, where he was filming a movie, and put in a call to Jane in Paris. When they arrived, a cardiologist told the family that it seemed unlikely an operation would be necessary. Peter returned to his filming, and Jane continued on to California to hit the trail for the Indochina Peace Campaign again. Henry's condition suddenly worsened and physicians decided to install a pacemaker.

When he was finally discharged from the hospital, Henry dragged around in a way that worried Shirlee. After watching him for several days, she took him back to the doctor, who discovered that the pacemaker electrodes were not reaching the lining of his heart. The flaw was corrected, and Fonda flew to California. He recuperated in Bel Air, working in his garden and tending the beehives he kept beneath his fruit trees. He eventually began to feel better, but Shirlee noticed a sea-change in her husband. He was no longer the confident, energetic figure she had always known. Almost overnight Henry Fonda had become an old man.

FIFTEEN

During her days as a radical, Jane had periodically toyed with script ideas that would have played up her unique situation. In one brainstorming session with feminist friends, for instance, there had been a discussion about filming "The Jane Dough Story," a skewed fable about a rich white girl who is captured by revolutionaries and becomes one of them. It was, in effect, the Patty Hearst story before Patty Hearst was kidnapped, except that the protagonist of this unmade movie would from the onset have been more radical than her captors because of her disgust with the wealth and privilege into which she'd been born.

Other than *Klute,* however, the films she had made during her radical years did not encourage her to return to the screen. *Steelyard Blues* had been a disaster, in part because it was released within a couple of weeks of her first trip to Hanoi. *A Doll's House* had also failed, in large part because of her insistence on bringing politics onto the set.

Jane had often wondered if she could be a star and still have standing as a "serious person." But now Hayden reassured her that it was possible to be both. The effort to further the cause of North Vietnam having come to fruition (Steve Jaffe recalls Tom and Jane following Hanoi's final offensive against the Saigon government on a large map filled with push pins and inked-in lines to indicate troop movements), they now began to talk about how politics and films might mix, and how the mixture might bring them back into the mainstream. They formed IPC Films (after the Indochina Peace Campaign) and explored the possibility of making "meaningful" movies in the future.

In the meantime, however, their financial situation was getting precarious. Hayden was spending his time conferring with former aides to Senator George McGovern and others about how he might enter the political arena, and the responsibility for making money was left to Jane.

Peter, for one, resented this. When he was in town, he would occasionally zoom past the Hayden-Fonda house in his car, roll down the window, and yell, "Hayden! Get a job!" But for Jane it was part of the bargain. In a 1974 meeting with Richard Rosenthal, she reviewed her will and, as Rosenthal wrote in a memo, "discussed placing Vanessa and Troi on equal footing. . . . [and] talked about making specific provisions for Tom." Then, as part of a general rundown, Rosenthal told her that she was being audited for her 1971 and 1972 federal taxes, and that she owed $15,000 in unpaid state taxes; she had only some $40,000 in cash left and was spending between $5,000 and $7,000 a month. "Unless there is a new project to generate meaningful income in the immediate future," he concluded, "there must be an effort to limit expenditures."

Jane worried that she might be blackballed. But unlike Peter, who offended everybody, she had always been careful, even in her most radical moment, not to trash Hollywood. Also, the great studios, the only institutions in Hollywood capable of enforcing such a discipline, had long since lost their power to control stars' lives. Almost immediately after making it known that she was ready for a comeback, she was offered the lead in *Fun With Dick and Jane*, costarring George Segal, about a middle-class couple who have everything but own nothing because it is all bought on credit. When the husband loses his job and creditors begin to swoop down on them, the wife has the inspiration that they should become high-class thieves.

The film was the perfect vehicle for Jane's return to the screen: it presented her in a role that harked back to her ingenue parts when she was still only Henry Fonda's charming daughter. She accepted a relatively low salary, primarily to prove, as she said later, that she could still be "funny and pretty."

As part of her promotion for the movie, she went on talk shows and revealed a new self. Instead of ranting about the Panthers or engaging in diatribes about the POWs, she now talked about middle-class concerns such as child care and the price of heating oil. She sounded like a candidate's wife—which by that time she was. Within weeks after the fall of Saigon, Tom Hayden had announced that he planned to run for the Senate seat held by California Democrat John Tunney, a moderate whose primary sin was having opposed the war in Vietnam too late.

Jane's dedication was one of her most attractive qualities, and she was indefatigable in her efforts to boost Tom. She signed for more film roles to raise money, and reached deep into her bank account to finance the campaign, giving it the class and credibility that only money could buy. She lined up Linda Ronstadt, Arlo Guthrie, Groucho Marx, and other celebrities to back Tom. Her biggest catch, though, was her father.

Worn down by her persistent assault, Henry had finally capitulated to Jane politically. A gaunt presence still weak from recurrent heart trouble, he campaigned for his son-in-law throughout the spring of 1976. Andy Ferguson, a young Hayden volunteer in charge of chauffeuring Henry from one private fund-raiser to another in Beverly Hills, was told that the Fonda patriarch chilled easily and that he should be sure that Fonda was always near a furnace, fireplace, or other heat source. Ferguson was also told to avoid frivolous conversation, although he learned his lesson the hard way one afternoon when he worked up the courage to ask a carefully framed question.

"Excuse me, Mr. Fonda," Ferguson began, "but I was wondering if you could tell me how much your film persona owed to John Ford."

"Look, kid," Henry snapped in response, "I don't want to make small talk. Just cut the film-school crap and drive, okay?"

At first, incumbent John Tunney took Hayden lightly. But toward the end of the primary campaign, as Jane's money and her relentless mobilization of Hollywood resources began to take effect, Hayden started to rise in the polls. Tunney tried desperately to beat him back, but Hayden managed to receive nearly forty percent of the vote; he raised such daunting questions about his opponent's competence that Tunney was soundly defeated in the general election by another amateur, the Republican candidate, Dr. S. I. Hayakawa.

In order to finance the campaign, Jane had agreed to do two films, *Comes a Horseman* and *Julia*. After the last bills were paid, Richard Rosenthal wrote her, "Our current cash flow problems relate directly to the fact that during the first eight months of 1976 nearly $400,000 of your funds were applied (directly or indirectly) to the campaign. . . . As I discussed with Tom, what all this means is that barring unforeseen income, we will have to run a pretty tight ship, at least until April, when you commence services on *Comes a Horseman.*"

The race against Tunney was not an end but a beginning. Almost immediately after the campaign was over, Tom and Jane began the Campaign for Economic Democracy. This membership organization was to be the SDS of the new age and also a vehicle for Tom's personal ambition. Among the political goals of the CED were rent control, government-sponsored child care, the public takeover of utilities, and establishment of police review boards. Hayden said that only what he called "economic democracy" could "save the free enterprise system from ruin."

They decided that they needed a retreat where they could have

CED meetings and functions in isolation. Rosenthal located 120 acres twenty minutes outside of Santa Barbara. High up in the mountains, the Laurel Springs Ranch featured breathtaking views of the Pacific. There were several cabins on the property, and a lodge, which Jane set out to rehabilitate; she had it outfitted with a windmill generator and solar panels so that it could function as a sort of research and demonstration project for CED ideas about alternative energy sources. Laurel Springs became a clubhouse and command post.

Jane and Tom were very upbeat, especially after *Fun With Dick and Jane* appeared and reestablished Jane as a star. She was on the cover of *McCall's, Ladies' Home Journal, Good Housekeeping,* and other magazines she had shunned in the past few years. "I'm told there is still a tremendous amount of hostility toward me," she said. "But I don't feel it nowadays. . . . When I went to work on *Dick and Jane* I really sensed that I had made it home. It was like we were right, we survived, we look good, we are validated."

As for Peter, he groused about Jane's "luck." He was filled with big ideas for movies that never seemed to pan out. In 1976, for instance, he and Bill Hayward had launched a new production company with considerable fanfare. After obtaining a financial commitment from the studios, they announced projects such as "The Last Western," to star Jimmy Stewart; an adventure film, "The Road to Dusty Death"; and a film about the Revolutionary War based on the Howard Fast novel *Conceived in Liberty.*

None of these would ever be completed, and the rambling description Peter gave of another project on the list, "Deleted Portions of the Zapruder Film, Part II," suggested why: "There's a guy in a window with four chicks. . . . He's got a bow, or a gun, or a knife. And they're nude or in garter belts. And this long hair Oriental biker is holding an AK-15, like the guy did in the Dallas jail. And there's a big cardboard cut-out of me draped in an American flag. . . . And it all builds up. The guy with the chicks finally pees out the window. A chick inserts a dildo. The camera pulls back from the falling cardboard [cut-out] and there I am with a gun. . . ."

Peter had courted the reputation of a rebel for so long that he now had to live up to his legend, even though his was a rebellion without any discernible cause. In 1973, when filming *Dirty Mary Crazy Larry,* a commercially successful movie he starred in but did not direct, Peter was clowning around in the front seat of a van shuttling cast members to the set. As a friend later reconstructed the incident, Peter was talking in a rush of profanity and someone said, "Peter! Please! There are ladies present!" As one person present recalls the scene, this brought a glint to his eye: "*Ladies present?* Well, if there are *ladies present,* they'll be interested in this." He stood up, dropped his pants, and put his naked butt on top of the seat, right in the faces of those in back. The women started shrieking, and one of them yelled, "Oh no, stop the car and let me out!" Peter put his pants back on and laughed the rest of the way.

It was a minor episode, perhaps, but it led to a disciplinary hearing before the Screen Actors Guild at which Peter was first defiant and then contrite. Close friends had become used to Peter's arrogant and provocative behavior. "He had a tremendous chip on his shoulder," says Bill Hayward. "He'd go into a film looking for trouble. He'd ally himself with the crew and find out what was bothering them. For example, a cameraman once complained to him that a certain producer was so cheap that he was forcing the crew to watch the dailies in black and white. Peter got mad and said to the producer, 'Well, I'm not showing up until the cameramen get color dailies.'"

To become known as "difficult" in the film industry was dangerous for an actor. But Peter had gone one step further, cultivating an identity that edged perilously close to "crazy." On one occasion, angry because of a billboard that Universal had put up to advertise one of his films, Peter sent a telegram to Lew Wasserman, head of the studio's parent company, MCA, and arguably the most powerful man in Hollywood. Peter preposterously threatened to put a hand grenade at the base of the offending billboard if something was not done. During another mood of rage, he called Universal executive Andy Albeck a Nazi because of his Germanic name.

But if Peter was a trial for those he considered authority figures, he was also a person of great appeal for those he saw as equals. He knew a good deal about a number of topics—music, geography, astronomy. His hypochrondria, a legacy from the days when his mother dragged him from one doctor to another, had given him a solid knowledge of medicine. Unlike Jane, who seemed to regard time as an enemy and did not enjoy meandering conversation ("That's it," she once said to a friend after catching herself beginning to enjoy a leisurely telephone call, "I'm hanging up because chatting wastes time"), Peter was compulsively gregarious and saw social occasions as opportunities for spontaneous explorations of the self.

He continued to make snide comments about Jane's reliance on Hayden. Yet he too had looked for someone who would give him unconditional emotional backing. In 1974, when he went to Key West to film *92 in the Shade,* he stumbled into a situation that one friend likened to a "sexual swap meet." The movie was being directed by novelist Thomas McGuane, who was in the middle of a torrid affair with one of the stars, Elizabeth Ashley. During the shooting, however, McGuane took up with another member of the cast, Margot Kidder, who ultimately bore him a daughter.

Watching these goings-on along with Peter was McGuane's wife, Becky, a short, vivacious blonde who resembled a young Barbara Stanwyck and was generally considered remarkable because of her tolerance of her husband's extramarital activities. ("I think it's wonderful," Becky had told Elizabeth Ashley after finding out about her affair with McGuane. "Normally he screws these dumb teeny-

boppers. I don't have those kinds of jealousies. I really do approve.")
Finally, Becky decided to take part in the game of musical beds
herself and went off for a time with another of the stars of the movie,
Warren Oates. When she came back, she and Peter got together.

He perversely insisted on calling her Portia, as if trying to rebap-
tize her as his woman. (Her full name was Portia Rebecca Crockett,
and she was a descendant of Davy Crockett.) What impressed him
about her was that she liked his boat. Late in 1976, when Peter and
Becky-Portia were married, one of his friends observed, "Becky is
like Jane—tough; nothing fazes her. She is the perfect person for
Peter. All those fantasies of incest, and he finally got to marry his
sister!"

Peter would always be Peter Pan—not willing to grow up, insisting
on maintaining a dual citizenship in the past and the present. His
sister, on the other hand, was settling into the role of Plain Jane.
Age lines had begun to show on her face, but a mature glamour had
replaced the unisex look she had worn at the beginning of her
radical period. Before, it had been a hard and calculating face. Now
it was softer, more appealing, and capable of a dreamy wistfulness.

Unlike other stars, Jane cultivated friends who were not in the
industry, the other activists in the CED. They cycled in and out of
the $40,000 home on Wadsworth Street in Santa Monica, which
she and Tom had helplessly watched appreciate to a worth of five
times that much in the California property boom of the late
seventies.

At first there had been problems fitting into the neighborhood.
Someone wrote with a finger in the dust of their car: "Jane Fonda is a
commie." And Troy (as it was now spelled) was caught selling
autographs he had begged from Jane so that he would have as much
pocket money as other show-biz kids. But Jane worked hard to
demonstrate that she was as bothered by problems of inflation and

pollution as anyone else on the block, and gradually the Hayden-Fondas were accepted. "It's important for me to live here," Jane said. "If you're a political organizer—which I am—you can't deal with people unless you share their problems."

She spent her days proving she was one of them by taking care of neighbors' kids along with her own; washing and wallpapering; and making fruit smoothies for Troy. All the time, she released a steady stream of explanation to whichever journalist happened to be sitting at the rickety kitchen table doing a story on what was cooking with the Haydens: "We don't have people who work for us. There's no one who does laundry. There's no nanny. There's no cook. We do all our own shopping. If you want to be responsible for your life, it means you have to be responsible for your whole life, not just the pretty parts."

Finally, after so many years, she was *real*. It seemed the perfect life, the perfect family. But one member of the group appeared out of place: Vanessa, who, in the words of a Fonda relative, "was often treated like part of another movie." Between the ages of two and nine she had spent half the year with Jane and half with her father, who was trying to reestablish himself in France. Then Vadim, feeling that Vanessa needed to be in one place, had moved full-time to the United States. But now that she was almost a teenager, she wanted, in her father's words, "something more than she got from Jane." There was an insufficient connection; Vadim thought it was an echo of Jane's own relationship with Henry.

Often Vanessa went to Peter's children, Bridget and Justin, for refuge. They were victims of divorce too. And each suffered from it. Bridget had been hurt when Peter tried unsuccessfully to get custody of her brother but not of her. Justin worshipped his father, yet was repeatedly wounded when Peter would promise to come for him on visitation days by nine in the morning and often not arrive until afternoon. Still, they felt part of a functioning unit. Vanessa told them that at her house, Tom and Jane and Troy appeared to be part of one family—the family of political aspiration and publicity photos—while she seemed to belong somewhere else.

Her mother was not unsympathetic. It was just that there wasn't time to attend to to a child's subtle needs. Each day, after finishing the household chores and the political organizing she said made her feel "whole," Jane hopped into her VW Rabbit and drove to Hollywood.

Julia, which was based on an alleged episode in the life of writer Lillian Hellman, had put her back in the mainstream. To promote the film, publicists played up the similarities between the life of a political woman of the thirties, the communist Hellman, and that of a political woman of the seventies, the radical Fonda. In an interview Jane made the mistake of saying that Hellman was a homely woman who nonetheless carried herself like Marilyn Monroe. She meant it as a compliment, but Hellman took umbrage; a chill remained between them for the rest of the project.

The role in *Julia* was important to Jane because it showed once again that the subliminal aspects of her association with radical politics might not be a hindrance to her career. Also, *Julia* taught an object lesson by bringing her into contact with an old friend. Vanessa Redgrave, who had just appeared in a documentary, *The Palestinians,* in which she danced and brandished a gun in support of the Palestine Liberation Organization, spent all her spare moments on the set obsessively proselytizing electricians and other technical people and trying to convince them to join her Trotskyist Workers' Revolutionary Party. Jane looked at this almost self-parodying activity and saw what she might have been if she had not met Hayden.

As she became a star again, Jane continued to think about making films of her own. Such an ambition would not have been possible a few years earlier, when her father's old nemesis, Darryl F. Zanuck, was head of Warner. Zanuck could sit down with a list of names of stars and directors he had under contract and match them with stories the studio owned, putting together the next year's entire production schedule in a couple of days. "Okay," he would say to his underlings, "we want three Bette Davises, four Cagneys, three Bogarts, two Errol Flynns."

But the industry was no longer ruled from the top down. Instead of being well-kept but impotent, as they had been in the old days, stars were now in control. Films were planned one by one in studios which fielded proposals from a galaxy of independent producers. The studios were not headed by individuals who rose to a position of power over a lifetime, but by young people often recruited from talent agencies because of their relationships with stars. They were individuals whose sensibility had been formed in (and by) the sixties and who paid attention to concerns other than the bottom line.

The man Jane chose to help build her production company, Bruce Gilbert, was an example of the new Hollywood executive. Bearded and soft-spoken, Gilbert had grown up in a well-off family in Beverly Hills and probably would have been a corporation lawyer if the sixties hadn't intervened. He had gone to school at Berkeley, majoring in developmental psychology and taking some film courses while dabbling in revolution as one of the footsoldiers of Hayden's Red Family.

In 1971, shortly after Hayden was expelled from the collective, Gilbert moved to Los Angeles to work on Daniel Ellsberg's defense. He got together with Tom and Jane, and they talked about movies, especially ones they could produce themselves. Gilbert had been affected by *Easy Rider* but in a different way from most people his age: he thought to himself, "Wait a minute. They can make that kind of picture and everyone goes to see it. Well, I can make something a lot more provocative with a lot more content and do it better."

After years of competition with Peter, these words were music to

Jane's ears, and when she set up IPC Films it was understood that Gilbert would play a role. While she was making *Fun With Dick and Jane* and *Julia* and Tom was running for the Senate, Gilbert gained experience for their future venture by taking a job as a story editor at a small film company. He read hundreds of scripts, and eventually came to the conclusion that the screenplay form was as difficult as haiku. The scripts that had good content were usually poorly structured; those that were technically accomplished usually had no substance.

Gilbert was no less a radical than Tom or Jane, but when it came to films, he agreed with Sam Goldwyn's remark that "messages are for Western Union." His idea was to make films that did indeed have a strong point of view, but that were above all dramatically sound and could appeal to a wide audience.

Their first feature came about as a result of Hayden's belief that with the defeat of the United States, there would be a domestic war over the meaning of the Vietnam War, and that they needed to enter the dialogue. Gilbert committed himself to the project. It was agreed that Nancy Dowd, who had worked on the FTA show and accompanied Jane to Norway for *A Doll's House,* would draft a script about a Marine back from Vietnam and the impact the war had on him and his wife.

Coming Home, as the work would eventually be titled, took five years to reach the screen. Dowd's version took the story in an eccentric direction, making it into a feminist fable about a relationship between the heroine, Sally Hyde, and another serviceman's wife, who develop an attraction for each other while working in a hospital for disabled vets.

Gilbert and Fonda didn't like the concept. To keep the project from stalling, they turned it over to Jerome Hellman to produce, and Hellman brought with him Waldo Salt, an accomplished screenwriter who had done the script for *Midnight Cowboy,* which Hellman had also produced. Salt turned *Coming Home* into the story of Sally

Hyde's sense of isolation after her macho husband volunteers for another tour in Vietnam, and her subsequent love affair with a paraplegic vet whose body is shattered but whose spirit is still intact.

At the time Salt was writing the script, he was helping Ron Kovic on the book that became *Born on the Fourth of July*. As Hellman says, "Ron was floundering and looking for a way out of his own problems. He frequently stayed at Salt's suite at the Chateau Marmont [in Los Angeles] and got emotional as well as literary support from him." The plan was for Kovic to be the technical advisor for *Coming Home*, but he completed his book and sold the screen rights to Al Pacino. Hellman and Salt felt betrayed, and for a time they worried that a competing project might keep their film from getting produced.

Originally, Jon Voight was supposed to play the martinet husband, but after five actors, including Jack Nicholson, turned down the role of the crippled veteran, he took that part instead. Both Voight and Fonda won Oscars for their roles in *Coming Home,* but the film itself lost out for Best Picture to *The Deer Hunter,* another Vietnam movie. Jane denounced the latter as "a racist, Pentagon version of the war," then admitted she hadn't seen it yet.

Coming Home marked Jane's emergence as the central female film figure of the decade. As critic Pauline Kael had once predicted, she had come to exemplify the tensions that characterized the seventies, just as Bette Davis had done in the forties, and Marilyn Monroe in the fifties.

The film also marked Jane's entry into the film industry as a businesswoman. She was not the first star to have a production company. John Wayne and others had done so in the 1950s, and Clint Eastwood had produced with notable success two decades later. But she was the first woman to make it big at a time when women were assuming once again the position as independent and powerful screen figures they had occupied in Hollywood before World War II.

Of the films Jane made in the late seventies, some were for other producers. *Comes a Horseman,* a western in which she played a tough ranch woman, was, scriptwriter Dennis Clark thought, an homage to her father. ("If you look at the film carefully, you can see Henry oozing out, either deliberately or genetically.") In *California Suite,* she played a hard-bitten, aggressive woman who was both a victor and a victim in the wars of sexual liberation.

But most of her energy went into IPC Films. Bruce Gilbert felt they had stumbled onto an important theme in *Coming Home:* the dilemma of an innocent who suddenly finds herself in the middle of what becomes a transforming experience. "Most people are just ordinary folks," Gilbert said in describing what he and Jane would parlay into a formula. "They come to conscience through many different roads, and it usually happens by something impacting upon them from the outside, events of one sort or another, personal and political." For Sally Hyde this experience had been the war; for Kimberly Wells, heroine of IPC's next film, *The China Syndrome,* it was the cover-up of a nuclear power accident.

The idea for *The China Syndrome* also came from Hayden, who had made opposition to nuclear power the centerpiece of the Campaign for Economic Democracy program. IPC Films had tried unsuccessfully to buy the rights to the story of Karen Silkwood, a young woman who died under mysterious circumstances after discovering safety violations in a Kerr-McGee nuclear power plant in Oklahoma. Then Gilbert heard that writer-director James Bridges had a script about a reporter who discovers the cover-up of a radiation leak at a power plant. Initially the protagonist was a man, but Gilbert got Bridges to rewrite the part for Jane.

Columbia did not like the title of the film, which came from an industry term for a meltdown so hot it would "reach all the way to China." Studio executives offered polls showing that most people assumed the "syndrome" was a disease of some kind. As alternative titles, they suggested "Power" and "Eyewitness." But Jane said she wouldn't promote a film with either of these titles. In a testament to her growing power, the original title stuck.

This was the first film her company produced by itself, without the partnership of an experienced industry insider like Jerome Hellman. Jane realized there was a lot riding on the outcome. The unconscious anxieties that had always plagued her sleep became active again; she had nightmares of drowning dogs and of Tom's leaving her.

Her nervousness seemed justified by the initial reviews of *The China Syndrome,* which were respectful but far from ecstatic. But on March 28, 1979, less than two weeks after the film opened, at the Three Mile Island nuclear plant near Harrisburg, Pennsylvania, an explosion and partial meltdown confirmed the premises of the script. It was a godsend. (Jane's costar Michael Douglas said, "It goes beyond the realm of coincidence. . . . It's enough to make you religious.") *The China Syndrome* was transformed from a slick, somewhat implausible suspense film into a prophetic *J'Accuse,* and Tom and Jane set off on a national tour attacking the nuclear industry and promoting "economic democracy."

The China Syndrome was a solid financial success, and soon after it was completed, Richard Rosenthal wrote Jane to summarize how far she had come since her decision to return to the screen: "Your fee for *Julia* only three short years ago was $350,000. Likewise for *Dick and Jane.* For *The China Syndrome* last year, your fee was only $500,000. . . . It is literally only in the past year with your price as an actress doubling to $1 million and our paying off past debts that it has begun to be possible to realistically anticipate your having the required capital to participate in the kind of investment situation that we would both prefer."

This was exactly what Jane wanted, for, as Rosenthal says: "From 1978, the focus was on money. That was the name of the game. The emphasis of the work I did for Jane was business, setting aside what we referred to beginning in 1978 as 'the campaign war-chest.' My understanding, although it was never made explicit, was that the objective was to elect Tom president."

It was a matter of making hay while the sun shone. As Jane said half humorously to a friend, "Tom says that in a few years I'll be old and wrinkled and they won't want me anymore. Now's the time we've got to earn money. We don't have any. And without money we're vulnerable."

They were putting money into the Laurel Springs retreat near Santa Barbara, making it into a summer camp for economically deprived children, but their biggest expense was the Campaign for Economic Democracy, whose annual budget had grown to some $500,000. The organization had become a force in California politics, with chapters up and down the state, and it entered into coalitions that helped elect "progressives" to offices in several cities.

One of the CED alliances was with California's eccentric governor Jerry Brown. Seeing in Tom and Jane potential allies in his quixotic new-age quest for the White House, Brown appointed Hayden to the state's Southwest Border Commission and its Solar Utilization Network in 1978. The posts might have had little power but they nonetheless gave him legitimacy as a mainstream political figure.

The CED was crucial to Tom's grand strategy, but maintaining it was expensive. (In 1976, one employee recalls, Jane was paying CED staffers $700 a month and telling them to confirm with the bank before cashing their checks, to make sure she had covered the payroll.) Brainstorming sessions were held at Laurel Springs in which Tom and Jane tried to think of ways to support the organization without relying on Jane's film income. One possibility explored was the printing business. Another was real estate, and they went so far as to look at a commercial complex in the Koreatown section of

Los Angeles. However, radical attorney Leonard Weinglass, an informal advisor, nixed this possibility by pointing out that it was a right-wing neighborhood and the people would regard Jane unfavorably.

Then Jane had an idea. Her role in *California Suite* had called for a bikini shot and she'd had to get into shape fast. Shirlee Fonda happened to be taking aerobics at Body Design by Gilda, and she brought Jane to the Hollywood studio for a quick tune-up. (Barbra Streisand, who also worked out at Gilda Marx's studio, asked Jane the first time she showed up, "How did *you* get here?") Jane quickly became addicted to aerobics. When she went on location for *The Electric Horseman,* she found there was no aerobics studio in the small Utah town. So, after each day's shooting, she taught classes herself for the women on the set.

This, then, might be the business they were looking for. Jane began taking private lessons with Marx's chief teacher, a woman named Leni Cazden, learning her routines and also studying how to be a teacher. She decided to make a go of it and hired Cazden to help set up the business—and, Marx later claimed, asked people who worked out at Body Design by Gilda to report on how the studio was equipped and furnished.

Having christened her business the Workout, Jane got started at her new studio in Beverly Hills. People looked in the windows (an activity referred to as "fun with Jane") and liked what they saw well enough to come in and take classes. Jane told friends: "We're going to beat them at their own game." The game was capitalism. She made the Campaign for Economic Democracy the sole owner of the Workout, and the Workout, which soon generated some $20,000 a month, made the CED rich.

It was, Jane would later say, the best time she could remember. Her life was absolutely full, and for her that was the best way to gauge happiness. Her friends were the "real people" of the CED "family"—organizers and activists. She saw herself like them, taking responsibility for her family and herself, enduring life's little crises and being buoyed by modest successes. "It was the great thing Tom did for her," a friend said. "He introduced her to normalcy and averageness."

What she and her husband were building together seemed to be summarized by Laurel Springs. The 120-acre retreat, soon to be bordered by Ronald Reagan's Western White House, had become so much a part of them that Jane had picked out a place on a bluff overlooking the ocean where she and Tom would be buried.

There were seminars attended by farm workers, CED precinct captains, and an assortment of refugees from the New Left who had attached themselves to Hayden. Every Easter there was a celebration for CED members and their families with an egg hunt for the kids (with Jane dressed up as the Easter Bunny) and secular services at which Tom delivered the homily, after which everyone joined in singing "Puff, the Magic Dragon."

It was also a place to bring kids for summer camp—the paying kids of Jane's Hollywood friends, and the underprivileged scholarship kids who helped make what was billed as an exemplary experience in "cooperation, democracy and social justice." Everything was political at the camp, one counselor inadvertently told a reporter, even swimming. Tom had to explain: "Swimming cannot be separated from larger concerns—the role of youth and the idea of competition."

Happy because of the life they were building, Jane realized she might be Tom's best asset but also one of his heaviest liabilities. Her past, like Tom's, was a "political problem" to be dealt with by gradual blurring and gauzy revisionism. On the one hand she gave interviews emphasizing that she had suffered for her principles ("I was blacklisted from 1970 to 1975 in the same way as the Jews during the McCarthy period") and that she had been in great danger ("I became a political activist at a time when I had friends who were murdered, people who were killed by the FBI. People disappeared. There were plans to kidnap my husband and castrate him in Mexico"). But she also implied that some of the things she had done during her radical period were wrong, although these mistakes could be understood and forgiven because of the psychic distortions caused by sexism: "During the first years of my political existence, I was so filled with self-loathing and contempt for what I represented that I couldn't function effectively. What got me into so much trouble was the attitude, 'I'm not left enough. I'm not militant enough.' More left rhetoric came out of my mouth during that time — I didn't even know what the words really meant. I was trying too hard to prove my credibility, to prove I was sincere."

The one setback in this campaign came in 1979 when Jerry Brown appointed Jane to the California Arts Council. She immediately put together a small staff at her own expense and, thinking she might turn the modest position into an influential one, even went to Mexico City to open negotiations with the wife of Mexican president José López Portillo on art exchanges between California and Mexico. But just before the Arts Council post came up for confirmation in the state Senate, Jane attacked Joan Baez for circulating a letter condemning the human rights abuses of the North Vietnamese. Hanoi Jane was back on people's minds, and the California Senate rejected the proposed appointment. She organized a letter-writing campaign accusing the senators of reviving McCarthyism, but the rejection was still a devastating defeat for her.

For the most part, however, Jane's attempts to project a more moderate image yielded results. The Hollywood Women's Press Club, which had given her its Sour Apple Award a few years earlier for "bringing disrepute to the entertainment industry," asked John Wayne to present her with its Golden Apple Award as Female Star of the Year. She began to climb up lists of the most admired women in America.

It was ironic, therefore, that at the moment she was being seen as an example of the modern, self-directed woman, she was most dependent on Hayden—for emotional validation and also for intellectual direction. "Tom's the intelligent one," she would admit somewhat sadly to friends. "I'm just a chameleon." A screenwriter on the set of *The Electric Horseman* saw her run to the phone when a television report flashed the news that the Chinese had invaded Vietnam. "Big stuff, huh?" the man heard her say to Tom, and then, after a pause, "So what's our position?"

Once told what the position was, she became an extremely effective political spokeswoman in public. A journalist who covered the nationwide tour Jane and Tom took for the CED in 1979 later reviewed her performance: "She begins by projecting vulnerability. 'I was very nervous thinking about talking to you tonight,' or: 'I'm not as nervous as I thought I'd be.' Sometimes she stammers slightly at the onset. Then she emotionally calls up, almost as if they were appearing by their own power, stories about this nuclear horror or that workers' rights outrage. Gradually she invests her call to arms with utter conviction. The audience feels that if *Jane Fonda* has found strength in politics, surely they should get out there and protest or continue the laborious organizing they've already begun."

Out of the limelight, though, the composure disappeared. People who got a rare look at Jane in repose saw someone with a driving need to be always in motion; a woman who seemed fearful that if she paused, something would catch up with her. In between CED speeches, she called often to check on the Workout, just as she called frequently to check on the CED from the sets of her movies. She constantly made lists; even when her body was still, her fingers played with each other incessantly. She always looked at Tom as if waiting for a cue. So what is our position on this issue? she seemed to be wondering. What is the line? What do we believe?

Her deference to and dependence on her husband were so extreme that some close to Jane wondered if she would wind up as a left-wing version of Pat Nixon, cheerfully loyal on the surface and resentfully depleted within.

Tom appeared to see none of this. He was confident almost to a fault. He believed that the zeitgeist was with him, and he looked for any scrap of evidence, however small, to confirm this opinion. A reporter was with him in 1980 when he was handed a poll showing that a majority of California voters were in favor of rent control, and watched him light up: "This is great! I *told* you rent control was a great issue. People think issues aren't going our way, that the right has all the issues. Bullshit!"

A few moments later he added, "It's coming. We're going to take over. The last few administrations have all been controlled by the generation of World War II. The next generation will be those who came to political life during Vietnam. My generation."

As the 1980 primaries approached, he scoffed publicly at the idea that he could ever be president. But privately he offered different scenarios by which it might happen: Kennedy–Brown–Hayden; Kennedy–right-wing reaction–Hayden. As a friend said, "He's convinced that he should and will be the key figure for social change in his lifetime."

SIXTEEN

For years, Peter's nomadic life had centered around the *Tatoosh*. It was more than a boat; it was a symbol of his unique status, of the freedom he had made out of his alienation and loneliness. "On this boat, my word is law," he said. "I pay no land taxes. I can enjoy real sovereignty."

But after his marriage to Becky, things changed. She wanted to remain close to Tom Jr., her son by McGuane. And so Peter bought a three-hundred-acre spread called Pine Tree near Livingston, Montana, right down the road from McGuane's Raw Deal Ranch. The large, lodgelike house was surrounded by forest. Inside, across from a huge stone hearth, was a lone picture on the wall—a still of Henry as Wyatt Earp. Near it, encased in glass, was the jacket Peter had worn in *Easy Rider*. His large collection of guns was spread around the living room—one of Earp's six-shooters from his days in Tombstone, the tiny derringer carried by the famous midget Tom Thumb; a pistol once owned by cowboy film star Tom Mix. For Peter, guns were not only objects of death and beauty but also symbols of power. "I'm a crack shot, man," he told a writer who asked him about his fixation. "Some people can put basketballs through a hoop. I can stick a bullet anywhere I point my finger."

At first he had grumbled about leaving the sea and talked about the ethical and environmental compromises involved in being land-locked. But soon he came to like Pine Tree and made tight associations with an artistic community that included, in addition to McGuane, writers Jim Harrison, Richard Brautigan, and William Hjortsberg, singer Jimmy Buffett, and actor Warren Oates. Jeff Bridges and Dennis Quaid would come along later, as would director Sam Peckinpah. The vaguely incestuous atmosphere, in which everyone seemed interrelated by a former marriage or love affair or deep friendship, recalled the Fonda–Hayward ties of Peter's youth. He called his new home a "Montana Bloomsbury."

While building a new "family" near Livingston, Peter was still trying to deal with his real family in Hollywood. As if seeking a medium that could straighten out their tangled relationships, he thought constantly about acting with Henry and Jane in films. About the time of *Easy Rider* he had optioned *Conceived in Liberty*, Howard Fast's novel about the Revolutionary War, for all of the Fondas. He had commissioned several scripts. Producer-director George Stevens was committed to the project. After Stevens died of a heart attack, *Conceived in Liberty* eventually fell by the wayside. Peter continued to look for possibilities that would unite two or more of the Fondas on the screen. Some of his ideas—such as the incest story with Jane—were too bizarre to succeed. In 1979, when Peter directed *Wanda Nevada,* he finally did cast Henry in a brief cameo role as a grizzled prospector. But this offbeat low-budget film was a box-office failure.

For a while Jane took up the same cause of developing a project for the three of them. She attempted to put together her own film about the Revolutionary War—"A House Divided" was the working title—in which Henry would have played a cobbler, Peter his apprentice, and she a barmaid in a tavern. But the idea never had the symbolic implications for Jane that it did for Peter, particularly after she had begun to feel more in control of her relationship with Henry. Soon she had a different agenda.

After making 9 to 5, a zany comedy about working girls that would gross over $100 million for IPC Films, Jane decided the time was finally right for her to act with her father. She had made their quarrel public twenty years earlier. In the years since, as her power increased and Henry's declined, the two had reached a rapprochement. But she still felt a need to close the gap between them that existed in the public mind. One way to do it was to win him the Academy Award he had never received and thus change the perception of her as a daughter (in John Houseman's phrase) from that of an Electra to that of a Cordelia.

She and Bruce Gilbert determined that they could stage a ritual closing of the Fonda circle by adapting *On Golden Pond*, a play about two elderly people, one of whom thinks he is close to death. That part would be played by Henry, and they ordered a script that would beef up the role of the daughter, to be played by Jane. Viewers who knew something about the family would be able to see the movie with a parallax view—watching Jane and Henry play the feuding father and daughter and also play themselves finding each other in the film's dramatic ending.

Peter had planned to shoot a film of his own, but while Jane was able to get clearance from the Screen Actors Guild to proceed with *On Golden Pond* despite a strike, he was not. "The strike has blown my company's projects out of the water," he said, sailing for Hawaii in the *Tatoosh*. But the significant fact was that Peter had been excluded from the touching family scene projected onto the big screen. When it came down to it, in film as in life, there were Henry and Jane, and Peter was still odd man out.

Henry was aware of how this special relationship looked to Peter, but he didn't feel he could do much about it. Under Peter's constant prodding, he was now able to say "I love you too" when cornered with a declaration of affection. But that was about it. He was tired of fighting his children, and he told one interviewer, "Frankly, I've never really dealt with personal problems at all. Eventually, if you sit there long enough, they just fall away."

Henry's attitudes were not the kind that encouraged loved ones to stick by him. His stepdaughter, Pan, Frances's daughter, had married an Italian diplomat and was not close to Henry. And his adopted daughter, Amy, who had grown into a pretty dark-haired woman, had made a life for herself in Colorado. Refusing to be wholly dependent on Henry, she had worked her way through college by baby-sitting and cleaning houses. At eighteen she married, and soon after she divorced. Amy saw Henry perhaps twice a year, and each time there was a distance between them she could not bridge. She felt as if she were in a Fonda limbo. Amy once screwed up her courage to tell him that after much torment she had made a decision to try to locate her blood parents. He had looked at her blankly and said, "Oh?"

If Henry was not emotionally demonstrative, however, he was loyal. During the filming of the television special *Gideon's Trumpet* at the Santa Ana Courthouse in 1980, he was signing autographs between takes when a large, menacing man came up and said, "How does it feel having a daughter who's a communist?" Although sick and frail, Henry jumped up and began jabbing a finger in the man's chest and yelling, "You take that back!" Finally the man stammered, "I'm sorry." Henry sat back down, finished signing his autograph, and then threw it at him.

And while he was not interested in playing the role of family patriarch, he did try to do his duty by his grandchildren. Because of his increasing closeness to Jane, he saw Vanessa and Troy fairly often. Peter's children, Bridget and Justin, had been with their mother the last few years, and for them, coming to Henry's house was a major occasion. Bridget, who had grown into a stunning blonde teenager, never talked to him about her increasing interest in acting. Yet she got an indirect lesson in the famed Fonda concentration by watching her grandfather paint with meticulous craftsmanship. Henry doggedly sat through Justin's Little League games and invited the boy for awkward visits at his house. (Asked what he did there, Justin replied, "Watch videos." Asked which ones, he said, "*Mister Roberts.*")

At a time when his contemporaries from the golden days of movies were fading off into retirement, Henry, still addicted to being characters other than himself, continued to work as much as he could. As when he was younger, he wondered if each new job would be his last. When he turned seventy-five, Jane arranged for her attorney to represent him. In their introductory meeting Henry offered a caveat, "I've got to tell you that I don't know if I'll ever work again." At about the same time, Peter brought a friend over to his father's house. Henry answered the door. Before Peter could make the introduction, Henry said "God damn it!" and stalked off. The friend asked what was wrong, and Peter replied, "Oh, he's pissed off because he's temporarily out of work."

Henry had continued to appear on the screen, often in mediocre films such as *Meteor, Swarm,* and *The Great Smokey Roadblock.* But he always added something to the good ones and never let the bad ones subtract from his integrity as an actor. He saved himself for stage plays—*The First Monday in October,* in which he played a Supreme Court judge, and *Gideon's Trumpet,* about a convict turned attorney who argued his own case.

He was always the consummate pro. David Rintels, author of *Gideon's Trumpet,* recalls him as old and frail when the play was turned into a TV docudrama. After a big summing-up scene, Henry was told to go rest while the jury's reaction was filmed. He insisted on staying to watch: "No, there are actors in that jury. They paid me the courtesy of listening to me and I'll do the same for them."

But by 1980 it became clear that Henry was fading. He had suffered renewed heart troubles and had undergone surgery to remove a benign tumor the size of a grapefruit from his diaphragm. Doctors had also discovered prostate cancer, which had metastasized. Although they felt they could slow the spread of the cancer, their patient was becoming increasingly debilitated.

On Golden Pond was his first meaty role in a good film in years and he was grateful, formally approaching producer Martin Starger at one point during shooting to say, "I want to thank you for this role. It's very important to me." And while he liked the part of Norman Thayer, he was annoyed by the psychodrama with which Jane surrounded it. However far he had come in his relationship with her, he still became uncomfortable when she tried to extort emotions from him. In one scene in the film she ad-libbed by reaching out to touch him. Later she said she knew this would take him by surprise. It did: his body shook visibly as he fought to control his emotions.

Jane kept trying to get close, to give the film some standing as autobiography. Henry kept trying to maintain artistic distance and retain the professionalism that meant so much to him. ("I was worried that I would be disoriented by our real-life relationship," he told one writer.) At times, Jane bored in so relentlessly that Henry rebelled. At one point he called her a sociopath, and only the soothing ministrations of costar Katharine Hepburn kept peace on the set. He exploded again during a close-up. Jane had already said her lines into the tightly focused camera and then stayed put, trying to get her face so near his that he would have to look at her while he said his lines.

"I don't *need* to see you," he rebuked her. "I'm not *that* kind of actor." The implication was that she *was* that kind of actor with that kind of need. Jane remarked later that at that moment she felt once again the nausea that had so often come over her when she was growing up.

But finally she broke Henry down. One of the crew recalls the moment when the script called for the father to touch his daughter for the first time: "She was crying and he was crying. All the rest of us were about to cry too."

After filming was over, Henry went back to his Bel Air estate and tried to putter with his little grove of fruit trees and his beehives. His lean body was stooped, his shoulders rounded; he seemed to have shrunk. He would run out of energy after a few minutes of gardening and soon he began to spend most of his time inside, painting and doing needlepoint, a hobby he had picked up from his friend Lucille Ball. Jane was so worried about his health that she asked Mark Rydell, director of *On Golden Pond,* to schedule a special screening for him. Henry arrived at the theater walking with the aid of two canes. Afterward, as he struggled toward Rydell, he stumbled and fell so that the director had to catch him. Henry whispered to Rydell, who was afraid the actor was dying in his arms, "Thank you for the most important film of my life."

On Golden Pond was a tremendous success, thanks in part to publicity which focused on the roman à clef of the Fondas' reconciliation. Seizing on a chance to show her deep love for the man who had always held her at arm's length, Jane took the film to Europe and Israel (a country that had become important to Tom's political plans), where she attended the premieres and gave emotional tributes to her father. The theme was always the same whether she was abroad or at home: The Academy Award was something her father was owed, and she was determined to make it happen for him. As word leaked out of how sick Henry had become, Jane's efforts became almost missionary. The film industry was being called on to administer its own version of extreme unction to one of its faithful.

Henry did get the Oscar. And Jane was there to accept it for him. Looking into the camera, she held up the statuette and said, "Oh

Dad, I'm so happy and proud for you." Then she addressed the audience: "My father didn't really believe that this was going to happen—but he told me a while back that if it did, he wanted his wife, Shirlee, to accept the award for him. But Shirlee wanted to be with him tonight, as is her way, and so I'm here. . . ."

That night Jane brought the Oscar to Henry's home, where he sat wrapped in blankets, a frail old man waiting for death.

A full-time male nurse accompanied him as he shuffled slowly from room to room with the help of a walker. Rapid weight loss had sunk his cheeks and made his eyes seem larger, although the clear slate-blue depths were occluded now. He was more silent than ever, as though he had exhausted his meager store of words. He spent time in bed lost in reverie, his face brightening only when Shirlee came into the room. He said that his life would have been different and better if he had met her first instead of last.

He had stopped painting in his last days, but his work was all around him—watercolor still-lifes of fruit; a London rooftop; a geranium on a chair—part of his effort to express himself in images as he never could in words. George Peppard, a good friend from his middle years, came to see him regularly; Barbara Stanwyck, one of his might-have-beens, brought him lemon cakes and other confections she knew he wouldn't be able to eat.

His oldest friend, Jimmy Stewart, visited three times a week. The two men, both nearly deaf, shouted laconically at each other about old times; the activity exhausted but also amused Fonda. Then they lapsed into the silences that each found so congenial and just sat there, monuments to the history of American film, content to be with each other. As Henry told a visitor, it seemed like yesterday that he and Stewart were starving young unknowns in New York, living at Casa Gangrene and working on model planes. He also recalled how, when they got hungry enough, they would crash parties to cadge a few beers and some food and then have contests on the long walk back to their apartment to see who would get farther in urinating his name into the snow.

Peter was at his bedside when he died on August 11, 1982. He remembered, "At the end, I looked into my father's eyes and kissed him on the forehead and told him I loved him. Then I prayed for him to let go." During the death watch, Jane had looked for a last sign or clarification, a final explication of the puzzle Henry had always been. She talked to him, trying to extract from him the essence of what he was experiencing as he began to fade. But sphinxlike, he resisted. "He didn't talk much when he was dying," she said afterward. "I kept wondering, Why can't he tell me what he's feeling? Then I realized that you don't do things at the end you do in your life."

Jane had left the hospital briefly on the morning of August 11, Shirlee later recalled, when Henry sat up in bed and stopped breathing. Summoned back, Jane arrived in such a rush that she did not put her car in park and a bystander had to jump in and put on the brake to keep it from rolling away.

For several days after Henry's death there was virtually an ongoing wake at the Bel Air house. Shirlee organized it, invited people and made them feel at home. Jane, who was sleeping in a spare room, walked around in a trance. Her primary identity for almost forty-five years had been that of daughter. It was as a daughter, loyal and caring, that she had distinguished herself in Henry's last months, and now she was left without that calling. As old friends circled through the house, Jane mechanically held meetings and made calls. She talked to Vanessa about the television coverage of Henry's passing, which reminded them both of the way the death of a president might be handled. Vanessa was confused: she couldn't be sure what she was sad about—the country's loss of a star or her own loss of a grandfather. Jane told her about the resentfulness she had often felt when she was young and saw her father treated like a national monument. Yet for Jane, if not for her daughter, there had finally been a perception of Henry as a real man, as well as a symbol, and a love that overlooked his limitations.

As the observance progressed—an observance that mourned the passing of a golden age of the American imagination as well as of a specific man—a few of those who had come to pay their respects became aware of a minidrama taking place behind the scenes. It involved Peter, who was trying to get something, anything—a favorite gun of his father's, some correspondence or personal memento out of his desk, a tangible relic. And Shirlee was saying no in a way that seemed to imply she might be acting in fidelity to an expressed wish of Henry's. At times the conflict would break through the decorous veil of mourning, with raised voices and sharply imploring words, as Peter assured her that he wasn't trying to rip her off and as Shirlee held her ground. One family friend said that "it seemed to go on and on."

Jane was the one who had engineered Henry's last days and possessed his death. Peter was present, but somehow outside the event, chronically unrequited, still complaining. He later noted that his close friend Warren Oates had mentioned him in his will in a touching way ("To Peter Fonda I leave nothing except for all my love") and that his own father had not given him even this. Feeling unloved all his life, he now felt at the age of forty-two that he had been orphaned.

"Every time my father would remarry," he said, "my new stepmother would tell me, 'You'll always have a room here.' Well, I'm still waiting for my room."

SEVENTEEN

On Election Night 1982, a few months after Henry's death, there was a victory celebration in the Santa Monica Hotel. A band was playing the soaring theme from *Chariots of Fire;* the glare from the lights made people squint at the television-news cameramen jostling for position. The size of the crowd and the press of media suggested that a candidate for governor or senator was about to claim victory. Indeed, the campaign just concluded had cost almost as much as one for high office, nearly $2 million of Jane Fonda's money, but the prize was only a seat in the state Assembly. Nonetheless, it marked a beginning for Tom Hayden. As he stepped to the platform, Jane smiling and waving at his side, there was a sense of transition. Trying to hush the crowd with a politician's calming hand gestures, he began to speak in the flat monotone that a generation of radicals had heard amplified by a bullhorn: "My victory marks the triumph of the politics of courage over the politics of fear."

It had been a tough race. Wherever he went during the campaign, Hayden had been shadowed by Vietnam veterans and Young Americans for Freedom. His Republican opponent had rented billboards all over the district and plastered them with the inflammatory statements ("We must abolish private property") Hayden had made in an earlier time. But in the end Hayden had prevailed because of a huge investment of money (it had been the most expensive state legislative race in U.S. history), because of his association with the Fonda glamour, and because of a clever campaign to overcome his large store of negatives.

The slogan on his campaign brochure was "Growing Up with America." The implication was that he and the country had gone through a troubled adolescence together and had now simultaneously become mature. For critics, however, his growing up had actually been a glossing over, and his radical past remained unassimilated. In this regard, his attention during the campaign had been focused with special intensity on the large bloc of Jewish voters in his district. Denying that they had ever supported the Palestine Liberation Organization, Tom and Jane had made a pilgrimage to Israel in 1980, when Tom was first considering running for office. They returned there soon after the invasion of Lebanon, which they said was inevitable because of PLO terrorism and the PLO's refusal to recognize Israel's right to exist. After her father's death, Jane returned once more to Israel to dedicate the Henry Fonda Memorial Forest outside Jerusalem.

The scramble for center ground continued unabated for two years. After the downing of Korean Air Flight 007, Hayden dumped Russian vodka at a rally in West Los Angeles. He said he was not opposed to the death penalty in all situations. While the new positions might have made him more palatable to the mass of voters, people who had followed his career noted that there was never an explanation of why exactly he had changed his old beliefs. And for his old leftist friends who had kept the faith, Hayden's new politics were simply contemptible. Said lawyer William Kunstler, who had helped defend him in the Chicago Seven trial, "I despise Tom for what he has become."

Some of Tom's own people, CED members, felt he had betrayed the outsider's crusade for the insider's ambition by running for the Assembly instead of continuing to organize around economic and environmental issues. He had a rationale for his decision: The sweeping election of Ronald Reagan in 1980 and the repudiation of liberals such as Edward Kennedy and Jerry Brown made it important for someone with his views to establish an electoral beachhead for the generation of the sixties. His old allies took this explanation with a grain of salt. One former CED member remarks, "Tom said it was important for the left to be elected. What he really meant was that it was important for *him* to be elected." Hayden himself inadvertently confirmed this interpretation in a somewhat grandiose statement after the vote was counted: "I wanted the democratic process to confirm my legitimacy."

It had confirmed even more his wife's dedication and single-minded drive. Lauren Weissman, her right-hand woman at IPC Films and a close friend, says: "Jane *made* it happen. I've never seen anyone give as much to another human being as she did to Tom. And I'm not talking just about money. It was time and influence too. She scheduled every piece of her day to help Tom. We shared an office and all I saw her do all day long was call her contacts and ask them to help. She made long lists and called [people] without embarrassment or shame. She was relentless. She was willing to do whatever was necessary to make the dream come true."

At the time of the 1982 election, everything seemed possible—a run for the House or even the Senate after a few years of legislative distinction; a national following as the first radical leader of the sixties to make a serious bid for power. In retrospect, however, the election would prove to be something quite different—the top of the Hayden–Fonda arc, and the beginning of their fall to earth.

The previous few years had been almost idyllic for Jane. As Lauren Weissman says, "I think it was the one moment in her life when she really felt whole." She believed she was part of a significant social movement that was making steady gains. The house on Wadsworth had become a sort of commune, with the people who shared Jane's dream coming by and sometimes staying over. There was a sense of élan, of belonging to an ideal family similar to the one Peter felt he had discovered in his Montana Bloomsbury.

But once she became the assemblyman's wife, intimate contact with the family of CED workers was no longer possible. The run-down house where they had lived for years had been fine for a pair of organizers, but it would not do for an elected official with ambitions for higher office. So Jane went shopping for a new house and found one for $2 million behind an electric gate in Santa Monica's best neighborhood. After redecorating the house in southwestern style, she arrived with some belongings in a rented U-Haul truck she drove herself—a final curtain call for Plain Jane.

There were some personal touches in the new home—a sideboard under the stairway crowded with so many photographs of Henry that it looked like a shrine; walls lined with Andy Warhol portraits of Jane. Yet it seemed a place where politics would be conducted. The bar in the living room was good for fund-raisers, and above it was a spacious balcony, perfect for speeches.

The mood of transition symbolized by the move to the new house was also apparent in Jane's professional life. She had been phenomenally successful over the past five years, as actress and especially as producer: IPC Films had made more than $500 million since *Coming Home*. (*On Golden Pond* had equaled the $100 million box-office gross of *9 to 5*). Success for a Fonda project now seemed almost automatic. It was only a question of what subject she and Bruce Gilbert chose to tackle.

The next film, they decided, would be either about a woman whose child dies of an environmentally caused cancer or about the depredations of multinational corporations. They decided on the latter because Hayden had read Paul Erdman's *The Crash of '79* and felt that the apocalyptic destructiveness of corporate greed was a concern whose time had come.

Film rights to the Erdman novel were not available, so Fonda and Gilbert, with help from Hayden, began to think up the story for what would become *Rollover*. Scriptwriter David Shaber, whom Gilbert brought in to shape the idea, thought from the beginning that the concept of a paralyzing economic crisis was inherently undramatic. But it was what they wanted, and there was no argu-ing. Jane pushed hard for the idea simply because it was Tom's. "In discussing the script," says Shaber, "She would throw around terms like 'corporate power' in a casual way. When she referred to the Trilateral Commission, this dreamy look would come over her face as if this organization had a shadowy shape in her mind. She really felt there was something terribly sinister there."

Gilbert decided it would help the movie if they did some field-work. They interviewed an investment banker in San Francisco and then flew to Washington to talk with staffers on the Senate Finance Committee. Finally, Gilbert got permission for them to look at the foreign trading room of Citibank in Manhattan. As Shaber recalls, "After we had wandered around for forty-five minutes, we came out and Bruce said, 'If there isn't a movie in that room, I'll eat this street.' They wanted a movie about corporate greed and the end of the world. It was a loser and somebody should have said no, but they were drunk with power. They'd made it work every time before. Why not now? There was no stopping them."

Almost as if subconsciously seeking failure, Jane, playing the part of a chairwoman of a board, did something she'd never done before: she based an aspect of her characterization on her mother (who had been, by her own definition, a businesswoman). Jane decided that her character's dressing room should be lined with gigantic mirrors, similar to the one she remembered Frances Fonda having. By summoning up the ghost of her mother, however, she was courting trouble for *Rollover*.

Tom wanted the heavies of the film to be the men in charge of American multinational corporations, men who in his thinking maliciously control the global economy. Gilbert, who was now feeling his oats as a Hollywood figure (one coworker says "he had become a radical in $200 pants and exactly the right loafers"), defied him by shaping the plot so that Arab businessmen were responsible for the global financial collapse dramatized in the movie. Jane was disturbed by this decision and even more upset when she learned that Gilbert, who had left his wife, had put his new girlfriend into a key role on the production team.

So when *Rollover* turned out to be a flop, there were massive recriminations. These meant the end of the "creative marriage" between Fonda and Gilbert which had lifted IPC Films to a commanding position in the industry. As Gilbert went his own way as a producer, Jane was left alone, bereft. "All my men betray me," she commented to a friend.

As Lauren Weissman says: "*Rollover* was just devastating. Prior to that, Jane felt she could have it all. She had set out to rehabilitate herself and done it. She had set out to create IPC Films and done it in a partnership with Bruce. She had set out to get her father an Oscar and done it. She had set out to help establish Tom a foothold in politics and done it. Then *Rollover* happened. For some reason there was a finality about it that prevented us from regarding it as just an isolated failure. She felt that it was symbolic, even if she wasn't sure what it symbolized."

Jane wouldn't make another movie for four years. Instead, she concentrated on expanding her exercise business. Her two workout studios in Los Angeles and the one she had established in San Francisco as the first step toward a national franchise were grossing some $2 million a year. *Jane Fonda's Workout Book* had sat atop the best-seller list for two years. The book sold some 2 million copies and earned more than $3 million in royalties. And in promoting *Workout,* Jane showed an almost flawless sense of professionalism, even when she went to France and appeared on the celebrated television show *Apostrophe,* one of the only Americans ever to be interviewed by host Bernard Pivot without an interpreter.

Initially Jane had resisted filming a video of her workout because she was afraid she would be seen as "a female Jack LaLanne" and her stature as a star would be injured. But the trauma of *Rollover* and the prospect of a financial windfall convinced her to take the chance. The video was an immediate success, selling more than 300,000 copies and proving that a cassette that was neither a film nor a filmed concert could be a best-seller.

Over the next two years, Jane kept turning out more books and tapes about fitness, including works directed at pregnant women and women on the edge of middle age. She had embedded herself in the middle-class consciousness in a way she could not have done through films alone. It was another of those pieces of "luck" Peter often remarked on: the fitness persona was an antidote to the lingering image of the radical.

Yet inside her expanding empire, employees accused Jane of hypocrisy. When one of her executives tried to get her consent for a raise for the clerical staff, for instance, Jane indignantly responded, "No secretary is worth more than $200 a week. That's tops." Even though Jane had recently completed *9 to 5* and was involved in an effort to spin off a television series from the film, the executive had to assemble data from the National Association of Secretaries to appeal the raise issue.

This was not an isolated instance. Some of the dancers on her exercise videos complained they had not been paid as performers. And women aerobics instructors in the San Francisco branch of the Workout charged Jane with sexism because she paid them less than she did male instructors. This eventually led to the closing of the branch and abandonment of plans to franchise the studio nationally.

Another failure came in 1984, when Jane started a line of what were supposed to be sexy workout ensembles. ("They show it off if you've got it," was the motto, "and hide it if you don't.") But the clothes were overpriced and the project failed abysmally, sending Capri, the small Long Island manufacturer Jane had chosen, into bankruptcy.

Jane had become more than a star. She was a one-woman conglomerate, a household word. But this megasuccess, which began to transform her from person into symbol, threatened exactly that sense of personal authenticity she had worked so hard to achieve. Moreover, it came at a time when she was still feeling the emotional aftershocks of Henry's death. ("All you have to do is mention the word 'dad' and I start to cry," she told one interviewer months after his passing.) Henry had been the one-man audience she had played to all her life. But his life had also been a cautionary tale about the consequences of emotional disconnectedness. As she continued to mourn him, Jane began to discover that in her own way, she was as disconnected as Henry.

She tried to organize the emotional relationships in her life the way she organized her work, by an act of will. But always there was a sense that she was acting out of conviction rather than feeling. She noted that Tom was geographically and emotionally distant from his widowed mother in Wisconsin, for example, and brought her to live with them and doggedly helped care for her until her death in 1985. "It was admirable," says a family friend, "but it was also very cerebral on Jane's part. She was talking about family in her political appearances, and this was an outgrowth of her political commitments at the moment."

But with her children the symbolic efforts didn't work. Tom was devoted to Troy, and flew home from Sacramento almost every night to see him. But his relationship with Vanessa, who resented his occasionally sarcastic comments about her mother's intelligence and fondness for a grand life-style, had moments of friction. Jane loved her daughter and wanted to be dependable for her in a way her own mother had not been. But she was also devoted to Hayden and this made for a conflict of interest. As a close friend and business partner says, "Jane always had the right idea. She *wanted* to do it right for Vanessa because of her poor relationship with her own mother, whom she referred to as 'a waste of time.' But her instinct for motherhood was often in conflict with her ambitions for Tom, which always won out."

"Well, she's *your* daughter," Hayden would tell Jane in moments of stress. Beneath the words was a veiled subtext: She is your daughter from a time before you were a serious person. Without always considering Vanessa's needs fully, Jane tried to bring the girl into line. A friend accompanying the family on the annual Christmas ski trip to Aspen observed a revealing moment between mother and daughter. Vanessa was not following the strict outline for the day's activities her mother had established. Jane tolerated her clowning around for a while, but then lost her patience and snapped at her, "Look, we're here to ski, not to have fun!"

Jane decided to deal with her daughter by trying to become her best pal and confidante. She would invite Vanessa's friends into the house and shower them with attention. "This was especially true of one black girl," says Lauren Weissman. "Jane was so pleased that her daughter had a black friend that she smothered her, and this of course alienated Vanessa from the girl."

Growing into young womanhood, Vanessa, who had the dark watchfulness of her father, was a rebel with a strong identity. Demanding and headstrong, she constantly talked about a career in show business and reproachfully told Jane that if she ever did become an actress, *she* would not have children.

She was resentful of the expectations that had been created for her. She was supposed to be the happiest camper at the Laurel Springs summer camp. When she arrived there after visiting her father in France, counselors would confiscate things Vadim had given her and make them communal possessions for all the children. Vanessa had to acquiesce wordlessly. It was also presumed that she would become involved in the Workout, which in fact she hated because it took so much of her mother's time. ("You couldn't drag Vanessa there with horses," says former instructor Paul Zotos.) And she was also supposed to be a model young progressive with politically correct opinions about Central America.

Feeling pressure to be a Fonda in her mother's mold, but not getting sufficient emotional backing, Vanessa became increasingly difficult. Jane worried that she might somehow have inherited a suicidal gene that skipped a generation from Frances, and sought advice from a doctor with the adolescent unit at UCLA's Neuropsychiatric Institute. Finally, she got Vanessa to seek early admission to college, and was pleased when she was accepted by Brown a year before her high school graduation. Vanessa's departure was emotional for Jane, but it removed a source of tension from the house.

While Vanessa was being brought up as another Fonda with large hungers and unmet expectations, Peter's daughter, Bridget, was spared some of this intensity. Because she lived with her mother after her parents' divorce, Bridget had grown up somewhat apart from the Fonda identity, even though she bore the famous name. A cool and confident young woman, she never had a problem being a Fonda daughter, or granddaughter or niece. As she said, "I always knew who I was. The question for me was who were *they?*"

In an echo of her father's experience as a boy seeing Henry menaced by lions in *Chad Hanna,* Bridget first really understood the power of film when she was seven and saw *The Hired Hand.* She grew bored and restless, and went to the theater lobby. After walking around awhile, she opened the doors to go back into the theater—at the moment her father was falling to the ground on screen, dying grotesquely from gunshot wounds.

Bridget also learned at an early age to take the company of movie stars for granted. Just as Peter had grown up with John Wayne and

Jimmy Stewart around, so Bridget had grown up assuming that there would be show-business figures such as Julie Christie and Dennis Hopper at her house. She had been with Hopper's family in New Mexico as part of the caravan traveling around America during the filming of *Easy Rider.* But she had not wanted to act until the end of high school, when she began appearing in school plays. Acting seemed a family business, even if no Fonda elder encouraged her to enter it.

She went to New York University, and studied acting at the Lee Strasberg Theatre Institute. She had the strong Fonda jaw and slate-blue eyes. Yet there was a distant, almost veiled beauty distinctively her own and a wary humor about the way her father and aunt had worn their hearts on their sleeves. Bridget determined not to do this; to play against what had become the Fonda grain. At one of their infrequent family gatherings, Jane had urged her to tighten her thighs by doing aerobics. Bridget later noted wryly that Jane had laughed hysterically at her reason for avoiding working out—"It sloshes my brain around"—thinking, incorrectly, that she was kidding.

Just before signing for her first screen appearance—in a dramatization of the *Liebestod* from *Tristan und Isolde* in the anthology film *Aria*—Bridget asked her father for advice about the business. Peter, in a quiet acknowledgment of his own fallen state, sent her to Bill Hayward.

While Jane's life was one of major milestones, each marked by a powerful man, Peter's life was a curve heading downward from *Easy Rider.* Friends and advisors had tried to get him to rehabilitate himself by accepting second or even third leads in good films, but while Peter would agree, he would not do it, letting them know when they pushed too hard that he was a Fonda and Fondas always got top billing. Bill Hayward tried to get him to recognize that he did not convey a swashbuckling presence and his strength was perhaps not in action roles but in psychological portrayals such as the one he'd done early in his career in *Lilith*. But Peter scorned what he saw as "Sensitive Sam" parts and insisted on being macho. And so he had once again entered the parallel universe of B movies.

He kept working, although work was not easy to find in American movies. He advertised motorcycles in Japan, where he was known as Peter Honda. He appeared in Japanese and German films. He made movies that most people saw first on the video rack.

Because of his reputation for being difficult, he often had to work hard even to get roles in mediocre films. His agent, Larry Kubik, had to pitch him several times to get him a role in *Split Image,* an unseen movie about cults. Even so, Peter proceeded to embroil himself in a conflict with the producer of the film, Jeff Young. In a showdown at his trailer, Peter had waved a loaded gun in Young's face, shouting, "The problem is that I'm a better writer than the writer on this film, a better director than the director, and a better producer than you!"

Friends and colleagues came to expect such outbursts because of Peter's continued investment in behaving like a sixties rebel. When he went into one of his tantrums on the set, someone would arrange to fly Becky in from Montana. She would calm him, and the film would be salvaged. As a friend of the couple said, "She spreads balm on Peter's wounds. She runs him, although she goes out of her way not to make it obvious."

He had become the butt of jokes. *The Village Voice* lampooned him cruelly in what it called "The Peter Fonda Workout": "Get up late. Smoke a joint. Call your sister. Beg for money." His hold on past grievances, all his life a defining characteristic, was beginning to slip. The gunshot scar that was his badge of honor had shrunk over the years and when he showed it to people now they could hardly see it.

Yet he was still filled with enthusiasm and big plans. Over the years he had managed a reconciliation with Dennis Hopper, and he believed he would be rediscovered, just as Hopper had been, and would someday earn the $2 million a film Hopper commanded. He reminisced with Hopper about the good old days when they had been so bad—as when they had carried LSD and marijuana into Europe for showings of *Easy Rider,* defying the law there as they had in America. He dwelled on the *Easy Rider* period as the time of his life. ("None of the Fonda films are remembered with such fervor," he said nostalgically. "None of my father's films and none of my sister's films.") He continued to put energy into a sequel to his epic of the counterculture. The script for which he had highest hopes was called "Biker Heaven." It would begin, he hoped, with Jack Nicholson in heaven watching news clips of the current American scene on television, becoming disgusted by the decadence and corruption, and coming down on a golden Harley to the place where Captain America and Billy had been killed. Then Nicholson would bring the heroes back to life from scraps of clothing and pieces of their motorcycle and they would hit the road again, searching for the American flag, which had been stolen from the people by "corporate types." Although Peter insisted that Nicholson was willing, he could not get backing for the project.

Peter's other major effort after Henry's death was trying to put together a film in which he would star with Jane. Working out of an office at Orion, he considered dozens of projects. One idea was a western; Jane would play Annie Oakley and he would play her younger brother, a famous bank robber who had become separated from her shortly after he was born. He optioned *Old Money,* a novel about a brother and sister who must deal with the crushing traditions they have inherited from their forebears.

Jane humored him. As Lauren Weissman said, "She wanted to help him out, but in the way a parent might help a child. She wants him to have the opportunities to develop in the ways she believes people develop."

PETER COLLIER

When asked about her brother, Jane would say that his career had flagged because he hadn't worked with top directors the way she had. Peter had another explanation: "Why aren't I offered good scripts like my sister? It's a male chauvinist industry. If all the heads of studios and producers were women, maybe I could have fucked my way to the top."

EIGHTEEN

If Jane had acquired enemies because of her political activities, she also had made friends along the way who retained deep and abiding ties to her. She tried hard to check her imperiousness. She was capable of impulsive acts of generosity, as when she subsidized the family of a woman friend whose daughter was stricken with childhood arthritis and required expensive medical care.

She had tried hard to give her life a specific gravity. Yet even those close to her wondered if any of her efforts were genuine. One woman friend compared Jane to a figure in Greek mythology, cursed by the very quality that gave her power: "She acts all the time. She doesn't want to but can't help herself. She conceals it pretty well, which I suppose is a tribute to exactly how good an actress she is. But you begin to notice after you've seen all the repeat performances. You recognize the Compassionate Friend who puts on the same long face, the same sympathetic eyes with a hint of tears welling up, the same heartfelt quaver in the voice. Then there's the 'I'm happy for you' Jane with the dazzling smile and twinkly eyes and the lilt in her voice."

On some level, Jane was aware of this lack of self, potentially a far more threatening problem than the stalling of her movie career after *Rollover* or the pressures involved with maintaining her business empire. Yet the knowledge that she was always acting did not torment her as much as it once had. The reason was Hayden. "It is great being married to Tom," she confided to Lauren Weissman, "because *no matter who I am,* he loves me." She said that Tom was her "reality."

And so she organized her life around Tom's political future, his next run for office. More than anyone else, she had been responsible for the creation of a new, political Hollywood in which a career was incomplete without a cause, and in which stars who were psychologically depleted by role-playing tried to discover their authenticity as people by grounding themselves in social movements. Now she tried to bend this new Hollywood to Tom's purpose by organizing the Brat Pack (or the Network, as they called it), a cadre of young Hollywood stars.

A starlet such as Ally Sheedy might find herself invited to an evening at Tom and Jane's with Bishop Desmond Tutu. She might be given an informal political catechism and afterward be asked to debut as a "political person" by hosting an evening for Hayden's ally California senator Alan Cranston. Soon she would be on her own, looking to Hayden and Fonda for political direction, a resource ready to be mobilized.

Yet these recruits sounded more like clones than political activists, people for whom politics was a fashion statement. "Jane's had more of an influence on me than anyone I can think of," said Sheedy. "If I can be anything like her, I'll have accomplished something." Actress Demi Moore agreed, saying of the Network: "It has expanded my knowledge of such issues as the protest against a new sewage plant in Malibu and the plight of black South Africans."

In the 1986 campaign, Sheedy, Rob Lowe, and other members of the Network traveled by bus up and down the state with Tom and Jane to campaign for an antitoxics ballot measure. It was the largest outpouring of celebrities since World War II — a juggernaut ready to back Hayden when the time was right.

While mobilizing stars and starlets, Jane was also associating herself with new causes that were more in keeping with the increasingly conservative mood of the eighties. She and Tom went to Poland and marched with Lech Walesa. She began a determined campaign in behalf of Ida Nudel, a Soviet refusenik whose plight she and Tom had heard about during their 1980 visit to Israel; Jane went to the USSR to meet Nudel and made a public plea for her release. She was on hand to greet Nudel when she was finally allowed to emigrate to Israel in 1985. Later Jane received an award from the American Jewish Committee. Such activities helped distance Jane and Tom even more from their past radicalism. Now they could appeal to the Jews who contributed big money to national Democratic candidates.

While Jane was fine-tuning her image, Tom was doing the same. He had played Little League baseball as a boy and now he made a publicized rediscovery of the sport. He went to Dodger games and attended Dodger fantasy camp in the spring. He got to know the team manager, Tom Lasorda, and began calling him "Uncle Tommy." He played for the Hollywood Stars, a team composed of people in the entertainment industry.

Hayden was a diligent legislator, putting in long hours and introducing a large number of bills. He fended off attempts by conservative colleagues to unseat him and was repeatedly reelected. He had always been a conspirator by nature, someone who did his best work behind the scenes, and gradually he gained respect as a Sacramento insider. But while this characteristic entrenched him in the Assembly, it did not win him the larger public following necessary for higher office. Evaluating his performance and prospects after several years in office, a friend said, "Tom's basic problem is that he can't be an up-front politician. He'll never look good on television, he doesn't work crowds well."

Hayden kept equivocating on the question of his next step because there seemed to be no other post he could win. Without forward momentum he was an ever more attractive target for attack. "You know, everyone used to knock me around for wanting to be a leader," he commented petulantly. "The Movement wasn't supposed to have leaders. But they never told the Vietnamese they couldn't have Ho Chi Minh, did they? Its about time we say it's okay to try to be one. Look, all I want is a chance, just a chance to make a little history."

But this chance seemed to be getting further away, not closer. His old friend and fellow radical Richard Flacks, who had helped Tom found SDS and who now taught at UC Santa Barbara, invited him to appear at a political science class. After listening to his speech to students, Flacks said, "He used to go into a room and turn kids on with his vision. . . . But this time he comes in and talks about the legislature regulating the conditions of people working on video terminals."

Somewhere along the line there was a split—between Jane's extravagant ambitions for Tom and his own more sober assessment; between her hopes and his sense of reality; between what was desirable and what was likely. Their closeness had always been based on shared vision rather than deep emotion. Once the vision fell out of focus, they began to lose contact. People who came to visit them at their new home got the impression that Tom and Jane were not sleeping in the same bedroom. Paul Zotos, an instructor at the Workout, says, "He'd make a big show of coming for the Christmas party. But otherwise you never saw them together. She took us out to dinner, and he wasn't there. We had a party, and she came alone. It suddenly dawned on me that she was sort of like one of the Kennedys. Everyone had this image of her, but basically she was kind of sad and lonely."

Speaking to writers, Jane continued to try to associate herself—and by implication, Hayden—with the moral values of middle

America, the America that had twice elected Ronald Reagan: "I'm not opposed to sex before marriage," she told a writer from *Ladies' Home Journal*. "Tom and I lived together for six months before the wedding. But I don't think a marriage can hold together if the partners are 'liberated' to the point of having other partners. Jealousy is a natural emotion, and when you deny feeling jealous in order to feel 'sexually liberated' I think you begin to form a callus over your heart. It would be hard to continue to live with the same openness and intimacy."

Yet as she was saying this, Tom was busy practicing sexual liberation himself. His actions were so blatant that some referred to Laurel Springs Ranch as his "stud farm." When people went there to hear some visiting intellectual or to participate in a seminar, they would find Jane taking notes with typical seriousness; Tom would be eyeing other women. On one occasion, when the political-education session had continued into the night, Jane, exhausted, began to nod off. Tom had been flirting so outrageously with Margot Kidder that everyone present, with the possible exception of his own wife, had noticed it. Tom looked at Jane and said curtly, "If you're tired, go to bed." After she had left, he continued his pursuit of Kidder, who later, according to a friend, said, "I know if I go to bed with him, Jane will know instantly."

While Jane was away filming the television movie *The Dollmaker,* a campaign aide to Hayden showed up at his house and found him inside with a pair of young women in bathrobes. All three, apparently, had just stepped out of the Japanese bath in the master bedroom. He says, "Tom didn't really bother to cover his tracks. We could never figure out if Jane knew and didn't care, or if she was just dumb."

From Lauren Weissman's perspective, Jane was far from dumb, although she often seemed willfully blind: "Sally Field and Jane and I were having a meeting trying to figure out a movie about a man who is husband to one woman and lover to another. We got to talking about what we would do in such a situation, and Jane said, 'If Tom ever had a lover, I would want to get very close to that woman. I would want to make that woman my best friend.' It was weird. I think she must have known he was screwing around with all these women and didn't want to admit it to herself."

By 1988 her relationship with Hayden had become a dark passage for Jane. "The marriage was over for a long time, but Jane didn't want to admit it," says Roger Vadim, a continuing observer of his former wife. "It was supposed to be the kind of marriage that leads to social good. For that reason, it went on and on."

Everything else in Jane's life seemed to be going sour too. Her recent film projects — *Agnes of God* and *The Morning After* — had not recaptured the momentum she lost with *Rollover*. She had met with Mexican novelist Carlos Fuentes and commissioned what became *The Old Gringo* for the new production company she formed after the dissolution of IPC Films. But the effort to turn Fuentes's book into a movie proved another disappointment. Attempts to get a script from the team of John Gregory Dunne and Joan Didion collapsed in acrimony. Burt Lancaster, scheduled to play a lead role, had to bow out and was replaced by Gregory Peck. Jane continued with the film, but she looked like someone just going through the motions.

In *Women Coming of Age,* the 1984 book she cowrote about the aging process, Jane had said, "In my mind, I've already laid the first brush strokes toward a picture of the woman I would wish myself to be in the twilight of my life. I see an old woman, walking briskly, out of doors, in every season. . . . Her face is lined and full of life. . . . Her husband often walks with her. They laugh a lot."

Yet now that she had passed her fiftieth birthday and was feeling even older than her years, she and Tom hardly ever saw each other, let alone laughed together. Friends said Hayden's drinking contributed to their marital problems, a claim he denied. Whatever the case, he was flippant when asked about the marriage. If he and Jane spent an evening together, Tom cracked, it was because their respective schedulers had made a mistake.

They had always had a great goal that brought them together— winning the war for Hanoi, electing Tom to high political office. But now this goal was blocked. Hayden felt that he was a man of history, yet after all of the revisionist versions of his past had been proposed and all of the money raised and spent, he still found himself mired in the state legislature.

Tom talked about how sick he was of being seen as "Mr. Jane Fonda"; how sick he was of her "Hollywood life-style." What had before been conveniences—the way she negotiated a clause in movie contracts so that producers had to have a Learjet available to bring him from Sacramento to her set—now seemed symbols of his predicament. What before had been signs of affection—the way she rushed out to buy him an elaborate boat for bass fishing when he mentioned that he liked the sport—now seemed an attempt to control him with possessions.

Hayden was also sick of the "Beauty and the Beast" jokes. One of his associates recalls accompanying the Haydens to lunch at a restaurant on La Cienega Boulevard to get a campaign contribution from the chairman of a southern California savings and loan. After listening to Jane's pitch, the businessman said he would donate $1,000, and added in what was supposed to be a funny aside, "But tell me, how come a sharp and attractive woman like you is married to this ugly son of a bitch?" Tom sat there biting his lip and trying to smile as his face colored.

One friend said, "Tom took it out on Jane by being cruel to her, taunting her about how beautiful other actresses they knew were; how good they looked. She told me that once when they were in bed he started talking about Jessica Lange, how firm and well toned she was." Demoralized by this, as well as by the shattering experience of a series of bad films, Jane tried to make herself better. After binge-ing on peanut butter and jelly sandwiches and ribs, she would check in at a southern California clinic and take weight off with ten-mile hikes and five-hundred-calorie days. For years she had advised women to "make friends" with their wrinkles. Now she had plastic surgery to get rid of hers.

In late 1988 she had breast implants. At first she tried to make people believe her new bustline was the result of weight training. But those close to her didn't buy it. An employee at the Workout says, "One morning we were up at the Santa Barbara ranch for our semiannual meeting and Jane shows up with these gigantic tits. She has on this little T-shirt and we're all saying, 'Do you see what I see? Are they for real?' It was dumb. She's in great shape, stronger than most people, and very shapely. She didn't need the make-believe boobs. She was getting hysterical over the marriage and everything."

Another friend saw her at a power lunch and was amazed: "She was in one of those dresses that cuts right above the nipples and she had these breasts sticking out. She was *sporting* them. She looked like an aged Barbarella."

Around this time Brooke Hayward got a call from her old friend. Jane asked how she felt, and when Hayward said great, Jane said incredulously, "How can that be? You're fifty-two years old. I'm feeling very different from great." Then she added, "But then I'm an actress and actresses have to be eternally young."

But hers was a crisis that was more than skin deep. "Jane said she was afraid she was losing Tom," says Lauren Weissman. "Actually she felt she was losing herself. She managed to keep this feeling at bay with all the frantic activity. For the last few years, she'd believed that the sum of all the causes she'd adopted would make a person. But with the relationship with Tom beginning to come apart, she saw this wasn't true."

Researching his memoir, *Reunion,* in 1987, Tom traveled across

America on a sentimental journey that recapitulated his rise to prominence as a leader in the Movement. One of the stops along the way allowed him to renew acquaintance with his first wife, Casey, who had been involved with him in the glory days of the civil rights movement. Told about this reunion, Jane reacted warily: "I know her, so I felt okay, although you know when he calls me and says they've checked into a motel together and says they've asked for separate rooms, part of me is saying, 'Yeah, sure.'"

According to what Peter told a friend, Jane eventually hired private eyes to check out Tom's women. Most were short-term affairs. Jane could live with that. But then came Vicky Rideout, an issues expert for the Michael Dukakis presidential campaign. Rideout had met Hayden when the Massachusetts governor made his forays through California. She was thirty-three, a five-foot-five blonde chain-smoker with a cum laude degree from Harvard. Tom did not treat her as another one-night stand.

During their Christmas vacation in Aspen in 1988, Jane told Tom to give up the other woman. Tom was unwilling to abide by the ultimatum. In February he got into his used Volvo station wagon and left the extravagant new house he claimed he had never liked, and took up residence in a modest Westwood apartment. Camera crews from A Current Affair blockaded the Santa Monica home, and helicopters hovered overhead. As one person said, "It was like Madonna's wedding or the death of Rock Hudson. That's what the great quest of Jane Fonda's life came down to—another Hollywood publicity ritual."

After the breakup, Jane initially resisted dividing her property with Hayden. Finally, to avoid a potentially nasty legal squabble, she agreed to give him an estimated $3 million, plus an annual allowance of $200,000. This out of the way, she then began to talk about what to do with what she called "the last third of my life." She discussed future movie projects such as a film about Czech president Václav Havel and an adaptation of Neil Sheehan's award-winning book about Vietnam, *A Bright Shining Lie*. But her career seemed to be waning, especially after the failure of *The Old Gringo* and *Stanley and Iris*.

In another context and a happier time, Hayden had inadvertently put his finger on her problem as an actress: "She's never going to play anything but Jane Fonda in a film. I'm convinced that this is all she is now. She's a more important character than any she'll ever play." And Brooke Hayward had passed this judgment of Jane as a filmmaker: "Thirty years ago, Jane and I used to sit around and complain about the dinosaurs of the industry who died and left no mark. She's like them. She will have been the richest and most powerful woman in Hollywood and have done nothing to improve movies. You remember nothing about the films she made except the way she looked."

But movies were not uppermost in Jane's mind after the split from Hayden. Her first instinct was to slough off another old skin and emerge anew once more. This attempt at a smooth midlife transit was accompanied by a media blitz, as if she were promoting a new film or a new cause. "I've reinvented myself again," she told one of the many journalists she spoke to in the months after the separation. But the question was, As what?

One role she tried was that of the jilted woman, sadder but wiser. When an interviewer asked her what, specifically, she had done to deal with the pain of divorce, Jane said, "I read Rilke—*Letters to a Young Poet*. I listened to Beethoven. I chose my friends very carefully. . . . It was as if each of these things were a stepping stone to healing and when I was healed I was much stronger than before the crisis."

Another part Jane considered was that of the woman who becomes resensitized to relationships as a result of emotional turbulence. She claimed that one of the benefits of the breakup was that she had drawn closer to Vanessa. "I didn't realize how wise she was," Jane said. "It was an interesting role reversal in which the kid became the parent."

In fact, however, Vanessa did not seem to be in a position to help herself, let alone her mother. A confused young woman who had been pushed into causes by her mother and Tom, but without ever really understanding their sense of mission, Vanessa had been disoriented by Jane's sporadic mothering. Observers felt that Vanessa had been glad about the split from Hayden. They believed Vanessa felt that Hayden had subtly abused her mother. Nonetheless, the end of the marriage caused a metaphysical lurch for Vanessa and seemed to increase her own sense of alienation. Vanessa's troubles worsened when she managed to make headlines of her own. Having come from Brown in Rhode Island to attend the New York premiere of *The Old Gringo,* Vanessa was arrested in a seedy New York hotel with her twenty-two-year-old boyfriend, who was allegedly trying to buy heroin. She was not charged in the incident and Jane immediately jumped to her defense, but the gap between the two women seemed to be growing.

Jane also tried the role of the mature woman who could now fulfill the quest for selfhood that had been subordinated for years by a selfish and unappreciative husband. The tabloids ran photographs of her sporting in a Mediterranean hideaway with a thirty-five-year-old Italian soccer player, Lorenzo Caccialanza. Later she began to be seen with a power consort, Ted Turner, who had read about the breakup of her marriage and said to an assistant, "Now there's a woman I'd like to go out with." The first time Turner called her, Jane told him she was still too bruised emotionally to go out with him. The second time he called, she said she was feeling better. Her employees, who sometimes referred to her as the "Queen of Hollywood" behind her back, joked about the possibility of a royal union between Jane and the King of Cable.

Jane understood that whatever role she played in the future, she had to maintain at least a rough linkage with the past. And so she gave interviews in which she looked back nostalgically to that moment in 1970 when she had set out to discover America and herself. With a kind of wonderment she said, "I was already thirty-two years old and I started over." She pointed out that she had been a "political person" before she met Hayden and would continue to be political now that he was out of the picture. But the concept "political" had become more ceremonial than activist: supporting the environment; supporting the countries of Eastern Europe disengaging themselves from communism. Privately, Jane even disparaged her own radical past. A person who sat near Jane and Ted Turner at a private dinner party in New York heard Turner ask Fonda about her Hanoi Jane period. Jane held him for a moment with her dazzling eyes and then smiled slyly: "You don't think I really meant all that, do you?"

Only Peter saw the real Jane. As the marriage with Hayden was unraveling, she had called him, and Peter, ever the loyalist, had come running. He was hurt that she didn't respect him more, and he sometimes referred to her as "Sister Dearest." Yet his romantic streak made him protective of her. Years earlier, he had gotten into trouble at the Denver airport when he took out a knife and defaced a sign reading "Feed Jane Fonda to the Whales." When he was arrested by airport security for disturbing the peace and damaging private property, he said, "She's my sister, and in my neck of the woods you don't get away with saying anything bad about someone's mother, grandmother, or sister." Now he talked in his hyperbolic way about what a pleasure it would be to put a bullet in the back of Hayden's head.

Peter tried to be perfect for Jane. He had tried to be perfect for his father too, but with Henry the irritant of his unhappy childhood had rubbed their relationship raw. With Jane, almost a maternal presence throughout his life, there was no such problem, and Peter, a stable figure in a crisis, was her constant comfort during the first painful weeks after the breakup. He took her to his Montana ranch, where they went fly-fishing and hiking, and returned with her to southern California. She said that she needed a man and that he was the only man she could trust. Sometimes she would have her secretary call around to acquaintances at two or three in the morning to find out where Peter was, because she was so lonely. Jane asked him to enter therapy with her and he reluctantly agreed. Once again, she raised the prospect of their appearing in a movie together.

Over the years, they had remade the Fonda family in their own image. But they had also exhausted the mystery in the name and made it a problem as well as an asset for those who followed them. Just as Jane's children had wrestled with their mother's celebrity, Peter's offspring had trouble with the Fonda heritage. Justin was studying acting in anonymity, avoiding any public showcase. Bridget, who was achieving a name for herself in movies including *Scandal* and *The Godfather, Part III,* said flatly that she could never be like her father or her aunt. Insisting that she wanted only to be an actress, she took her grandfather, the man Jane and Peter had struggled against all their life, as her inspiration: "My dad and Jane are very out there, very intense. What drives them is very different from what I saw in Henry. He was cool. He didn't show a lot of things, and that's the way I am."

In a way, this comment was a measure of the whole Fonda saga: a Hollywood story no matter how much Henry and his children had tried to transcend the land of tinsel and glitter. It began with a quiet midwesterner who stumbled into the Dream Machine at a golden time when legends were being made, who gained movie immortality because people looked at him and saw the face of America. Through no effort of his own, Henry struck a chord in moviegoers, and that was what Hollywood was about.

His son, graced with hints of the Fonda presence, and with an opportunity to equal Henry's achievements, could not subdue his abrasive, needful nature. Success was elusive for Peter. As the character he played in *Easy Rider* says, he blew it.

Henry's daughter fared better, managing to become one of Hollywood's most powerful symbols in the pivotal era when the Dream Machine turned into the Deal Machine. But while she might be the Queen of Hollywood, Jane yearned for authenticity as a person. The real object of her quest seemed continually to slip through her fingers.

It is fitting that at the end of the story, as at the beginning, there were just Jane and Peter, alone together. The backdrop against which they played out their lives, the suicide of their mother, was an act of rejection from which they never recovered. So consumed by her own troubled soul that she could not acknowledge her children's needs, Frances had begun an unending circle of narcissism in which they were still trapped as adults. They had made families of their own and implicated them in their crises, yet Peter and Jane had never escaped membership in the primal family dominated by a mother too frail to make it and a father bigger than the life he gave them. And after thirty years of headlines, they remained orphans of the storm, still living in a world made up of only two estates—victims and survivors.

"Jane and I are like army buddies," Peter told people. "When we meet we say, 'Here we are again. My God, what we have gone through together!'"

AUTHOR'S NOTE

Early in 1970, when I was an editor of the New Left magazine *Ramparts*, I got a call from Jane Fonda. She said she had read and been moved by a piece of mine about Indian affairs. She said further that she was ending her long European exile with Roger Vadim and had come home to the United States hoping to "get involved." Would I take her to Alcatraz Island and introduce her to some of the dissident Indians who were staging an occupation there? Naturally, I said yes.

She arrived in San Francisco on a foggy morning a few days later, fresh-faced and self-confident, taller than I had expected, her hair cut in a boyish shag. As we stood on the wharf waiting for a boat to take us to Alcatraz, Jane stared out at the old maximum-security prison floating ominously in the bay. She said she felt she had been away from America too long; she was glad to be back home where it was "happening." I joked that perhaps she had waited too long: the sixties, after all, were over. A look of apprehension crossed her face and she said, "Oh, I hope not!"

We made small talk as we sailed out to the island and the slogans the Indians had painted on the rock cliffs came into focus. Jane discussed her unsatisfactory recent trip to India, where she had found only grinding poverty instead of the spiritual enlightenment she had expected. She talked about the Black Panthers and antiwar activists with whom she had become acquainted in the last few weeks as if they were as exotic as the tribes she was about to meet.

As we landed, she scrambled up the dock and began introducing herself. The older Indians looked at her curiously. It occurred to me that they might be among the few groups in America who didn't know who Jane Fonda was. But she made immediate contact with the young people, especially the Sioux whom she quickly and correctly identified as the radical core of the Alcatraz occupation. When I left the island later that day, she was off in their corner of the old prison exercise yard smoking dope and listening to their stories.

In the next couple of weeks, I talked to her a couple of times on the phone, helping plan the itinerary of her cross-country trip to discover radical America. A few days after she had left on her odyssey, I got a letter from Winnemucca, Nevada. "My head has been turned 90 degrees," she wrote in a backhand scrawl. She said the next time we ran into each other she was sure she'd have some stories to tell.

That next time never came, as Jane quickly became enveloped in a radical apotheosis of her own design. Over the next few years, as she became a radical icon, I continued to watch her progress out of the corner of my eye.

During this time, I was working with David Horowitz on a series of biographies of families of wealth and power. In writing these books, we were interested in how generational linkages were forged and broken, how individuals raised with certain expectations cope with their history and heritage. Because of my brief contact with Jane years earlier, the Fonda family remained in the back of my mind. I took note of their feuding and reconciliation, of the way they dramatized their discontents in the public arena. The Fondas were interesting not only because of this fractiousness and the spectacle of Jane's ongoing self-creation, but also because of the tragedy that seemed to haunt them and the nagging sense of incompletion that appeared to alloy all of their achievements. It occurred to me that in their own way the Fondas were as archetypally American as the Rockefellers, Kennedys, or Fords, and that it would be interesting to write about them someday.

I could not have done so, however, without the efforts of David Horowitz, my longtime friend and collaborator. He did most of the dozens of interviews that form the spine of the research for this book, and in terms of authorship he should be regarded as my silent partner.

I am indebted to Phyllis Grann and Karen Mayer of Putnam's, and especially to Andrea Chambers for her good eye and steady hand during the editing of the manuscript. I also thank Dolores McMullan for her help with the photo research, and Jim Denton of the National Forum Foundation, who provided support, possibly without knowing it, for this project. And of course I send my love to Mary Jo, Andrew, Caitlin, and Nicholas, who are clearly the best of the Colliers.

NOTES

‖‖‖‖‖‖‖‖‖‖‖‖‖‖‖‖‖‖‖‖‖‖‖‖‖‖‖‖‖‖‖‖‖‖‖‖‖‖‖

Greenwich, 1950

Page

11 "She had a strange look": Interview with J. Watson Webb.

11 "I hate the East": Henry Fonda, as told to Howard Teichmann, *Fonda: My Life* (New York, 1982, paperback), p. 198. (This book will be referred to as "Teichmann" in succeeding notes.)

12 "Hank doesn't satisfy": Fred Lawrence Guiles, *Jane Fonda—The Actress in Her Time* (New York, 1982), p. 32.

12 "I can't fight this": Interview with J. Watson Webb.

13 "Just look at me!": Guiles, p. 34.

13 Jane watching Frances: Jane later told Vadim, "I was upstairs with Peter, whom I didn't allow to leave the room. For an entire hour, I heard my mother calling us, but I didn't budge. Finally, one of the nurses told my mother it was time to go back. 'Oh, no,' my mother said. 'Not yet. I must talk to her.' And she cried out my name again. I left my hiding place and watched out the window as the car made a U turn and disappeared." Roger Vadim, *Bardot, Deneuve, Fonda* (New York, 1986), pp. 272–273.

14 "At least I can go potty": Interview with J. Watson Webb, one of Frances Fonda's closest friends. He helped reconstruct the events leading up to her death.

14 "Mrs. Grey": James Brough, *The Fabulous Fondas* (New York, 1973), p. 124.

One

20 "Oh, God": Teichmann, p. 100.

23 "Fathers are men": Brough, p. 6.

23 Henry at the bordello: Teichmann, p. 30.

24 "It comes once in a lifetime": Charlotte Chandler, *The Ultimate Seduction* (Garden City, NY, 1984), p. 249.

24 Lynching of the black man: Henry Fonda interview, *Playboy,* December 1981, p. 98.

25 "Henry is a man reaching": "The Flying Fondas and How They Grew," *Time,* February 16, 1970, p. 59.

26 "Absolutely not!": Teichmann, p. 31.

27 Henry not talking to his father: Later Henry said of this period: "I rarely saw anybody in my own family. And when I did see my father, it was a tense situation between us, and we didn't speak. He had been overruled and I was living in his home and not doing what he wanted me to." Mike Steen, *Hollywood Speaks: An Oral History* (New York, 1974), p. 18.

27 "There was one scene": John Springer, *The Fondas: The Films and Careers of Henry, Jane and Peter Fonda* (New York, 1970), p. 27.

28 "Sir, I've come to give notice": Teichmann, p. 36.

28 "Please, God": Henry Fonda interview, *Playboy,* p. 100.

28 "I've told my mother": Teichmann, p. 38.

29 The University Players: For a detailed history of this group, see Norris Houghton, *But Not Forgotten* (New York, 1951).

29 Henry's "Elmer" character: Ibid., p. 58.

30 "The fight, to female inexperience": Ibid., p. 68.

30 "He wiped us all off the floor": Joshua Logan, *Josh: My Up and Down In and Out Life* (New York, 1976), p. 216.

30 "Henry was very flattered": Interview with Delos Smith.

31 "It took every penny": George Stevens, "Why I Will Not Marry Maggie Sullavan Again," *Photoplay,* May 1936, p. 103.

31 "I was perfectly capable": Ibid.

31 "By the time I'm thirty-five": Brough, p. 37.

32 "You would have thought": Brooke Hayward, *Haywire* (New York, 1977), p. 185.

33 "What do you mean, hired?": Ibid., p. 189.

33 "I don't suppose": Teichmann, p. 59.

34 Henry's fall: Interview with Cesar Romero.

34 "The two of them fought": Houghton, p. 161.

34 "What! Marry Fonda?": Ibid., p. 255.

35 Harris's affair with Sullavan: Teichmann, p. 69.

36 "His first marriage": Merv Griffin, *From Where I Sit* (New York, 1982), p. 75.

36 "Don't despair": Chandler, p. 231.

37 "It won't cost you": Hayward, p. 135.

38 "No sense in using": Teichmann, p. 104.

38 "Eventually this thing": Don Shay, *Conversations* (Albuquerque, NM, 1969), n.p. This document is in the Library of the Academy of Motion Picture Arts and Sciences, Los Angeles.

39 "Dad, that's what'll happen": Henry Fonda interview, *Playboy*, p. 107.

Two

42 The Sinclair campaign: See Neal Gabler, *An Empire of Their Own* (New York, 1989, paperback) pp. 311ff; also Upton Sinclair, *The Autobiography of Upton Sinclair* (New York, 1962).

43 "Nothing is unfair": Gabler, p. 315.

43 "If Katharine Hepburn and I": Sara Hamilton, "The Stormy Heart of Margaret Sullavan," *Photoplay*, June 1936, p. 118.

44 "I thought these two guys": Interview with Henry Jaglom, to whom Welles made this remark.

44 "Anybody that would stick": Teichmann, p. 111.

44 Li'l Abner modeled on Fonda: David Shipman, *The Great Movie Story* (New York, 1970), p. 203.

45 Sullavan and Wyler: Axel Madsen, *William Wyler* (New York, 1973), p. 110.

45 "Hello, Peggy": Teichmann, p. 112.

45 "They approached each other": Hamilton, "Stormy Heart," p. 118.

47 "George, don't you think": Guiles, p. 4.

48 "Frances came on the set": Interview with J. Watson Webb, to whom Annabella made this comment.

48 "When a woman wants a man": Guiles, p. 4.

48 "Arriving New York soon": Interview with J. Watson Webb, whom Frances told about the telegram.

48 Henry and Frances's wedding: Jack Smalley, "Henry Fonda's New Love Story," *Photoplay*, December 1936, p. 72.

49 "The Maggie Sullavan Club": Madsen, p. 163.

50 "Jane came this close": Interview with Michael Parks.

50 "He was as warm": Teichmann, p. 128.

50 "There was a group": Interview with J. Watson Webb.

51 "They used to tell me": Chandler, p. 232.

51 "I think it's absolutely beautiful": Shay, n.p.

51 "What's all this shit": Steen, p. 40.

51 "Nature gave him": Springer, p. 93.

52 "I know he's": Leonard Mosley, *Zanuck* (New York, 1984), p. 182.

53 "a narrow bastard": Interview with J. Watson Webb, to whom Fonda made this comment.

53 "I hear from Leland": Teichmann, p. 136.

54 "Times pass": Springer, p. 24.

54 Kidnapping rumor and FBI: Henry Fonda FBI file, obtained by the author under provisions of the Freedom of Information Act.

55 "Hank is in fine form!": Frances Fonda to J. Watson Webb, n.d.

56 "He wants": Stevens, "Why I Will Not," p. 38.

Three

58 "She loved the stock market": Interview with J. Watson Webb.

58 "You can come out now": Springer, p. 20.

61 "Say, are you Henry Fonda's twin?": Interview with Rupert Allen.

61 "The School graduates": Henry Fonda to J. Watson Webb, n.d.

62 "Probably something like sweetheart roses": Henry Fonda to J. Watson Webb, August 31, 1944.

62 "I am living": Teichmann, p. 163.

63 Island-hopping operation: James Poliny, "Mr. Roberts Is a Banker Now," *Collier's*, December 15, 1951.

64 "Chad?": Teichmann, p. 173.

65 Playhouse parties: Interview with Eve Johnson.

65 "Maria has the face": Interview with Rocky Cooper.

66 "She was very un-Hollywood": Interview with Jack Hathaway.

66 "She could talk": Guiles, p. 5.

66 "Frances seemed lonely": Interview with confidential source.

66 "always in another room": Interview with Bill Hayward.

67 Jane crying at birthday parties: Lillian Ross, *The Player* (New York, 1962), pp. 93ff.

67 "quick to laugh": Interview with Ned Wynn.

67 "Whenever she wanted": Interview with Eve Johnson.

67 High jinks at Tigertail: Interviews with Maria Cooper and Sue Sally Hale.

68 "Jane ruled": Interview with Eve Johnson.

68 Pedro and Pancho episode: Ron Rosenbaum, "Dangerous Jane," *Vanity Fair,* November 1988, p. 144.

68 "Jane pretended": Interview with Ned Wynn.

68 "I was shy": "Flying Fondas," p. 59.

69 "She was finely tuned": Interview with Eve Johnson.

70 "George wouldn't have wanted": Interview with J. Watson Webb, Jr.

70 "Now listen": Interview with Eve Johnson.

70 "He used to go": Interview with Rocky Cooper.

71 "Through his quiet": Springer, p. 134.

71 "We were all afraid": Interview with Brooke Hayward.

72 "Hank, I'm really sorry": Logan, p. 259.

72 "When I act": Stephen Farber and Marc Green, *Hollywood Dynasties* (New York, 1984), p. 143.

Four

75 The Fondas and the Haywards in Greenwich: Interview with Brooke Hayward.

76 "My name is Jane": Thomas Kiernan, *Jane: An Intimate Biography of Jane Fonda* (New York, 1973), p. 42.

76 "Peter was gifted": Interview with Brooke Hayward.

76 Selznick's yacht in Greenwich: Peter Fonda interview, *Playboy,* September 1970, p. 100.

77 Henry at the table: Interview with Bill Hayward.

77 "I imagined": Phyllis Batelle, "The Unknown Jane Fonda," *Ladies' Home Journal,* October 1985.

78 "The children were aware": Interview with Brooke Hayward.

78 Henry banging his head: Interview with Rocky Cooper.

78 "Even when I was with my father": David Levine, "Fonda, Fonda, Fonda," *US,* March 30, 1982.

79 "he was being told": Interview with Bill Hayward.

80 "Frances, I want a divorce": Teichmann, p. 210.

80 "If anyone mentions": Ibid., p. 211.

81 "If I had been living": Interview with Brooke Hayward.

81 "I was just curious": Guiles, p. 33.

82 "This is the best way": Brough, p. 124.

82 "How weird": Teichmann, p. 219.

83 "A guy's got to keep going": Kiernan, p. 47.

83 "When he was out there": Interview with Eli Wallach.

83 "If only I had been": Michael Freedland, *Jane Fonda* (New York, 1988), p. 15.

83 "They say suicidal persons": Interview with Rocky Cooper.

84 "It was dramatic": Teichmann, p. 225.

84 "I didn't like her": Ibid., p. 202.

84 "It probably had very profound": Batelle, "Unknown," p. 74.

85 "Your mother was crazy": Michael Leahy, "My Family Hid the Truth from Me," *TV Guide,* October 28, 1984.

85 Peter shooting himself: The incident is discussed in detail by Peter in an interview in *Playboy,* September 1970, pp. 97–98.

Five

88 "It is not that you": *Letters of Scott Fitzgerald,* ed. Andrew Turnbull (New York, 1963), pp. 64–65.

89 "I never heard": Farber and Green, p. 148.

89 Henry signing of *Variety* ad: Henry Fonda FBI file.

89 Henry "graylisted": Interview with Richard Schickel.

90 "Stop crying": Teichmann, p. 258.

90 Henry and Wyeth: Chandler, p. 247.

91 "Love, Mom": Teichmann, p. 239.

91 Peter and .22 rifle: Interview with Bill Hayward.

91 "Jane's main thrust": Interview with Brooke Hayward.

92 "I know the *line*": Farber and Green, p. 150.

92 "There is a deep, deep sadness": Kiernan, p. 71.

93 "at one time or another": Ibid.

93 Jane's eating disorders: Jane Fonda, *Jane Fonda's Workout Book* (New York, 1981), pp. 14ff.

94 "She began to show up": Interview with Brooke Hayward.

94 Jane and Brooke Hayward in Hollywood: Ibid.

95 "Jane was a beach wonder": Interview with Jack Hathaway.

95 "Why should I look": For an account of the confrontation between Fonda and Ford, see Josh Logan, *Movie Stars and Real People* (New York, 1978), pp. 238ff.

97 "You understand": Brough, p. 147.

97 "All the marriages": Kiernan, p. 71.

98 Peter's sexual initiation: Rex Reed, "Holden Caulfield at 27," *Esquire,* February 1968, p. 73.

98 "presented as perfect": Peter Fonda interview, *Playboy,* p. 96.

98 "I've known that": Teichmann, p. 259.

99 Jane describing the pleasure of sex: Interview with confidential source.

99 Henry's fling with Ekberg: Afdera Fonda, *Never Before Noon* (New York, 1986), p. 8.

99 "It would have been all right": Afdera Fonda, p. 7.

102 "How'd I do?": Kiernan, p. 59.

102 "While Daddy was onstage": Harrison Kinney, "*McCall's* Visits Henry Fonda," *McCall's,* September 1956.

103 "It was one hour out": Interview with Anthony Perkins.

103 "You're no good": Teichmann, p. 271.

103 "I see that": Afdera Fonda, p. 50.

104 "Oh, wow!": Reed, "Holden Caulfield," p. 71.

105 "She was mad": Interview with Rupert Allen.

105 "For dinner they had": Kiernan, p. 82.

106 "I think he was": Afdera Fonda, p. 56.

107 "the Anything-Goes Girl": Freedland, p. 30.

107 "She had a reputation": Kiernan, p. 72.

107 "She was going out": Interview with Michael Thomas.

107 AWOL weekend: "Flying Fondas," February 16, 1970, p. 60.

108 "Get your ass out of here!": William Gibson, *The Seesaw Log: A Chronicle of the Stage Production* (New York, 1959), p. 283.

109 "How does it feel": Afdera Fonda, p. 71.

109 "There was such panic": "Flying Fondas," p. 60.

Six

113 "I'd known her": Interview with Brooke Hayward.

114 Actors Studio: For a summary of Strasberg's career and the development of the Method, see Cindy Adams, *Lee Strasberg: The Imperfect Genius of Actors Studio* (New York, 1980).

115 "If she'd been Jane Doe": Interview with Thomas Kiernan, who studied at Actors Studio at the same time Jane did.

115 "Before . . . I was one person": Kiernan, p. 95.

116 "Most of us": S. J. Wolf, "Henry Fonda Gives a Recipe for a Hit," *The New York Times Magazine,* April 20, 1948, p. 20.

116 "going underwater": Interview with George Peppard.

NOTES

117 "What have you ever done": Rex Reed, "Everybody Expected Me to Fall on My Face," *The New York Times,* January 25, 1970, p. D22.

117 "I was into Salinger": Interview with Henry Jaglom.

118 "She was there to be seduced": Interview with Robert Lawson.

118 "Jane was so insecure": Kiernan, p. 115.

118 "And of course Henry's disapproval": Interview with Alexander Whitelaw.

119 "You've *got* to drive me": Ibid.

119 "When I marry": Kiernan, p. 101.

119 Jane's makeover, and suggestions: Jane discusses the attempt to alter her physically in *Workout,* p. 17.

119 "I think it is getting," and the account of the end of the relationship: Interview with Alexander Whitelaw.

120 "In a way": Interview with Anthony Perkins.

121 Peter at Bill's wedding: Hayward, pp. 44–45.

124 "You know, Hank": Teichmann, p. 293.

124 Peter's $150 loan: Peter Fonda interview, *Playboy,* p. 100.

Seven

127 "I have a hunch": Martin Kasindorf, "Fonda: A Person of Many Parts," *The New York Times Magazine,* February 3, 1974, p. 16.

127 "Even if": Interview with confidential source.

127 Jane's introduction to Everett: Interview with Anthony Perkins.

128 "We talked for a while": Kiernan, p. 117.

128 "Timmy was a troubled guy": Interview with Anthony Perkins.

129 Jane naked on the street: Vadim, p. 212.

129 "You're afraid": Brough, p. 185.

129 "What have you done": Kiernan, p. 122.

129 Henry and Avedon photograph: Interview with Peter Basch.

130 "I am still fighting": Guiles, p. 82.

130 "she went from extremely loose": Interview with Brooke Hayward.

131 "Andreas was the guy": Interview with Dan Petrie.

131 "We'd be lying around": Kiernan, p. 129.

132 Voutsinas's ankle-wrapping: Shelley Winters, *Shelley II* (New York, 1989), p. 469.

132 Jane's opinions on Henry and Peter: Vincent Canby, "The Fondas," *Los Angeles Times,* July 1, 1962.

133 "Daughter?": "Flying Fondas," p. 62.

312

134 "Under his tutelage": John Houseman, *Final Dress Rehearsal* (New York, 1983), p. 227.

134 Jane's "slave-girl mentality": Sheilah Graham, *Confessions of a Hollywood Columnist* (New York, 1969), p. 232.

134 "That woman": Interview with Robert Lawson.

134 "A new talent": See Stanley Kauffmann, *"The Chapman Report," The New Republic,* November 24, 1962.

135 "I've never seen": Farber and Green, p. 152.

135 "You too?": *Los Angeles Times,* December 6, 1964.

135 "It gets boring": Freedland, p. 11.

136 "You'll have to go": Guiles, p. 73.

136 "You expect me": Interview with confidential source.

137 Schickel's view of Peter: Interview with Richard Schickel.

137 Peter and Jim Mitchum: Peter Fonda interview, *Playboy,* p. 102.

138 "Just to get up": Kiernan, p. 153.

140 Crist review of *Joy House*: Ibid., p. 163.

Eight

143 "Miss Fonda will never": Roger Vadim, *Memoirs of the Devil* (New York, 1975), p. 147.

143 Jane saying she'd been warned: Vadim, *Bardot, Deneuve, Fonda,* p. 213.

143 "You've seduced her": Ibid.

144 Jane's melodramatic confession: Vadim, *Memoirs,* pp. 147ff.

144 Vadim and Jane in bed: Vadim, *Bardot, Deneuve, Fonda,* pp. 215ff.

145 Jane in Moscow: Ibid., p. 228.

146 "He's known beautiful women": Kiernan, p. 174.

146 "Ah, yes": Tom Burke, *Burke's Steerage* (New York, 1976), p. 101.

147 "Good God, no": Kiernan, p. 170.

147 "One did not visit her": Interview with Brooke Hayward.

147 Jane turning down *Doctor Zhivago*: Interview with Dick Clayton.

148 "I hate the French": Vadim, *Bardot, Deneuve, Fonda,* p. 235.

148 "Each wife": Interview with Roger Vadim.

148 "There was certainly": Kiernan, p. 181.

149 Vadim and Selznick: Interview with confidential source.

149 "She's too young": Vadim, *Bardot, Deneuve, Fonda,* p. 244.

150 "What is going *on?*": Interview with Henry Jaglom.

151 "This turned him off": Interview with confidential source.

152 Peter "tweaking" Henry: Interview with Bill Hayward.

152 "Okay, I can understand": Peter Fonda interview, *Playboy*, p. 98.

152 Peter on Arizona location: Interview with Burt Kennedy.

Nine

155 "went all out": Vadim, *Bardot, Deneuve, Fonda*, pp. 257–258.

155 "a new way to live": Thomas Thompson, "A Place in the Sun All Her Own," *Life*, March 29, 1968, p. 72.

156 "Well, this is very good soup": Interview with Alexander Whitelaw.

156 "Henry is a very moral man": "Flying Fondas," p. 62.

157 "Well, I loved them all": Graham, p. 224.

157 "I got you a great girl": Interview with Robert Ellis Miller.

158 "one of the most embarrassing": Interview with Richard Shickel.

158 "You can't do that!": Otto Preminger, *Autobiography* (Garden City, NY, 1977), p. 221.

159 "Suddenly I busted through": For Peter's detailed description of his first LSD experiences, see Reed, "Holden Caulfield," p. 70.

160 "four years at a good psychiatrist": Graham, p. 228.

160 Escondido Beach episode, and trip to Baja California: Interview with Robert Walker, Jr.

161 Peter and AIP: Peter Fonda interview, *Playboy*, p. 86.

162 "I don't believe it": Ibid.

162 Twenty-five acid trips: Ibid., p. 104.

162 "I really dig": Reed, "Holden Caulfield," p. 75.

163 "I think the whole obsession": Kiernan, p. 212.

163 "You know, John": Interview with John Phillip Law.

164 Jane shivering: Interview with Roger Vadim.

164 "How can you respect me?": Vadim, *Memoirs*, p. 166.

164 Jane's dreams of dead dogs: Freedland, p. 111.

165 "They say that pot": Lorraine Gauguin, "Ms. Jane Fonda's Causes and Effects," *Views and Reviews*, Summer 1973, p. 6.

165 "Your war": Vadim, *Bardot, Deneuve, Fonda*, p. 246.

166 "I discovered it was my morale": Freedland, p. 140.

167 "Politically, I can prove": Peter Fonda interview, *Playboy*, p. 98.

167 "They just put Nixon": Vadim, *Bardot, Deneuve, Fonda*, p. 283.

168 "Jane has a baby girl!": Interview with Delos Smith.

Ten

169 "I've reached the age of thirty-one": Vadim, *Bardot, Deneuve, Fonda,* p. 234.

170 "He was just cast aside": Interview with Brooke Hayward.

171 "I hate it": Vadim, *Bardot, Deneuve, Fonda,* p. 296.

171 "Their peculiar marital situation": Interview with Brooke Hayward.

171 Viva: See Viva, *Superstar* (New York, 1970). Thomas Kiernan (pp. 240ff) was the first to note that episodes in Viva's book have a resemblance to events in the lives of Fonda, Polanski, and the other stars she came into contact with in southern California in 1969 as part of Andy Warhol's group. In an interview for this book, Viva herself (Susan Hoffman) coyly disclaimed any autobiographical intent in her novel.

172 "It doesn't matter": Kiernan, p. 237.

172 "Where's Jane?": John Phillips with Jim Jerome, *Papa John* (New York, 1986, paperback), pp. 290–291.

174 "Listen, man": Peter Fonda interview, *Playboy,* p. 88.

176 *Easy Rider* cemetery scene: Howard Junker, "Maui Boogie," *Rolling Stone,* May 13, 1974, p. 30.

177 "*Easy Rider* will not become a classic": Guy Flatley, "Henry Fonda Takes Aim at . . . ," *The New York Times,* October 18, 1970, p. D13.

178 "When I read them": Shay, n.p.

178 "Jesus Christ": Henry Fonda interview, *Playboy,* p. 136.

179 Jane's fan letter: Chandler, p. 241.

179 "What has he really done": Interview with Brooke Hayward.

179 "I couldn't tell reality": Reed, "Everybody," p. D22.

180 "The feminine and soft side": Interview with Jay Cocks.

181 "like living with a Martian": Reed, "Everybody," p. D22.

181 Warhol at dock: Vadim, *Memoirs,* p. 166.

182 Jane's visit to attorney's home: Interview with Richard Rosenthal.

183 "You don't mind": Reed, "Everybody," p. D22.

184 "We're close now": Jane was always guilty of premature closure with her father. In an interview that appeared in the December 1981 *Playboy,* Henry was asked if he had grown closer to his children over the years. He began his reply: "Not really . . . "

184 "freaking out": Interview with John Larsen.

184 "He was in his bathrobe": Interview with Mary Cronin.

185 "Everybody asks me": Interview with Jay Cocks.

185 "Well, if that's the way": Ibid.

Eleven

190 "I realized that": Jeffrey Klein, "The Essential Tom and Jane," *Mother Jones,* February 1980, p. 40.

190 "I always had": Reed, "Everybody," p. D22.

191 *Ramparts* story: Peter Collier, "The Red Man's Burden," *Ramparts,* February 1970.

193 "Jane is not": Interview with Brooke Hayward.

193 "I don't know what I can do": Kiernan, p. 285.

194 "You listen to her": Henry Gris, "What Scares Me About Peter and Jane," *Coronet,* September 1970, p. 44.

195 "When I left the West Coast": John Frook, "Nonstop Activist," *Life,* April 23, 1971, p. 52D.

195 "I would think": Freedland, p. 160.

196 "She'd be talking": Interview with Josette Roe.

197 "I can't, Mark": Interview with Mark Lane.

197 Jane and the Panthers: Interview with Robert Williams; also conversations between David Horowitz and Huey Newton, as related by Horowitz to author.

197 "her instincts": Interview with Mark Lane.

198 "A lot of them": Interview with Steve Jaffe.

198 "Here's a woman": Interview with Richard Rosenthal.

198 "Sorry, but I was": Flatley, "Henry Fonda," p. D13.

199 Confrontation between Henry and Jane: Teichmann, p. 325.

199 "My instinct": Gris, "What Scares Me," p. 46.

199 "This is my authority": Sandra Sheney, "Peter Fonda: An Interview," *Playgirl,* March 1974.

199 "teach revolution": *People,* July 22, 1974.

200 "I was going to send Jane": Junker, "Maui Boogie," p. 31.

200 "Once I got a call": Interview with Steve Jaffe.

200 "She was a queen bee": Interview with confidential source.

200 "Jane was very well organized": Interview with Steve Jaffe.

201 "My biggest regret": Interview with Robin Mencken.

201 "Because if I don't": Interview with Steve Jaffe.

201 "I came to New York": *Interview,* March 1984.

202 "If you are absorbing": Interview with Henry Jaglom.

203 "She was so militant": Interview with Mark Lane.

Twelve

205 "You let my poppa sleep": Interview with Roger Vadim.

206 "I have no desire": Kiernan, p. 325.

206 "There are other things": Interview with Richard Rosenthal.

206 "What I'm trying": Interview with Joe McDonald.

207 Jane reproaching Lane: Interview with Mark Lane.

207 "She was able to commit": Interview with Henry Jaglom.

207 Fonda–Sutherland rendezvous: Donald Sutherland interview, *Playboy*, October 1981.

208 "My wife and I": Ibid.

208 "Donald was crazy": Interview with confidential source.

208 "Well, maybe": Interview with Steve Jaffe.

208 "We're not going": Kiernan, p. 331.

209 "It came suddenly": Interview with Francine Parker.

209 "living in the world of Roger Vadim": "Growing Fonda of Jane," *Time*, October 3, 1977, p. 90.

210 "Jane started surrounding": Interview with Peter Boyle.

211 "Interestingly enough": Jane Fonda, "I Want to Work with Women," *The New York Times*, October 31, 1971, sect. 2, p. 17.

211 "She was into feminism": Interview with Alan Myerson.

211 "There were all these factions": Interview with Peter Boyle; also interview with Howard Hesseman.

211 "whenever you talked": Interview with Lauren Weissman.

212 "I've seen Peter": Interview with Dennis Clark.

213 "It was like watching": Interview with Jay Cocks.

213 "The movie had everything": Interview with Verna Bloom.

214 "Here, this is your fault": Interview with Bill Hayward.

214 "You'd hear him": Interview with confidential source.

214 Rumors of drugs on Maui: Junker, "Maui Boogie," p. 31.

215 "There'll be a mass panic": Burke, p. 103.

215 "Peter felt": Interview with confidential source.

Thirteen

217 "Godard is the only person": Kiernan, p. 344.

217 "Godard really hates": Guiles, p. 185.

218 "The Oscar is what": Kiernan, p. 355.

218 "I'm sorry I blew the line": Interview with Richard Rosenthal.

NOTES

219 Bookstore episode: Interview with Robin Mencken.

219 "By the spring of 1972": Interview with confidential source.

220 Hayden as New Left figure: See Tom Hayden, *Reunion* (New York, 1988).

220 "That was sort of crazy": Craig Unger, "Tom Hayden's Original Sin," *Esquire,* June 1989, p. 184.

221 The Red Family: For a retrospective analysis of the Red Family from a former member of the collective, see Harold Jacobs, "Tom Hayden: The Waning of a Politics of Vision," *Tikkun,* May–June 1989.

221 Jane's "lowest period": D. R. Katz, "A Hard Act to Follow," *Rolling Stone,* March 9, 1978.

223 "I felt a current": Rosenbaum, "Dangerous Jane," p. 208.

224 "Their real solution": Katz, "Hard Act," p. 44.

224 Tom's visit to Jane's house, and Jane's weeping: Hayden, p. 446.

225 "Jane Fonda felt": This and the citations from Jane's Hanoi broadcasts that follow are from transcripts collected by the U.S. Government Foreign Broadcast Information Service.

227 "I'll be handling": Interview with Steve Jaffe.

227 "It was like a movie": Interview with Roger Vadim.

228 "I appreciate": Interview with Mark Lane.

228 "He hated Hayden": Interview with confidential source.

228 "If it had been the fifties": David Talbot and Barbara Zheutlin, *Creative Differences* (Boston, 1974), p. 136.

229 FBI surveillance of Jane: For details, see Guiles, pp. 165ff.

229 "working on political speeches": Thomas Kiernan, *Jane Fonda: Heroine for Our Time* (New York, 1982, paperback), p. 286.

230 "Sometimes I just want": Interview with Roger Vadim.

230 "We are campaigning": Kiernan, *Jane Fonda: Heroine,* p. 287.

Fourteen

231 "I guess one": Interview with Steve Jaffe.

233 "Because he's always afraid": Interview with Verna Bloom.

233 "Hers is not my way": T. Thompson, "Fonda at 68," *McCall's,* September 1973.

234 "Fucking lie!": Henry Fonda interview, *Playboy,* p. 131.

234 "I have the feeling": Peter Fonda interview, *Playboy,* p. 98.

234 "Henry wasn't the sort": Interview with Bill Hayward.

235 "Cyrano's restaurant": Interview with Dennis Clark.

NOTES

235 "For Peter": Interview with Robert Walker, Jr.

235 "Imagine if you're married": Interview with confidential source.

236 "Can this really": Interview with Ellie Walker.

236 "Yes, but it isn't right": Aljean Harmetz, *Rolling Breaks* (New York, 1983), p. 155.

236 "Jane loved it": Interview with Lauren Weissman.

236 "liars, hypocrites, and pawns": Gauguin, "Ms. Jane Fonda's," p. 6. In *Reunion* (p. 455), Hayden chivalrously claims that it was actually he who used this phrase.

236 "Tortured men": Gauguin, "Ms. Jane Fonda's," p. 6.

237 "I had a broken arm": *Los Angeles Times*, April 13, 1973, p. 3.

237 "I've heard the whole story": Sheney, "Peter Fonda."

239 "These young American politicians": Vadim, *Bardot, Deneuve, Fonda*, p. 316.

239 "He was a man": Mel Gussow, "Fonda Set to Open in Darrow," *The New York Times*, March 25, 1974, p. 41.

239 Fonda's illness during play: Interview with David Rintels.

Fifteen

241 "The Jane Dough Story": Interview with Robin Mencken.

242 "Hayden! Get a job!": Interview with confidential source.

242 Rosenthal memo: Richard Rosenthal to Jane Fonda, May 6, 1974. Rosenthal sued Jane after their relationship was abruptly terminated in 1980, and this memo is part of court record CV84-1620RMT, U.S. District Court, Central District, California.

244 "Excuse me, Mr. Fonda": Interview with Andy Ferguson.

244 "Our current cash flow": Richard Rosenthal to Jane Fonda, February 11, 1977. This letter is part of court record CV84-1620RMT, U.S. District Court, Central District, California.

245 "I'm told": Talbot and Zheutlin, p. 136.

245 "There's a guy": Junker, "Maui Boogie," p. 30.

246 "Peter! Please!": Interview with confidential source.

246 "He had a tremendous chip": Interview with Bill Hayward.

247 Hand-grenade threat: Interview with confidential source.

247 Peter calling Andy Albeck a Nazi: Interview with Larry Kubik.

247 "That's it": Interview with Lauren Weissman.

247 "I think it's wonderful": Elizabeth Ashley, *Actress* (New York, 1978), p. 148.

248 "Becky is like Jane": Interview with confidential source.

249 "It's important for me": Harmetz, p. 155.

249 "We don't have people": Ibid.

249 "something more than": Interview with Roger Vadim.

251 "we want three Bette Davises": Mosley, p. 393.

252 Dowd script: Interview with Richard Rosenthal.

253 "Ron was floundering": Interview with Jerome Hellman.

253 "a racist, Pentagon version": *People*, March 10, 1979.

254 "If you look": Interview with Dennis Clark.

254 "Most people": Bruce Gilbert interview, *Cinéaste*, 6, no. 4 (1975), p. 257.

255 Jane refusing proposed titles: Ibid.

255 "It goes beyond the realm": Guiles, p. 260.

255 "Your fee for *Julia*": Richard Rosenthal to Jane Fonda, July 30, 1979. This letter is part of court record CV84-1620RMT, U.S. District Court, Central District, California.

256 "From 1978": Interview with Richard Rosenthal.

256 "Tom says": Ibid.

257 "How did *you*": Interview with Gilda Marx.

257 "We're going to beat": Interview with Richard Rosenthal.

258 "It was the great thing": Interview with Lauren Weissman.

258 "I was blacklisted": Gail Sheehy, "Hers," *The New York Times*, January 10, 1980, p. C2.

259 "During the first years": Talbot and Zheutlin, p. 136.

259 Jane's attack on Baez: D. Seligman, "Echoes," *Fortune*, July 30, 1979, p. 52.

260 "Tom's the intelligent one": Interview with Lauren Weissman.

260 Big stuff, huh?": Interview with confidential source.

260 "She begins": Klein, "Essential," p. 42.

261 Jane as Left-wing version of Pat Nixon: Ibid.

261 "This is great!": Joel Kotkin, "Tom Hayden's Manifest Destiny," *Esquire*, May 1980, p. 48.

261 "He's convinced": Klein, "Essential," p. 46.

Sixteen

263 "I'm a crack shot": Peter Fonda interview, *Playboy*, p. 279.

264 "Montana Bloomsbury": For a portrait of Peter in Montana, see Toby Thompson, "The Disappearance of Peter Fonda," *Esquire*, March 1984.

264 Peter's American Revolution project: Interview with Bill Hayward.

265 "The strike has blown": *Variety,* August 14, 1981.

266 "Frankly, I've never really dealt": Kiernan, p. 75.

266 Amy Fonda: See Riva Le Blanc, "The Fonda Nobody Knows," *Redbook,* May 1979.

266 "How does it feel": Interview with David Rintels.

266 Henry and his grandchildren: Interview with confidential source.

267 "I've got to tell you": Interview with Richard Rosenthal.

267 "God damn it!": Interview with Larry Kubik.

267 "No, there are actors": Interview with David Rintels.

268 "I want to thank you": Interview with Martin Starger.

268 "I was worried": Chandler, p. 241.

269 "She was crying": Interview with Gary Daigler.

271 "At the end": Thompson, "Disappearance," p. 220.

271 "He didn't talk": Sally Ogle Davis, "Jane Raw," *Los Angeles,* October 1989, p. 144.

272 "it seemed to go": Interview with Lauren Weissman.

272 "To Peter Fonda I leave": Thompson, "Disappearance," p. 220.

272 "Every time": Ibid.

Seventeen

273 "My victory marks": Jerry Gillam, "Hayden Declares Victory," *Los Angeles Times,* November 9, 1982, p. 1.

274 Hayden and Fonda on Israel: *Los Angeles Times,* July 13, 1982.

274 "I despise Tom": Unger, "Tom Hayden's," p. 186.

275 "Tom said it was": Interview with Michael Dieden.

275 "I wanted the democratic process": Hayden, p. 447.

275 "Jane *made* it happen": Interview with Lauren Weissman.

276 Tom and *The Crash of '79*: Interview with Michael Dieden.

277 "In discussing": Interview with David Shaber.

278 "*Rollover* was just devastating": Interview with Lauren Weissman.

278 Jane's business success: See Julia Vitulo-Martin, "The Business Education of Jane Fonda," *Fortune,* February 20, 1984.

279 "No secretary is worth": Interview with Lauren Weissman.

280 "All you have to do": Christopher Andersen, "Jane Fonda: I'm Stranger Than Ever," *Ladies' Home Journal,* October 1989, p. 115.

280 "It was admirable": Interview with confidential source.

281 "Jane always had": Interview with Lauren Weissman.

281 "Look, we're here": Ibid.

282 "You couldn't drag": Interview with Paul Zotos.

282 Jane seeking doctor's advice: Interview with Lauren Weissman.

284 "The problem is": Interview with Jeff Young.

284 "She spreads balm": Interview with confidential source.

285 "She wanted to help": Interview with Lauren Weissman.

286 "Why aren't I offered": Thompson, "Disappearance," p. 218.

Eighteen

287 "She acts": Interview with confidential source.

288 "It is great": Interview with Lauren Weissman.

288 "Jane's had more": For Fonda's impact on stars and starlets, see *Glamour*, April 1988.

289 Tom fine-tuning his image: See Joe Domanick, "Middle Age Crazy," *Los Angeles*, June 1989.

289 "Tom's basic problem": Kotkin, "Tom Hayden's," p. 51.

290 "You know": Ibid.

290 "He used to go": Domanick, "Middle Age," p. 145.

290 "He'd make a big show": Interview with Paul Zotos.

291 "I'm not opposed": Batelle, "Unknown."

291 "If you're tired": Interview with confidential source.

291 "Tom didn't really bother": Interview with Richard Wellig.

291 "Sally Field and Jane and I": Interview with Lauren Weissman.

292 "The marriage was over": Interview with Roger Vadim.

292 *The Old Gringo*: For background on the making of the film, see Pete Hamill, "Mexico in Flames," *Premiere*, October 1989.

292 "In my mind": Jane Fonda with Mignon McCarthy, *Women Coming of Age* (New York, 1984), p. 14.

293 "But tell me": Interview with confidential source.

293 "Tom took it out": Interview with Lauren Weissman.

294 "One morning": Interview with Paul Zotos.

294 "She was in one": Interview with confidential source.

294 "How can that be?": Interview with Brooke Hayward.

294 "Jane said": Interview with Lauren Weissman.

296 "She's never going": Katz, "Hard Act."

296 "Thirty years ago": Interview with Brooke Hayward.

296 "I've reinvented myself": Michelle Willens, "Starting Over," *US*, November 13, 1989, p. 61.

296 "I read Rilke": Davis, "Jane Raw," p. 139.

NOTES

297 "I didn't realize": Willens, "Starting Over," p. 62.

298 "I was already thirty-two": Levine, "Fonda, Fonda, Fonda."

298 "political person": Andersen, "Jane Fonda," p. 117.

298 "You don't think": Interview with confidential source.

298 "She's my sister": Freedland, p. 227.

298 "Jane and I": Sidney Skolsky, *Don't Get Me Wrong—I Love Hollywood* (New York, 1975), p. 229.

INDEX